2/02

Once Upon
an American Dream

CultureAmerica

Karal Ann Marling & Erika Doss, *editors*

Once Upon an American Dream

THE STORY OF EURO DISNEYLAND

Andrew Lainsbury

 University Press of Kansas

© 2000 by the University Press of Kansas

Published by the University Press of Kansas (Lawrence, Kansas 66049), which was organized by the Kansas Board of Regents and is operated and funded by Emporia State University, Fort Hays State University, Kansas State University, Pittsburg State University, the University of Kansas, and Wichita State University.

Library of Congress Cataloging-in-Publication Data

Lainsbury, Andrew, 1967–
    Once upon an American dream : the story of Euro Disneyland / Andrew Lainsbury.
        p.   cm. — (Culture America)
    Includes bibliographical references (p.) and index.
    ISBN 0-7006-0989-X (cloth : alk. paper)
    1. Euro Disneyland (Marne-la-Vallée, France)—History. 2. Walt Disney Company—Finance. 3. Popular culture—France—American influences. I. Title. II. Series.
    GV1853.4.F82E95   2000
    791'.06'844363—dc21   99-37813
                                          CIP

British Library Cataloguing in Publication Data is available.

Printed in the United States of America
10 9 8 7 6 5 4 3 2

The paper used in this publication meets the minimum requirements of the American National Standard for Permanence of Paper for Printed Library Materials Z39.48-1984.

The greatest desire an artist knows is to create a world of his own where everything is just as he imagines it. To build such a world is never work: it is a refreshment to the spirit. It is an escape, a holiday from the strain of the world of everybody else.

—Aubrey Menen

Contents

Acknowledgments

This project could not have been completed without the support of many people. I take great pleasure in thanking them here for their countless contributions to my research.

The Graduate School at the University of Minnesota provided me with a fellowship to begin my graduate education in 1991. The American Studies program awarded me travel funds to deliver papers in Rhode Island, Colorado, and Pennsylvania. But it was the CLA Honors Division at the University of Minnesota that first took a chance on me: their grant of four hundred dollars for an undergraduate project requiring research at Walt Disney World in Florida was an important factor in my decision to pursue the study of American popular culture.

Many others lent strength to my interest in theme parks. Special thanks go to Tina Lee, my Montessori school friend, who invited me to Japan for unforgettable tours of Tokyo Disneyland; Mark Matten, who explored Ocean Park and Hong Kong's many other amusement areas with me; Cheng and Elaine Tan, who took me to see the pleasure gardens of Singapore; Jenni Phillips and David Waithaka, who rarely let me miss a state fair; and Sue Larson, who has made the Minnesota Renaissance Festival an annual event in my life.

Friends at Euro Disney have also proven to be invaluable. Janette Bubinak, Danny Johnson, Marcey Lieberman, Rita Malanga, Michelle Massie Katstra, Amy Wehrung, and Lisa Weiss have filled my mailbox with relevant newspaper clippings, articles, videotapes, photos, and books since their return to America. Nigel Bratcher, Sebastien Frank, Paul Jones, and Kai Schomann—still "working for the mouse" in France—have answered many questions I didn't think to ask while I was there. Barb Coleman, Chris Gordon, Susan Green, Pat Hemmis, Gail Jardine, Kathy Meyer, Erin Mullen, Ted Nobui, Caitlin Patterson, Amy Shapiro, and John and Babby Schwarz have supplemented this information with even more, offering themselves as sounding boards for ideas that were still in formation.

The people I spoke with at the Walt Disney Company made many contributions to this project, too. Special thanks go to Marty Sklar, vice-chairman and principal creative executive at Walt Disney Imagineering, who made it possible to interview members of the Euro Disney design team and other in-house planners: Stewart Bailey, Tony Baxter, Susan Bonds, Barry Braverman, Bobby Brooks, Wing Chao, Ron Chesley, Bill Cottrell, Rolly Crump, Marvin Davis, Tim Delaney, Glen Durflinger, Morgan "Bill" Evans, Tom Figgins, Bruce Gordon, John Hench, Eric Jacobson, Ward Kimball, Joe Lanzisero, Sam McKim, Tom Morris, David Mumford, Jan Sircus, Eddie Sotto, Card Walker, and Bob Weis. Their insights changed the way I thought about Disney theme parks.

The encyclopedic knowledge of the Collections Management team at Walt Disney Imagineering—Denise Brown, Mike Jusko, and Randy Webster—made doing primary research both compelling and fun. David Smith and Robert Tieman of the Disney Archives provided sheaves of information. And Arline Chambers, my Disney liaison, deserves special thanks: her many hours of hard work setting up interviews, museum visits, and "power lunches" around Los Angeles, not to mention her unbridled enthusiasm for my project, went over and above the call of duty.

The members of my dissertation committee—Bill Beyer, Roland Delattre, Judith Martin, and David Noble—have also proven to be invaluable. Their careful readings of chapter drafts and their incisive questions challenged me to consider my work from new angles. My thesis adviser, Karal Ann Marling, has been especially generous. Her sharp eye and detailed knowledge of Disney art improved this project immensely. Her insights helped me to develop and articulate my own perspective on popular culture. And her words ("I wouldn't pass up a year in France!") convinced me to take a one-year leave of absence from graduate school in order to work at Euro Disney when the opportunity arose. A portion of my dissertation appeared as an article entitled "Imagineering Euro Disneyland" in the *Columbia Journal of American Studies* 3, no. 1 (1998), pp. 20–35.

Erika Doss, co-editor of the University Press of Kansas's CultureAmerica series, also merits special recognition. By offering astute comments and opening up new areas of inquiry for me to explore, she has elevated my understanding of theme parks—and American culture as a whole. Nancy Scott Jackson, Susan Schott, Rebecca Knight Giusti, Sara Henderson White, and Kerry Callahan of the University Press of Kansas have been amazing as well: their unflagging enthusiasm and support of this project have made working on it a true pleasure.

But my greatest debt is to my family, who made everything possible. Without their encouragement, their generosity, and their sense of humor, it's hard to imagine that I could ever have finished. My father, Freeman, clipped newpaper and magazine articles on Disney topics that I certainly would have missed. My brother, Dan, got me neat Disney gifts that weren't available to the general public. My sister, Mary, taped numerous programs that applied to my project and dragged me to Valleyfair or the movies whenever writer's block set in. And my mother, Fran, was endlessly supportive. By reading my work, taking me out to lunch, and cheering my every accomplishment, she helped to make a difficult process much, much easier. For all of these things and many others, no words of thanks will ever suffice.

Introduction

In the darkness of a cool spring evening in 1992, Michael Eisner, chairman of the Walt Disney Company, looked out into the star-studded crowd that had gathered in front of Le Château de la Belle au Bois Dormant (Sleeping Beauty's palace) in France. Roy Disney Jr., vice-chairman of the Walt Disney Company, and Robert Fitzpatrick, president of the soon-to-be opened Euro Disney Resort, stood on either side of him, beaming with anticipation. The moment they had all awaited was only a heartbeat away. As Eisner produced a pair of jumbo scissors with which to snip the red ribbon stretched out before him, a dramatic hush fell over the scene: all eyes were riveted on the man who was about to make history by bringing a Magic Kingdom to life in the ancestral homeland of Walt Disney. "Et maintenant," Eisner proclaimed in his very best French, "Je déclare Euro Disney officialement ouvert!" A jubilant Mickey Mouse, dressed in a tuxedo, emerged from the palace and waved park guests in to explore his world of fantasy and fun. A fireworks display from ten different locations lit up the sky in a burst of colors. And a swelling chorus of music warmed the air with melodies from familiar fairy tale films.[1]

It was a spectacular sight. I remember feeling many different things as I watched from the living room of my Minneapolis apartment: nostalgia and pride that my favorite childhood entertainers were alive, well, and seemingly more popular than ever; wonder that the Walt Disney Company had managed to cut through countless levels of red tape and resistance to bring a multibillion-dollar theme park to life in the Old World; and curiosity with how this new "American" enterprise would fare with highly skeptical French—and European—audiences. But more than anything, I felt a sense of gnawing anticipation, for I had recently been offered the chance to join the ranks of Euro Disney "cast members" who were so happily marching across my television screen.

That's right: I had a job offer in hand from the Euro Disney Resort (which included the Euro Disneyland theme park and a 5,200-room hotel district). Just months before, I had flown out to California to interview for a management position at the new European Disney venture. The title of my post, "Stagiaire Professionel," sounded rather important, in a vague sort of way— especially when pronounced with a nasally French accent. It didn't indicate what sorts of things I might be doing to earn my paycheck, but that didn't matter. Not really, anyway. The thought of going to work at one of the most publicized and hotly contested leisure developments around intrigued me. I wanted to understand French and European hostility to the Euro Disney enterprise and find out if there was any truth to charges that it represented American cultural imperialism at its worst. I wanted to know why the Walt Disney Company had persisted in building the park despite fierce resistance. Most of all, I wanted to see how the Walt Disney Company was coping with what seemed to be a new outbreak of anti-Americanism on the rapidly transforming landscapes of Europe. Given that I had passed the previous eight months as a first-year graduate student in American Studies, this chance to be part of an evolving work of popular culture overseas was simply too much to resist.

Little did I know at the time that I would one day be writing this book. I was unprepared for all of the compelling stories I would find at the world's newest Magic Kingdom. I was unprepared for one other thing, too: the life of a "Stagiaire Professionel." Much to my horror, it became apparent during the first few days of orientation that my Euro-chic title did not carry the same degree of prestige in France as it had in Minnesota. A tour of the Hotel Disneyland, where I would initially be stationed, revealed armies of other "Stagiaires Professionels." And the jobs they were doing—from food service and housekeeping to carrying luggage—were decidedly unglamorous. It was time to face the facts. I would not have an assistant, an office with an Eiffel Tower view, or my own desk. I would not even have access to the office supply cabinet. (In an effort to keep costs under control that first year, hotel management informed new recruits that we were to furnish our own pens at work.) It was becoming dreadfully clear that my hopes of rubbing elbows with power brokers in Euro Disney's executive dining room were not to be. The smoky little vending machine nook in the basement—the one with two wobbly tables and no chairs—was where I'd be grabbing my grub between shifts.

Disappointment does not begin to describe how I and other wide-eyed American transplants felt about our new station in France. Some would-be Euro Disney "professionals" ultimately turned around and went back to the United States rather than bus tables at one of Euro Disney's fabulous themed eateries. (The Walt Disney Company graciously reimbursed them for their airfare.) Heaven knows, I thought about bailing too. I hadn't carried a double courseload to finish my master's degree a year early—or begged for a leave of absence from graduate school—for this kind of career development. There were plenty of jobs washing dishes back home on the other side of the planet. Mickey Mouse and his relentless smile were really beginning to tick me off.

The frustration was unsettling—and not just because of the cosmic injustice of it all. Things like this were simply not meant to happen at the Wonderful World of Disney, even the one in France. This was supposed to be a place of endless promise, where fantasies came true for deserving souls, where all surprises were good ones—not a place that handed out elf costumes or hairnets to aspiring executives. After all, hadn't Disney magic

3

made Dumbo fly? Didn't Davy Crockett, Cinderella, and all the other Disney characters (except the truly evil ones) have cool theme songs and live happily ever after? Either Walt Disney had knowingly pumped me—and millions of others worldwide—full of sugar-coated tales that had no basis in reality (a thought I couldn't stomach), or he truly believed that wonderful things would happen to those who dared to dream. I reminded myself that Disney storytellers frequently insert scenes of great emotional distress (like Bambi's mother being shot by a hunter) at the beginning of tales to intensify the sweetness of happy endings. It was out of curiosity more than anything else that I decided to stick around at Euro Disney, just in case this grim beginning gave way to a more intriguing storyline.

It is a decision I do not regret. The year I spent at Euro Disney stands out as one of the most challenging and unforgettable experiences of my life, largely because of the other "Stagiaires" with whom I worked. They came from all corners of the globe: France, Italy, Sweden, New Zealand, Nigeria, Brazil, China, Iran. Some were fresh out of school and looking for adventure. Some were recent retirees. Others were working to feed their families. Some were friendly and outgoing, the model of Disney politesse. Others were haughty and unpleasant. Everyone spoke some degree of French (it was required for employment at Euro Disney). But as I quickly found out, different dialects, accents, and levels of fluency hampered easy communication with guests—and with each other. The making of a truly multinational team, much less a whole vacation resort, was much more complicated than I had ever imagined.

With each passing day on the front lines, my colleagues and I struggled to keep up with a never-ending flow of requests, problems, and outbursts from diverse groups of visitors. We prepared and delivered fruit baskets to the rooms of VIPs. We tracked down lost luggage. We parked cars. We booked meetings. We provided tours of Euro Disney's facilities to travel agents. We reunited lost children with their parents. And we endured the wrath of irate guests screaming at us in unrecognizable languages. My perspective on Disney art gradually began to shift. No longer was it a distant source of entertainment, as it had been throughout my childhood: the Disney experience was something that I was helping to create. And I was developing a rich appreciation for how difficult that was. I knew all too well that the many outdoor flower arrangements did not replant themselves each night during the freezing winter months and that the thousands of hotel-room minibars were not refilled daily with the stroke of a magic wand. Some poor shmo like me was doing it for little thanks and even less glory. The truth of Disney CEO Michael Eisner's words had become clear. "Fantasy is very hard work," he commented in a magazine interview. "To make something fun is hard. It's gratifying. It's satisfying. But fun? No."[2]

Six months into my tour of duty at the Hotel Disneyland, something unexpected happened: I was offered a different "role" in the Euro Disney "show." The Entertainment Division urgently needed someone to play Prince Charming, and one of its scouts recruited me for an audition. I landed the part with no special talents at all—other than my ability to fit into the costume, carry a glass slipper, and wave. After some coaching in the basics of ballroom dancing and autograph signing, I found myself catapulted into a large pumpkin carriage with a pretty Scottish cast member who was outfitted as Cinderella. The daily parade was followed by as many as six back-to-back performances in "Le Livre Magique de Mickey," an elaborate stage show that recounted the tales of "Cendrillon" (as she is known in France), "Blanche Neige" (Snow White), and "La Belle au Bois Dormant" (Sleeping Beauty) in front of the palace in Fantasyland.

The experience had a tremendous impact upon me. It changed the way I looked at—and thought about—Disney art. By stepping inside the Disney version of Cinderella and helping to animate it for tens of thousands of park guests each day, I learned to appreciate the complexity of creating and sustaining fantasy experiences without "cassant le rêve," or shattering the dream. Most importantly of all, I was able to see firsthand what Disney entertainment meant to European audiences. The flashing cameras, the waving adults, the fierce hugs of children—and yes, even the waggling feet of would-be princesses seeking a chance to try on the glass footwear I displayed—were all unmistakable signs that Disney art was filled with meaning for people on both sides of the Atlantic.

Someone, I decided, needed to tell the story of Euro Disneyland. The real story—not the same old one being trumpeted in newspapers and academic journals around the world, which blistered the park as a "Cultural Chernobyl" and a "Tragic Kingdom" long before it ever opened. Someone needed to fill in the many blanks left by journalistic reports that cutely proclaimed: "The Mouse Isn't Roaring" and "Euro Disney Attendance is Disappointingly Mickey Mouse." Someone also needed to examine why Euro Disneyland had become the target of media scorn in the first place, with TV shows like *Saturday Night Live* and others taking merciless jabs at it. While some of the lampooning was undeniably inspired (*The Simpsons* poked fun at the struggles of an ill-conceived theme park named "Euro Itchy and Scratchyland"), the majority of it was more tiresome than enlightening. Each instance, nonetheless, fed into a growing wave of anti–Euro Disney sentiment that seemed determined to seal the fate of the troubled vacation complex—or at least turn it into an international joke.

THE WONDERFUL WORLD OF DISNEY CRITICISM

None of this is to suggest that the Euro Disney Resort was the target of some spontaneous conspiracy. But the zeal with which journalists, academics, and other self-appointed guardians of European culture pounced on the development is a phenomenon that cannot be ignored. Their frenzied determination to expose Euro Disney as a doomed effort to export U.S. entertainment prevented them from seeing—and reporting on—the many fascinating stories woven into the very fabric of the park. Historical, cultural, aesthetic, geographical, and other concerns were swept aside in favor of stirring the kettle of public opinion with sensational headlines. All the while, people everywhere followed the controversy to find out how soon this ill-fated Magic Kingdom would be closing its gates once and for all.

In many ways, it was a classic Disney drama. Would Eisner and his undefeatable Hollywood dream-weavers be able to recover from this latest plot twist? Would Mickey Mouse, traditionally cast as the sympathetic hero, go down in smoke once and for all? It seemed that everyone wanted to know. And many around the world were quietly—or not so quietly—rooting against Mickey, in the hope that the Walt Disney Company had finally met its match. John Huey, the managing editor of *Fortune,* said it best: "The ugly truth is that when Eisner's unbroken string of successes at Disney began to unravel in 1992 with the Euro Disney crisis, a lot of people, both inside and outside Hollywood, were happy to see it, particularly the culture press, which viewed the fact that it happened in Paris as proof that God still prefers live ballet to the audio-animatronics of the Country Bear Playhouse."[3]

While cultural protectionism may explain some anti–Euro Disney sentiment, much of it was also rooted in a more general disapproval of the Walt Disney Company. John Hench, a former colleague of Walt Disney's who at age ninety still oversees the design and development of theme park attractions in Disney's Imagineering unit, has observed a dramatic shift in people's perceptions of the Walt Disney Company over the years. In contrast to the early days, when Walt Disney and his alter ego, Mickey Mouse, were seen as underdogs fighting more powerful studios to secure their place in Hollywood, Hench noted, today's Walt Disney Company appears to have been recast as the evil giant in a very public performance of the "David and Goliath" story.[4] For many, Mickey Mouse has morphed into a symbol of corporate power and greed.

This should not be totally surprising. Disney's recent acquisitions—from record companies, cable channels, and sports teams to the American Broadcasting Corporation (ABC)—have transformed it into what one writer has described as "the world's greatest media empire."[5] And many have come to distrust it for precisely that reason. Witness the Southern Baptist Convention's boycott on all things Disney for moving away from "family values"; the protests surrounding the proposed Walt Disney's America theme park just outside of Washington, D.C. (which was finally abandoned after waves of negative publicity); or the rumors that Eisner was considering a purchase of America Online in a bid to dominate the Internet.[6] Or simply access the Massachusetts Institute of Technology's April Fool's Day Web page (1998), which sneered at Mickey's increasing muscle with a biting headline: "Walt Disney Corporation to Acquire MIT for $6.9 Billion."[7] Each of these instances (not to mention the widespread horror when Eisner cashed in on $565 million in Disney stock options at the end of 1997) reflects the alienation that many have begun to feel toward a once-beloved institution of American culture.[8]

So ready are some to leap on the anti-Disney bandwagon that proper impulse control—and fact checking—fail. Greg Burkman, writing in the *Seattle Times,* wrongly attacked the Mouse for a film that was actually produced by 20th Century Fox. "I don't consider the actual story that inspired Disney's historically bankrupt 'Anastasia,'" he sneered, "to be matinee fare."[9] More recently still, *TV Guide* greeted the May 1998 opening of Disney's Animal Kingdom with a raspberry in its weekly "Cheers & Jeers" column for "exploit[ing] its many TV properties in a shameless fashion to mark the event."[10] Eisner responded to such criticism on NBC's *Today Show.* "When you try to do something good that appeals to families and goes toward the light," he reflected, "there's the dark that tries to come after you."[11] The remark, which cast critics as villains, did little to win them over. But it illustrated the resounding truth of a comment penned by writer Liane Bonin. "Disney is a company racked by self-doubt," she noted, "knowing that any step forward, no matter how well calculated, is likely to be criticized."[12]

Trend analyst Faith Popcorn has described the phenomenon of targeting large corporations—like the Walt Disney Company—as "Icon Toppling." In her book, *Clicking* (1997), she argues that contemporary consumers have become more sophisticated and suspicious in their thinking about the world. This wariness, she claims, has sent tremors through the worlds of politics, business, culture, and everyday life:

> We no longer sheepishly follow authority, accept the old rules, or only buy name brands. The larger the entity, the more suspicious or resentful we are. Even institutions that have been around for a long time can't bank on touting their heritage anymore. Too many companies earned our trust and then abused it. Ford and GM thought they could get away with shoddy products, and for a while they did. But after too many lemons rolled off the line, consumers got wise. Winning us back hasn't been easy, and we'll never blindly trust these and other corporate turncoats again.[13]

Advertising columnist Mark Dolliver expressed a similar viewpoint in *Adweek*. "Though most Americans never bought the idea that small is beautiful," he commented, "they're keen on a corollary notion: Big is ugly."[14]

Dolliver's observation, however, is not limited to those in the United States. People the world over have grown suspicious of large multinational corporations, especially American ones, because of their potential (and perceived desire) to dominate and destroy all in their path. So when word got out that the Walt Disney Company was planning to build a new theme park in Europe, many were eager to believe the worst. Some looked askance at Mickey and Company, sneering at the latest effort to export U.S. entertainment. Others organized protest rallies and hanged Disney characters in effigy in a desperate bid to demonize the Mouse before the world media. Still others, like the extremists who planted bombs outside the park prior to the grand opening,

9

resorted to terrorism. To all those who resisted, the very idea of installing an "American" theme park in Europe was at once maddening and terrifying.

The Euro Disney Resort, described by one scholar as "the central symbolic event representing the omnipresence of American mass culture beyond its own national borders," is more than this.[15] As geographic historian John Dorst has pointed out, casting the terms of discussion in this way has limited the consideration of much larger issues. "To judge from the popular rhetoric," he observed, "it is merely a matter of whether the European 'invasion' by Disney heralds the ultimate Americanisation, which is to say, degradation, of European national cultures."[16] Dorst's suggestion that Euro Disney should not be dismissed as an example of U.S. imperialism is important. After all, the Walt Disney Company can no longer be classified strictly as an "American" corporation. More importantly still, imperialism can no longer be viewed as a uniquely "American" strategy: it has become a global *corporate* phenomenon. Nationalist critiques that fail to consider such complexities are both flawed and misleading.

This book represents an effort to crack open the Euro Disney controversy by demonstrating that Europe's Magic Kingdom is much more than a tragic experiment in exporting U.S. culture. It pushes beyond questions of imperialism to consider a host of other historical, cultural, and artistic issues that have thus far escaped discussion: How did the Walt Disney Company arrive at the idea of building a new theme park in Europe? Why did Disney executives decide to locate it in France? How did political negotiations affect the design and development of the theme park and hotel district? How was the Euro Disney Resort promoted to continental audiences? What were the reasons behind its widely publicized financial struggles? And what might be the role of Euro Disney and the Walt Disney Company in the twenty-first century and beyond?

The Euro Disney Resort reveals much about the audiences it serves, the ways they were, are, and imagine themselves to be. It also reveals much about the people who struggled to bring it to life. Proceeding from Alexander Pope's argument that the proper study of humankind includes the examination of humans as well as what they have made, this project treats the Euro Disney Resort as an important cultural creation, capable of being "read," analyzed, and interpreted in the broad context of American—and human—history.[17] It investigates Euro Disney from a multimedia perspective and examines its connections with other Disney (and non-Disney) parks around the world to construct a comparative and cross-cultural history of the development. In so doing, this book aims to cast light on the social and cultural iconography of the multifaceted work of art that is Euro Disney while highlighting the many ways in which Walt Disney's conviction that "It's a Small World" is expressed to diverse audiences in a new setting at the tourist heart of Europe.

A BRIEF OVERVIEW

This book is composed of five parts, which together tell the tale of successful venture capitalism against a backdrop of European turmoil. It considers both how and why the Euro Disney Resort came into being—and survived—as Europe reinvented itself, changing from a collection of warring nation states into a more cohesive economic community, capable of competing on a global scale. Chapter 1, "A Disneyland for Europe," considers how Disney executives set the wheels in motion for a new continental pleasure garden. By examining the search for a site, the intricacies of political negotiations, and the agreements that were made with local and regional government authorities, it demonstrates how the Walt Disney Company secured a place for itself in the multinational land that produced the fairy tales (and the castles) that originally inspired Disney lore.

Chapter 2, "Designing the Euro Disney Resort," focuses on how Disney Imagineers reinvented the theme park for Europe. Drawing upon interviews with the Euro Disney Imagineers (or theme-park designers), it sheds light on the many conversations that shaped and ultimately defined the character of Europe's first Magic Kingdom, while revealing the Euro Disney Resort to be a strikingly original creation.

Chapter 3, "Marketing a New Magic Kingdom in Europe," considers the ways in which the Euro Disney Resort was promoted, from television and radio to corporate sponsorship agreements. By uncovering the media synergies in Euro Disney's publicity campaign, this chapter demonstrates what *Los Angeles Times* reporter Christopher Woodyard meant when he commented that "Disney knows how to market the heck out of everything."[18]

Chapter 4, "Rescuing the Euro Disney Resort," examines the many struggles of the controversial theme park development in its early years—and the steps that executives took to overcome them. By considering the impact of new attractions, pricing structures, advertising strategies, and a financial rescue package made possible by a consortium of lenders and Prince Al-Waleed Bin Talal Bin Abdulaziz Al Saud of Saudi Arabia, this chapter demonstrates that many parties had a vested interest in saving what had become known as the "Tragic Kingdom."[19]

Chapter 5, "It's a Small World, Inc.," broadens the view of the Disney operation in Europe—and around the world. It shows how the Euro Disney Resort has served as a catalyst for other new pleasure gardens and draws a critical distinction between the concepts of cultural globalization and cultural homogenization. This chapter also looks toward the future to consider the impact of the Walt Disney Company in the wake of its merger with media giant Capital Cities/ABC. In so doing, it sets the stage for an ongoing discussion about Disney's role in the global marketplace and its ability to promote a sense of internationalism in world cultures.

In all, *Once Upon an American Dream* traces the journey of the Euro Disney Resort from New World to Old World. It is a tale filled with drama, controversy, and unexpected plot twists. Its cast of characters is made up of people from all over the world.

But the story is far from over. Nobody knows whether or not there will be a happy ending in Disney's grand tradition. And nobody knows what Walt Disney would think of the park that was created in his honor. "There's enough ugliness and cynicism in the world," he once commented, "without me adding to it."[20] The Euro Disney Resort stands as a tribute to the artistic vision of Walt Disney, his desire to entertain family audiences, and his special talent—in the words of Yale's William Lyon Phelps—for "endearing America to the hearts of foreigners."[21]

1   A Disneyland for Europe

On August 12, 1985, Walt Disney Productions announced its decision to build a European theme park in the sugar-beet fields of Marne-la-Vallée, France. After years of searching for the ideal location and negotiating with the governments of prospective host countries, a conclusion of sorts had finally been reached. But this was just the first in a series of events destined to have a lasting effect upon the Walt Disney Company and the landscapes of the Old World.[1] France's Socialist leader, President François Mitterand (pronounced "Mickeyrand" by critics wary of his pro-Disney stance), was certain that the impact would be positive: he greeted news of the Disney decision with glee, noting that the Euro Disney Resort would create many new jobs and expand tourism in his country. Ignacio Fuejo, deputy secretary for tourism in Spain (France's main contender in the battle to host the new theme park) was less gracious. "They made a mistake in choosing France," he remarked. "The weather is dreadful in Paris."[2]

Fuejo's disappointment was understandable. For years, he and other Spanish officials had worked tirelessly to attract the project. The jobs, the tourist dollars, not to mention the prestige of a new Disney theme park, had promised to do wonders for an ailing economy. It might even have established Spain as a major force in the rapidly integrating European community. But all such hopes had been crushed in an instant. France, not Spain, would be home to the newest Disney kingdom.

The decision had not been easy. Disney executives had invested years combing over feasibility studies, exploring sites, and talking with political leaders all over Europe. They measured differences in climate and geography, studied the vacation habits of people in major cities, and evaluated existing infrastructures to identify the best place to anchor the Euro Disney Resort. Each step of the way, their efforts were complicated by translation barriers. Different languages, currencies, cultures, and worldviews challenged Disney officials to draw meaningful comparisons between possible venues and reminded them how such variables might impact the overall flavor of the new theme park.

Writer Alan Brown's prediction that "Euro Disneyland will never have it so easy [as Tokyo Disneyland]" was more accurate than anyone might have imagined.[3] After all, this park would not have the luxury of settling into a relatively homogeneous foreign landscape. The Euro Disney Resort would face the much greater challenge of making itself at home in a truly multinational setting. That meant contending with diverse audiences, expectations, and reactions. Naturally, some opposed the Euro Disney development: their stories were given broad coverage in the international press. Many others championed the project, including five successive premier ministers of France, who did everything short of selling their souls to nail down the deal.[4] The struggles that surrounded the making of the Euro Disney Resort merit close scrutiny. By mobilizing people on both sides of the Atlantic to reexamine traditional notions of art, entertainment, and America's influence in global commerce, they sent a powerful message to the world that Euro Disney would be much more than a fourth edition of "the happiest place on earth."

DISNEY AND EUROPE

Disney CEO Michael Eisner is frequently credited with—or blamed for—concocting the idea to build a Disney theme park in Europe. In fact, it was Walt Disney who first dreamed up the plan, after witnessing the success of his first venture in Anaheim, California.[5] Disneyland, which opened its gates in 1955, had been inspired by Copenhagen's Tivoli Gardens, the quaint charms of Paris, and continental chateaux such as Chambord, Vaux-le-Vicomte, and Pierrefonds.[6] What better gift for the land that had nourished his imagination, Disney felt, than a pleasure garden there of his own design? A Disneyland for Europe would honor his ancestral connections with the Old World and celebrate his memories of serving in France as a World War I ambulance driver. But it wasn't until long after Walt Disney's death in 1966 and the immediate record-shattering success of Tokyo Disneyland, nearly twenty years later, that his company decided to act on the dream. "We knew then," remarked Disney executive Dick Nunis, "that we had to go to Europe."[7]

Preliminary feasibility studies for a Disney park in Europe revealed some rather encouraging facts. For starters, researchers discovered that Orlando, Florida, was the third most popular travel destination for Europeans visiting the United States: it ranked after New York and Los Angeles, respectively, and just before San Francisco and Washington, D.C. (Walt Disney World, which had transformed Orlando into one of the fastest-growing cities—and by far the largest hotel market—in the United States, was largely responsible for putting this once-sleepy Florida community on the map.)[8] Another finding was equally impressive: that European tourists were visiting a Disney park in America at the rate of some 2 million per year. This number jumped to 2.7 million in 1990, and these guests spent upward of $1.6 billion on Disney merchandise.[9]

The magnetic pull of Disney theme parks among continental audiences could hardly be denied. Or could it? That Europeans were visiting the Magic Kingdom in surprising numbers seems perhaps less indicative of Disney's particular appeal than of the appeal of the United States in general. Many, no doubt, had been enticed into making the transatlantic voyage by other uniquely "American" attractions as well, from Graceland to the Grand

Canyon. Furthermore, the popularity of such favorite European tourist spots (including Disney theme parks) arguably rested on the fact that they were rooted in another landscape—a whole world away. Transplanting one to the Continent would not address the European desire for total immersion in Americana.

Nonetheless, Disney executives commissioned further analyses to forecast the advisability of bringing such a venture to Europe. The demographic picture alone filled them with confidence. Western Europe, roughly half the size of the United States, boasted a population of some 370 million people (as compared to America's 250 million). In such a concentrated market, officials had no problem imagining a steady flow of visitors to a European Disney park, year-round. The relatively high standard of living and substantial amounts of legally mandated leisure time (usually five weeks in France and Germany) brightened the picture even more—to say nothing of Disney's solid reputation in Europe.[10]

For more than half a century, Disney films and products had enjoyed great success on the Continent. Characters like Dingo (as French audiences know Goofy) and Topolino (Mickey Mouse's nickname in Italy) were huge celebrities there, a fact that prompted writer Charles Vial to finger Europe as the "continent of [Disney's] greatest cinematographic success."[11] Whether or not Europeans truly embraced Disney art more heartily than Americans is of little consequence. An estimated 25 percent of all Disney magazines, T-shirts, and souvenirs went to Europe. And if corporate projections were to be trusted, Walt Disney Productions stood to make as much as $1 billion per year in added revenues from a new park.[12] The plan to move forward with Walt Disney's vision under the leadership of Michael Eisner and Disney president Frank Wells promised to be a sure-fire success.

But Eisner and Wells had much more in mind than a standard theme park. They envisioned hotels, restaurants, movie studios, office buildings, and a host of other lucrative overlays. Christopher Woodyard, a reporter for the *Los Angeles Times*, suspected early on that the park was part of a broader plan to gain a strong foothold on the Continent. "This development is very important for Disney," he noted, "because in order to reach the entire industrialized world they absolutely have to have a major facility in the heart of Europe." Wells admitted his eagerness to set up shop on the other side of the Atlantic. "If you look at the projections," he remarked, "the enormity of growth in Europe exceeds that of any other geographic section of the world."[13] Eisner agreed, describing the park as "the Walt Disney Company's most important project until the year 2000."[14]

ADIOS SPAIN, BONJOUR FRANCE

Originally, the search for a suitable location included more than 1,200 different sites scattered throughout Europe.[15] France, Spain, Portugal, Germany, Italy, and Great Britain were all early contenders. But the Disney task force (headed by theme park boss Dick Nunis, Jim Cora, and Arvida chairman Chuck Cobb) quickly eliminated most of them as unworkable. England, for example, was scratched off the list because the largest available site was a measly three-hundred-acre tract outside of London. Italy was withdrawn from consideration because the largest parcels of land near major population centers were disrupted by mountain ranges. And Germany was nixed when it was determined that most Germans prefer to spend their vacation time in other countries. But size, topography, and European vacation patterns were not the only factors considered. Disney planners looked at climate, accessibility, land availability, governmental cooperation and stability, existing infrastructures, and the presence of a willing labor force and strong tourist base.[16]

Erasure from the narrowing list of prospects caused hard feelings among certain members of the European community. Great Britain was especially miffed when Disney executives decided to pursue sites on the other side of the English Channel. More than five years after being dismissed, reports in the *Times* of London mocked Disney's "excuse" that the Docklands of London had presented "various problems" for a joint theme park and resort venture.[17] A 1993 story in the British journal *New Statesman and Society* would later scowl that "Britain might have made a better fist of [Euro Disney] than France, if the success of [British theme park] Alton Towers is anything to go by."[18]

Aside from such grumbling, the whole of Europe remained interested in where the next Disney park would be built. By March of 1985, Disney executives had whittled down their selection of host countries to two: Spain and France. Each locale had distinct advantages. Spain, with its more balmy climate, offered the appeal of Disney's warm-weather parks in California and Florida. France, with its proximity to major population centers, promised a steady flow of tourist traffic. At first, Disney officials focused their attention on the Mediterranean town of Toulon in the south of France, not far from Marseilles. Its beauty and moderate climate made it a leading contender until engineers discovered a thick layer of bedrock under the soil—a feature that would have made construction a costly nightmare. Alicante, another tempting site located along Spain's Mediterranean coast, was also dismissed in the end, due to the strong mistral winds that trouble the region for several weeks each year.[19]

By 1985, both Spain and France were eagerly bidding for the right to host Disney's next theme park, with sites located just outside of Barcelona and Paris, respectively. And neither country was prepared to take no for an answer. Spain's minister of tourism and transport expressed the determination of his country's government in September. "We want to obtain Disneyland at any price!" he remarked.[20] With expectations that a multibillion-dollar theme park would help to lower high jobless rates, increase foreign exchange revenues, and fuel its efforts to become the nerve center of Europe, each side saw the new leisure development as the opportunity of a lifetime. Disney's track record for theme parks had been proven in California, Florida, and Japan. And, Disney's overall popularity was apparent all over Europe. Its future success was never held in doubt.[21]

In a desperate bid to outdo each other, officials from both Spain and France rolled out the red carpet to Walt Disney Productions. Each country extended a wide selection of sweeteners, ranging from financing deals to tax breaks, transportation networks, and even free land. Disney officials were in the enviable position of being able to stand back and let the two potential hosts present increasingly generous offers. But Spain's director of tourist promotion, Ignacio Vasallo, downplayed the idea of a bidding war to the press:

> Actually, it's more a question of choosing between two concepts than choosing between two countries. If they opt for an amusement park project in an area of concentrated population and relatively high income level, they'll go for Paris. If they want a big thematic complex, complete with other attractions such as golf, a yacht basin, beaches, convention facilities and a massive flow of tourists, with the touristic infrastructure already there, then Spain is the choice.[22]

Ultimately, Vasallo was wrong: Disney officials opted to build the large "thematic complex" he described, but decided against Spain. Despite its mild and sunny climate, its proximity to the Balearic Islands, its access to three major airports (Barcelona, Valencia, and Alicante), and a motorway that would have linked it with the rest of Europe—not to mention a local Catalonian government known to be more flexible than that of its Gallic neighbor—Spain emerged as first runner-up in a winner-takes-all game.

A major reason why Disney strategists chose the French site was its location. Because a projected 90 percent of all visitors to the park would be European (with the French accounting for 55 percent of the total, Germans another 14 percent, and the British another 8 percent), a central position on the Continent seemed crucial. Estimates showed that more than 50 million people lived within a 2-hour drive of the French park site; more than 68 million people lived within a 4-hour drive; more than 109 million lived within a 6-hour drive; and some 310 million were within a 2-hour flight. In addition, its proximity to the Eurotunnel (the transit passage being built beneath the English Channel) would put the park within a 2.5-hour traveling distance for British visitors coming from London's Waterloo Station as of 1993.[23]

Spain, in contrast, was far from Europe's center. It used a different rail line from the rest of Europe, and it lacked a nationwide highway network. Disney executives, curiously unmoved by the example of how Walt Disney World had created a new tourist hub in the geographical cul-de-sac that was central Florida, feared that locating a new park off the beaten path would restrict both attendance and revenues. Initial first-year forecasts of 6 million visitors to a Spanish Disney park (as compared to the 11.7–17.8 million projected for France) helped to seal the deal.[24] The rainy weather and often frigid temperatures of northern France were seen as a small concession overall. "If Tokyo had not taught us that the parks are weather-proof," noted one insider, "we might have chosen to go to Spain because of the warmer climate."[25]

The other main selling point of the French site was its position in relation to the city of Paris. According to Disney Vice President Dick Nunis, the choice came down to "the proximity of major airports, good roads, and of course, the attraction of Paris itself."[26] More than twenty million visitors each year passed through the City of Lights, making it Europe's single greatest tourist magnet. With this gushing flow of traffic, not to mention a residential population of ten million that was known to be "Disney-friendly," France seemed the perfect choice.[27] Cultural critic P. J. O'Rourke even remarked on the Gallic affection for Disney art in a 1983 commentary on the World Showcase at Florida's Epcot Center. "I don't know why Mickey Mouse isn't in the 'France' exhibit," he noted. "You see him all over Paris, where he is considered an existential figure of stature equal to Camus or Jerry Lewis."[28] So assimilated into French life was "Monsieur Mouse" that many children there did not even view him as an American creation.

SLIPPING FRANCE A MICKEY

On December 15, 1985, four months after the park site had been selected, Disney CEO Michael Eisner and France's Socialist prime minister Laurent Fabius signed an official letter of intent for the Euro Disney Resort. Several prominent newspapers celebrated the event. The French Socialist daily *Le Matin* featured Mickey Mouse dancing across its front page, and another newspaper, *Libération*, added his familiar mouse ears to its logo for the day. It seemed that all of France delighted in what one government official referred to as "the largest investment in recent history in France." *Time* magazine supported this conclusion, reporting that "while anti-Americanism has welled up in other areas of French life, no one ever seemed to have anything against Mickey Mouse."[29]

But some did. In fact, the "ravenous rat" had become the target of several vocal groups, including farmers, timber workers, and small villagers unhappy about losing their land and gaining Disney as a neighbor; carnival workers and small park operators worried about the possibly disabling competition; and Left Bank intellectuals concerned about the threat of American cultural imperialism running rampant across the French countryside.[30] The backlash against Mickey Mouse and the vulgar materialism that he was seen by some to embody was further heightened by a number of popular French magazines, which ran stories forecasting only gloom and doom. One such journal pictured a monstrously large Mickey on its cover, smiling as he hovered Godzilla-like over the Parisian cityscape, ready to destroy all in his path. Another showed him in the cockpit of an American fighter plane over Paris with a caption reading: "Invasion Site."[31] To some French, Mickey Mouse had become a rodent in need of extermination.

Mickey's status as a mercurial symbol in French life cannot be overestimated. His celebrity was seized upon by opponents to the Euro Disney project, who needed a central icon around which   23 they could wrap anti-Disney—and ultimately, anti-American—sentiments. But his widespread fame also invested the theme park with a sort of immediate credibility and cultural authority among Disney consumers in Europe. The smiling face of Mickey Mouse, in its ability to mean many different things to many different people, proved to be a versatile and polarizing force in France. By providing a strong visual hook to supporters and detractors alike, it effectively branded the Euro Disney Resort as something much, much more than another leisure park.

Most deeply affected by the decision to locate Euro Disney in France were the people who lived and worked in Marne-la-Vallée and its surrounding communities: Bailly-Romainvilliers (population 609), Chessy (1,137), Coupvray (2,403), Magny-le-Hongre (338), and Serris (925). Because family connections to the land stretched back generations in many cases, their emotional distress was profound. The malaise stemmed from two factors: the intended use of the property and the unmistakable sense that they had been sold out by their own government. Locals did not understand how the sacrifice of excellent country land, which had been used by farmers and hunters throughout the ages, could possibly be justified. The very idea of developing the site into a fantasy theme park—an American one, no less—seemed both wasteful and blasphemous.

Longtime residents were also upset by their government's seeming indifference toward its own people. Not only had French officials failed to consult or inform them on the proceedings that would drastically change their lives, they also had demanded total and immediate cooperation with efforts to accommodate Disney. That the people of these small villages had no say in the matter of their own future became evident when the state revealed its plan to purchase—or, if necessary, seize—their property "in the public interest" under the law of eminent domain. The sense of betrayal generated by this act fueled strong feelings of hostility toward the French government and the proposed Disney park.

Bruno Aube, president of the one-thousand-member Association for the Protection of People Concerned by the Euro Disney Development (APPE), which was established to defend the interests of locals, was appalled by France's lack of concern for its people. He remarked on the irony of seizing French land for the business interests of a country that espoused its belief in justice for all. "In a liberal society," Aube noted, "this is a strange procedure. It is a procedure completely opposed to American attitudes on rights and property." Given that laws of expropriation are alive and well in the United States, Aube's comment was misinformed. But it did effectively question whether or not the spirit of this measure—which provided for the purchase of land at normal market price so that it could be used "for a military base, a railroad, or a nuclear power station"—was being violated if invoked to build, of all things, a commercial theme park. Aube promised that APPE would "impose itself" as a partner in the Euro Disney project by seeking assurances that those who lost their jobs would receive proper retraining, by demanding that any needs created by the project (such as new roads and more police) would not cause an increase in taxes, and by initiating legal proceedings whenever possible.[32]

Residents of the five rural towns neighboring the park site also established a union to resist the ill effects of the Disney development: the Syndicat d'Agglomeration Nouvelle des Portes de la Brie (SAN). Headed by Charles Boetto, its mission was to protect village life as they knew it against the impending flood of tourists and other "delinquents."[33] "We want to become a city that welcomes Disney parks," noted Boetto, "and not the city of Disney parks."[34] A local mayor agreed, stating that he would refuse to serve as the elected official for any town known—officially, or otherwise—as "Mickeyville." But their battle would be a difficult one. In the next few years, the population of the five villages would swell to more than triple as Euro Disney employees and others moved into the area. And their combined land holdings would be reduced dramatically. Bailly-Romainvilliers alone would lose two-thirds of its total acreage to the development.

Across the landscape of Marne-la-Vallée, opposition to the park was visible. Locals put up signs along roadways and stuck pitchforks through effigies of Mickey Mouse at public demonstrations. Anti-Disney graffiti and posters were plastered on public walls everywhere. Some pictured Mickey Mouse in a trench coat, grabbing his crotch Michael Jackson–style, in open defiance of local politesse. Others featured a saddened mouse reacting to signs that read "Stay Home, Mickey." Perhaps the most scathing of all showed Uncle Scrooge, the miserly millionaire duck (known as "Picsou" in French), with his feathered fists clenched. The bubble over his head read: "I don't give a damn for the locals. I buy land, I buy villages. I buy the residents. I buy everything." It wasn't long before angry villagers snidely began referring to Euro Disneyland as "Euro Picsouland."[35]

But not all local residents joined in the crusade. Philippe Mancel, mayor of Serris, observed the futility of trying to block the new development. "One realizes it's a lost cause to be against Euro Disneyland," he commented.[36] Michel Colombe, mayor of Bailly-Romainvilliers, concurred, adding, "We prefer to get maximum benefit from an operation that, in any case, will be imposed."[37] And Olivier Bourjot, the mayor of Chessy, where most of Euro Disney would be located, suspended judgment. "According to the newspapers," he noted, "Chessy will soon be the richest community in France. But I will wait to see before I believe it."[38] Jean-Claude Thoenig, an expert on French local politics, observed that Euro Disney had served as a much-needed catalyst for developing the region east of Paris and argued that even if the park failed, the new infrastructure would benefit local residents. "It would have been done anyway—the western suburbs are saturated," he commented, "but [development] would have taken a great deal longer."[39]

A final group protesting the Disney development was made up of traveling carnival and small park operators, who blasted the park as a threat, an environmental hazard, and a "dagger in the back." Marcel Campton, president of the Syndicate of

Amusement Parks of France, worried that Euro Disney's presence in France would wipe out small traditional fairs and threaten the lifespan of France's parks. He also feared that the pollution generated by such a massive development, from litter to exhaust fumes and water contamination, would take its toll on the region. But the thing that disturbed Campton most was the sense that he and his countrymen had been misled by their own government. Claiming to have been assured by French officials in December 1985 that "nothing would be signed" with Disney on the theme park deal, he was shocked to learn later that month that Fabius and Eisner had moved forward and concluded an official preliminary agreement.[40]

MICKEY MOUSE DEALINGS

On March 16, 1986, all plans came to a halt with the defeat of Prime Minister Laurent Fabius's Socialist government in the general elections. People across France and Europe wondered if the political upset would spell the end of the Euro Disney Resort. For Disney executives, the consequences were potentially serious. All of the time and energy they had invested in negotiations (with some thirty-six different offices from France's state and local governments) had come to naught. The many agreements and compromises the two parties had hammered out, but not yet made official, vanished into thin air with the newly deposed administration. Worst of all, it happened only two days before the scheduled signing of the final contract. Negotiations would have to be reopened from scratch—if, in fact, the new government was willing to support the concept of a Disney theme park at all.[41]

Of course, it was. Disney executives had taken precautions to make certain of this before the election. In fact, the moment Fabius's chances of reelection began to look bleak, Disney vice president Dick Nunis and his team hopped a plane to Paris to meet with Jacques Chirac, the Parisian mayor, who was favored to be named the next premier of France. Chirac, who had served as prime minister previously (under President Valéry Giscard d'Estaing, 1974–1976) and run unsuccessfully against Mitterand in the 1981 elections, came from a different political perspective than his Socialist counterparts. But he was still very much in favor of the Euro Disney project, which promised to reduce France's chronically high unemployment rate of 10 percent.[42] At his meeting with Disney officials, Chirac promised that if elected, his new conservative government would be just as enthusiastic about the theme park as Fabius's. He even suggested that certain measures would be taken to cut through the red tape in France's notorious bureaucracy.[43]

One such measure was the appointment of a single chief negotiator to represent the interests of France. Jean-René Bernard, a high-ranking official who had previously served as France's ambassador to Mexico, was selected to fill the newly created role of "premier minister." He became, in the words of Disney historian Ron Grover, "the glue that kept the French team together."[44] At the first official meeting between the two sides, which took place at Vaux-le-Vicomte (a seventeenth-century castle Louis XIV had used as a model for Versailles), officials from France and the Walt Disney Company agreed that the letter of intent signed three months earlier was ambiguous and without great meaning. Both parties wished to honor the spirit of the agreement, but believed that more specific provisions would have to be spelled out.

During almost fifteen months of talks, mediated by interpreters, the deal nearly fell apart several times. But in the end, Prime Minister Chirac made good on his promises to the Walt Disney Company. On July 11, 1986, less than four months after his election, the regional council for the Île de France area approved plans for the Euro Disney Resort by an overwhelming vote of 112 to 20. Only members of the Communist Party opposed it: they objected to the idea of spending any governmental money on such a park before providing for more immediate public needs.[45] But these protest votes were washed away in the flood of political support for the Euro Disney Resort.

On March 12, 1987, Michael Eisner officially named Robert Fitzpatrick president of Euro Disney. Fitzpatrick, who had been president of the California Institute of the Arts (a school founded by the Disney family in the 1960s to develop the visual and performing arts) since 1975, had also served as the director of the Los Angeles Festival, as dean of students at Johns Hopkins University, and as a Baltimore city councilman.[46] These experiences, plus other unique qualifications (such as a graduate degree in medieval French literature, fluency in French, and marriage to a native Frenchwoman) made him a natural choice to be Disney's cultural ambassador to France. "He is not an American like the others," remarked one of his European colleagues. "He has read Balzac and he knows that Spain is down to the left on the map."[47] Fitzpatrick would play an important role in selling the Euro Disney project to continental audiences and in helping American planning teams to avoid political and cultural land mines in the start-up process.

On March 24, 1987, less than two weeks later, Michael Eisner and French prime minister Jacques Chirac met at the Hôtel Matignon to sign a $7.5 billion final contract for the Euro Disney Resort. The ceremony was attended by a flock of right-wing, pro-business heads of relevant regional authorities. It was, and still is, considered to be a landmark event of the Chirac administration, an inspired capture of major foreign investment that promised to create tens of thousands of jobs for France.[48]

THE ART OF THE DEAL

A top priority of Disney executives during negotiations in Europe was to avoid repeating past mistakes—especially those made while dickering with Japanese officials over terms for Tokyo Disneyland. Disney execs wanted much more than a forty-five-year contract that limited them to 10 percent of admission fees, 5 percent of food and merchandise sales, and 5 percent of licensing fees.[49] Disney officials wanted a piece of the action this time, a chunk of the ownership interest. They could not bear to sit back

29

and wring their hands again as hundreds of millions of dollars in profits that might have been theirs flowed into other pockets. The "risk-free" financial agreements for Tokyo Disneyland, which had come to be regarded as one of the greatest blunders in Disney corporate history, stood as a painful reminder that overly cautious deal making begat even more cautious profits.

Disney executives, however, had more in mind than simply "righting" past wrongs this time around. With plans to open a third Florida theme park in December 1989 (the Disney-MGM Studios would cost some $500 million), they simply had to strike a good deal in France.[50] So they created two separate French owner companies: Euro Disney SNC (a finance vehicle that would own the park for the first twenty years) and Euro Disney SCA (the public holding company that would own it thereafter).[51] French officials, however, thwarted the Walt Disney Company's attempts to maximize its ownership interests in the development by limiting Disney's shares to less than half the total. The Walt Disney Company complied and reduced its stake in Euro Disney SCA accordingly, to 49 percent (a full 49 percent more than its ownership interest in Tokyo Disneyland).

But the Walt Disney Company's profit margin was not limited to its ownership interests. It also arranged to receive royalties on the sale of tickets, food, and souvenirs (in the same percentages as at its Tokyo theme park). These were projected to bring in $350 million each year over and above the revenues generated by licensing, management, and incentive fees. The greatest "profit" of all, however, took a nonfinancial form: decision power. Because of a wrinkle in French law that allowed majority votes by shareholders to be overruled in certain circumstances of ownership (of which this was one), the Walt Disney Company retained 100 percent control of Euro Disney SCA.[52] So despite its limited ownership in the park, its control over the operation and development of the Euro Disney Resort would be virtually limitless.

Yet such benefits of ownership and control cannot be fully appreciated outside of all the other concessions made by the

French government. Foremost among these was a generous financing deal that enabled the Walt Disney Company to minimize its investment (and therefore, its risk) in the multibillion-dollar park. The French government provided a $960 million twenty-year loan at low, subsidized interest rates of 7.85 percent. It secured another $1.6 billion in floating-rate loans from a syndicate of forty-five banks. And it offered an additional $1 billion in loans from the state-owned Caisse des Dépôts. The rest of the money, some $400 million, came from special partnerships formed to buy properties and lease them back. In the end, the Walt Disney Company put up only $250 million for 49 percent of the equity capital in the company that would operate the park and 17.5 percent of a French partnership that owned the land.[53]

The French government also practically made a gift of the park site, selling 4,841 acres of land to the Walt Disney Company at 1971 farmland prices: only $5,000 per acre—a mere fraction of its then market value.[54] The low purchase price had the added benefit of ensuring that property taxes would start from a low base. Even more importantly, the French government granted the Walt Disney Company the right of first refusal on the sale of about 10,000 acres surrounding the park site, which enabled it to prevent parasitic hotel and leisure developments from springing up and restricting future development, as happened at the Disneyland park in Anaheim, California. In short, any outsiders wanting to build in this "exclusion zone" would first need the permission of the Walt Disney Company, which would be able to sell (or not sell) chunks of it to developers at any time, for any price.[55]

Another set of perks addressed Euro Disney's need for new auto routes and mass transportation systems that would connect the rural site with the rest of France and Europe. State and regional authorities of the French government agreed to extend the RER suburban railway lines another six miles from Paris to the Euro Disney Resort at a cost of $125 million. They also agreed to put in a new North-Atlantic line of its 156-mile-per-hour Train à Grand Vitesse (TGV) that would, by 1994, connect Marne-la-

Vallée with Brussels, Geneva, and the future Eurotunnel.[56] France even provided a custom-built RER and TGV interchange station only 150 yards from the entrance gate to Euro Disneyland.[57] Finally, it paid an additional $105 million to build six-lane highways that would link the park with Brussels, Frankfurt, and nearby Charles de Gaulle airport.

The French government provided other deals as well. It coughed up $400 million to install water, electricity, telephone, and other basic services. It cut the 18.6 percent value-added tax (VAT) on Euro Disneyland's ticket sales to just 7 percent. It even agreed to outside arbitration (rather than the French court system) for any disputes that might arise involving the park.[58] In its issue of October 9, 1989, the *Times* reported that the Walt Disney Company was making out like a bandit:

> Clear winner is the parent Disney corporation. It takes half all dividends, and royalties and management fees which from 1996 will exceed pre-tax profits. Obvious loser, in cash terms alone, is the French government, which pumped in soft loans and obligingly provided the surrounding transport network, including a Channel tunnel link.[59]

French journalist Gilles Smadja expressed similar disapproval in a book he penned, entitled *Mickey: The Sting* (1988), which denounced the French government for spending such huge sums on park-related infrastructure.[60] Bernard Poupard, a writer for the French magazine *Études*, was equally angered by the concessions. "What [has] pushed the State, the Region, the Department to offer such a red carpet to the Americans?" he demanded. "Everything is happening as if Disney was invited [to France]."[61]

The answer to Poupard's query is straightforward: the Euro Disney development, which dwarfed every other tourism project in European history, promised to be one of France's biggest economic bonuses ever. In the eyes of French officials, the inducements were but a small price to pay for a vacation complex that would reduce unemployment and increase tourist revenues by a full 10 percent.[62] Projections indicated that Euro Disney would create as many as 30,000 new construction jobs, 12,000 on-site positions, and another 30,000 jobs in off-site servicing. And these figures were likely to be low, given that Japan's smaller Disney development had created more than 150,000 jobs in the greater Tokyo area.[63] John Forsgren, Euro Disney's chief financial officer, explained that the generosity of the French government could be attributed to one factor. "This financing arrangement has been possible," he observed, "because Disney has a solid track record."[64]

WHO'S AFRAID OF THE BIG BAD MOUSE?

In addition to the cries of resistance coming from journalists and affected groups in the Marne-la-Vallée area were snorts of disgust from members of the Left Bank intellectual elite, who enjoy much more of a voice in the mainstream press than their U.S. counterparts. They denounced the park as "the fifty-first American state" and "a black stain on the soul of France."[65] Such "champagne socialists," as one wry observer referred to them, defamed the Euro Disney venture by painting it as "the encroachment of an alien civilization next to the city of enlightenment" and "the mother cell of an American virus that would taint the blood of French culture."[66] Writer Alain Finkielkraut described Euro Disney as "a terrifying giant's step toward world homogenization" and lamented that it would crush the imaginations of France's children, reducing them to spectators and consumers of American entertainment.[67] Novelist Jean-Marie Rouart concurred, arguing that the park represented the transformation of culture from craft into industry. "If we do not resist it," he warned, "the kingdom of profit will create a world that will have all the appearance of civilization and all the savage reality of barbarism."[68] Others were even more bitter. "I hope with all my heart," admitted Jacques Juillard, an editor for *Le Nouvel Observateur*, "for a May 1992 that will set fire to Euro Disneyland."[69]

Perhaps most damaging of all were the words of Paris theater director Ariane Mnouchkine, who labeled Euro Disney "a cultural Chernobyl," an epithet that would be quoted again and again in press reports of the developing venture.[70] That Mnouchkine, a personal friend of Euro Disney president Robert Fitzpatrick, made such a remark to the media undoubtedly stung. But it also came as a terrible surprise. Not long before, she had accepted his invitation to visit Disneyland in California and, by all accounts, had had a nice time. Mnouchkine had even stopped to pose for a picture with Mickey Mouse. When her damning words hit the press, Fitzpatrick admitted, he almost fell off his chair.[71]

Mnouchkine's comment reflected a fear that the new theme park would contribute to the "Coca-Colonization" of French landscapes.[72] But it also seemed to betray a belated guilt for having had fun at a place designed and operated by American capitalists. To admit enjoyment was to admit defeat in the continuing battle to assert a superior cultural identity. *Time* reporter Richard Corliss mocked Mnouchkine and other hateful critics. "Few sights," he wrote, "are as droll as that of the European intelligentsia trying to have a rotten time. . . . Where their children (who buy 10 million copies of *Le Journal de Mickey*) see a mouse, French intellectuals smell a rat."[73] Another writer found the explosive scorn of these critics laughable. "The fact that Mickey and Minnie manage to draw against them the holy alliance of right-thinking progressives and conservatives ought to bring them the Oscar for humor," he noted. "When the grumpy Allan Bloom compares Disneyland to Plato's cavern, that hell of ignorance and servitude, I have to laugh. . . . Along with the hate that the little mouse (or the rat, as its detractors call it) awakens, wrapped in a ridiculous and overweening elitism, there also figures a raging and sometimes ravaging provincialism."[74]

Most French intellectuals ignored the relentless optimism of Disney officials and condemned the new theme park venture as another example of U.S. pop culture: glitzy, sugar-coated, and ultimately empty.[75] Writer Jean Cau scorned the would-be park as "a horror made of cardboard, plastic and appalling colors, a construction of hardened chewing gum and idiotic folklore taken straight out of comic books written for obese Americans."[76] British writer Stephen Bayley echoed Cau's disdain:

> There is no gainsaying the optimism, commitment and quality of Euro Disney, a brilliantly buffed-up exercise in professional leisure management, but equally the fastidious aesthete is lost for words at the grotesque vulgarity of it all, a vulgarity doubly damaging because it is so effortless to consume. . . . It is all so undemandingly mindless, the Prince of Wales might have been the master architect. There is no grit in the mechanism, no flies in the soup, no truculent waiters, no exaltation, no boredom. Forget exploration or hazard; Euro Disney offers a version of culture with the effect of intravenous Valium and elevator music.[77]

"Euro Disney is kitsch; it is bad art," Bayley went on to conclude. "This is not to say that it will not be immensely popular because, as H. L. Mencken knew, no one ever went bust underestimating the public's taste. With its roster of postmodern architects and its seductive catalogue of risk-free themes—no Liverpool dockside or Naples back alley here—Euro Disney takes underestimation to new heights."[78]

Many such critics were careful to point out that their revulsion for the "Euro Dismal" project, as they gleefully called it, was not rooted in anti-Americanism, but rather in a general distaste for mass-produced simulations of reality.[79] It just so happened that most of these originated in the United States. Jean-Francois Revel, author of *Ni Marx, Ni Jesus,* argued that anti-Americanism had never truly been a popular sentiment in France. "French society has never been viscerally american-ophobic," he explained. "It has always borrowed from the vitality and the creativity of our 'allies.'"[80] But most intellectuals were fundamentally unable to

35

imagine either of these qualities in a Disney park. Dennis Lacorne of *Esprit* expressed his intolerance with more than a little sarcasm:

> It is now possible to precisely measure France's cultural de-lay, since 31 years have elapsed between the creation of Dis-neyland in Anaheim, California and the decision to implant in France one that will never be anything, to use the expres-sion of Jacques Juillard, but "the copy of an imitation."[81]

French writer Frederic Ferney seconded this statement by argu-ing that "in the Pirate Cave or on Main Street, simulation op-poses representation. The image is no longer the reflection of reality, it masks the absence of reality."[82] That Disney parks in America were "false" worlds seemed true—and horrible—enough to many French. But the idea that Euro Disney would be nothing more than a replica of these already false places in the United States made it even more deplorable in intellectual circles.

While many in France were scrutinizing the would-be theme park as an important cultural phenomenon, Disney executives tried to position it as simple family entertainment. "We're not try-ing to sell anything but fun," commented one corporate insider.[83] Michael Eisner invited skeptics to visit the park before attacking it and offered cheerful reassurance: "If they bring their children to Disneyland, they'll have a good time."[84] Fitzpatrick concurred, refuting the argument of a Paris museum director who had claimed that no connoisseur of the high arts would ever hop on a train to Marne-la-Vallée to see Mickey Mouse. "Diversion is also a form of culture," he responded. "The French know it well. Have they forgotten?"[85] Even Christian Cardon, head of the interminis-terial government delegation supervising the Disney project, sided with Mickey's team. "French culture cannot be threatened by Disney," he asserted. "Just because an amusement park will open, university students are not going to stop studying Sartre."[86]

Others responded to French resistance with frustration. One

spokeswoman for Euro Disney demanded: "Who are these

Frenchmen anyway? We offer them the dream of a lifetime and lots of jobs. They treat us like invaders."[87] James Lileks, an American columnist, agreed. "If I were Donald Duck," he wrote, "I'd wonder how to give someone the middle finger when I only had four of them. . . . Most nations would be happy to have a $4 billion enterprise set up shop within their borders, but not France." He did, however, acknowledge that not everything from the United States was worthy of critical acclaim:

American culture can be loud, brash, full of rude animal energy, a monster truck climbing over local folkways. But Euro Disney won't do anything that wasn't begun long ago. It's not like we forced the French to adore unwashed has-beens such as Mickey Rourke or insisted the government give medals to gibbering idiots like Jerry Lewis. They are perfectly able to ruin their culture without Disney's help.[88]

Views like these must have been music to the ears of Euro Disney planners. "All these critiques regarding so-called threats to French culture seem a little theatrical to me," remarked Fitzpatrick. "Some in France would like to put up a Maginot line of the imagination. To them, I respond, you have held on more than one thousand years and resisted many invasions, if today you fear the arrival of a mouse, it's your problem."[89] Even Revel supported the claim that Euro Disney would not mark the end of civilization in France. "If French culture can be squashed by Mickey Mouse," he wrote, "or more exactly by simply moving Mickey geographically, it would have to be disturbingly fragile."[90]

EMBRACING THE MOUSE

Despite the much-publicized resistance toward the new theme park, Disney executives were not fatalastic. "In America," noted Fitzpatrick, "one easily accepts that which comes from other   37 cultures. . . . In France, one reflects, one debates. It's curious, this difference of mentality. When I am in the United States, I am expected to make conversation. In France, to participate in debates. This reflection in loud voices, this French manifestation, it's also a way to absorb things. That's why all this contestation which regularly manifests itself in certain newspapers doesn't frighten me."[91] Eisner agreed that the situation was less perilous than it sounded. Remarking on a possible $3 billion theme park that the Walt Disney Company had recently walked away from building in southern California, he noted: "We've had less problems in France than we had in Long Beach."[92]

But the confidence of Disney executives was bolstered by something else. The public opinion polls conducted by Michel Giraud and the regional council of the Île-de-France indicated upward of 86 percent approval for the new park, confirming their hunch that Disney supporters greatly outnumbered opponents.[93] Never doubting for a moment that the people of France—and Europe, as a whole—would be ready and willing to plunk down their francs, marks, pounds, and lira when the gates opened, they forged ahead with plans to build the greatest Disney theme park ever. Fitzpatrick explained away some of the bad press it had received. "In France, more than the United States," he argued, "there's a small group, an arts mafia, who sees anything popular, anything American, as endangering French culture. Don't think that's the French public view."[94] Guy Sorman, a French economist and author, seconded his assessment, asserting that "anti-Americanism in France only mobilizes the elites. The people, they have always loved Walt Disney."[95]

But were the social classes at odds over Disney art? French minister of culture Jack Lang, a man so powerful that he controlled the government's second largest budget, questioned the validity of such a conclusion:

I challenge this distinction between the people and intellectuals. That is as insulting to one as to the other. The people are not sheep and are capable of responding with enthusiasm to works of beauty and great artistic quality. Many French artists aim toward an immense public without resorting to demagoguery or vulgarity. I admire the genius of Walt Disney, but I must admit that my preference goes to the America of Faulkner, Coppola, Pollock, and not to one standardized America. I prefer America the audacious, I prefer its innovation to the America of clichés and a consumer society.[96]

Lang was "a man with a past," so to speak, of protecting French culture from American "corruption." In 1981, he boycotted the American film festival in the name of "superior French cinema interests." In 1982, he addressed the world conference of UNESCO in Mexico by stating that "[w]e are calling a veritable crusade against . . . financial and cultural imperialism." And in August 1985, he explained that "if there is an American cultural 'invasion' in Europe, it is the Europeans, and especially all the French, who are responsible due to their passivity."[97] As a result, it came as little surprise when he not only declined the honor of cutting the ribbon on Euro Disneyland's opening day, but announced that he had no intention of even attending the ceremony.[98]

Yet Lang's asserted disgust with "standardized" American culture deserves closer examination. For, like Mnouchkine, he too had been guilty of enjoying its pleasures. At a ceremony for Sylvester Stallone, who was being awarded the Chevalier of Arts and Letters (the same honor bestowed upon Walt Disney in 1935) for his contributions to cinema, a beaming Lang decorated the action star. One spectator who observed Lang posturing before television cameras commented on the irony of seeing France's most aggressive watchdog of culture hobnobbing with Rambo. "Envy and snobbery often go together," he noted.[99] But Lang defended himself in an interview. "I have never, never denounced 'the cultural invasion' of Europe by America," he claimed. "This expression, which is not mine, horrifies me. . . . I am one of the principal supporters of modern American culture."[100]

Lang's behavior typifies France's longstanding love-hate relationship with American popular culture. For decades, the French have been endlessly fascinated with all things American: Clint Eastwood westerns, Levi's blue jeans, Madonna videos, Marlboro cigarettes, and McDonald's cuisine have made themselves as much at home in France as in the United States. Yet many patrons of Americana have claimed to detest these things, even while pushing their francs across the counter to acquire them. Reporter Richard Corliss put things in perspective:

> [W]hen the French select Mickey Rourke as a patron saint and Mickey Mouse as the antichrist, they are simply proving their obsession with things American. U.S. pop is their guilty pleasure. The French love American culture even as they love to hate it. Four of their five top-grossing films are from Hollywood, tepid versions of U.S. game shows blanket French TV, and it isn't just American tourists who patronize the Burger King restaurants on the Champs-Élysées. . . . The naysayers—those who approach someone returning from a visit to the site and ask, with anticipatory glee, "Well, is it grotesque?"—are simply not Euro Disney's customers. One must remind them that this is an amusement park, a place of diversion for children and their indulgent parents. Attendance is not mandatory.[101]

Philosopher Michel Serres summed up America's place in French society. "It is not America that is invading us," he noted. "It is we who adore it, who adopt its fashions and above all, its words."[102]

Many in France made no secret of their enthusiasm for Euro Disney and American culture in general. Unmoved by the warnings put forth by figures such as Socialist deputy Max Gallo, who predicted that the park would "bombard France with uprooted creations that are to culture what fast food is to gastronomy," they looked forward to Euro Disney's opening and indicated that they would come in droves.[103] The covers and headlines of European newsstand items said it all: "In Paris Today à la Mode Means à l'Américaine," "Culture: Let's Not Fear America," and "The French Love the United States."[104]

One French writer, André Glucksmann, fiercely defended Euro Disney, proving that not all intellectuals looked upon it as Armageddon. "This may come as a surprise," he wrote, "but I don't feel attacked either by an outside enemy or by a hostile foreigner. Disney does not violate our secular culture; he lands in good company, with Charles Perrault and the Brothers Grimm. Europe sent beautiful words across the Atlantic, its fairy tales, Pinocchio, Alice; they came back in pictures. This heartening toing and fro-ing is only the last of a long series." Glucksmann did not stop there:

> Hollywood is the high place not of America's cultural imperialism but of Europe's! The Old Continent sent Charlie Chaplin, Fritz Lang, Marlene, Garbo and many, many others who "colonized" the imagination of the New World. So forgive us for being wild about MGM-Universal-Warner Bros, about Broadway, about Satchmo singing, after Lotte Lenya, "Mack the Knife." We are only taking back our due, plus, as a premium, Orson Welles, Marilyn, Tex Avery, brothers, sisters. And Walt Disney.[105]

According to Glucksmann, the Euro Disney Resort was anything but a foreign intrusion. It was a cultural reclamation, a continental homecoming, and a greatly desired *import* of Americanized fun. "Kindly seven dwarfs, make yourselves at home," he concluded, "here you will never be invading, just coming home."[106]

Glucksmann also took issue with the "aristocratic disdain" of intellectuals and their charges that Euro Disney would "irradiate millions of children . . . whiplash their imaginations and manipulate their dreams."[107] "The serious minds who head off . . . on crusade are missing the provisional and imaginary side of the place," he explained. "The visitor himself does not confuse

41

the dream and the reality; buying his admission ticket, he knows well that he who laughs on Sunday, works on Monday. The stroller will not marry Cinderella or live in Sleeping Beauty's castle. Sometimes he allows himself a little humor and savors, along with his popcorn, this 'end of history' that so causes professors to cogitate and split hairs."[108] French film director Philippe Labro echoed this sentiment. "A child's imagination," he noted, "is . . . subject to all kinds of influences but it is also limitless. Let's have a little faith in children's intuition and intelligence."[109]

Peter Mikelbank, a reporter for the *Washington Post*, characterized the people of France in less than flattering terms. "The French are a confounding people," he wrote. "Arrogant, charming, childish, melancholic, and poetic; delightful, rude, intuitive, didactic, proud, petulant, principled, wildly xenophobic, and they've lacked humor since Molière. They are often contrary for its own sake; in France, you can toss a coin and come up with a controversy. And there are few topics as controversial in France as the state of the country's culture."[110] However overwrought this generalization may be, it does shed light upon the complexity of cultural identification in France. Adam Gopnik, writing for the *New Yorker*, insisted that the French are not chauvinists. "But," he hastened to add, "they remain chauvinists about their judgment. Increasingly, their judgment is all the culture they have."[111] Lileks was even more merciless: "The French are different. . . . [They] bring such panache, hauteur and high-mindedness to disliking the rest of the world that you get the impression they have actually accomplished something of significance since 1789."[112]

Popular culture scholar Todd Gitlin put the ongoing debate about Euro Disney in proper perspective. "American popular culture doesn't erase all vernacular alternatives," he noted. "The new semiculture coexists with local cultures more than it replaces them."[113] In other words, Euro Disney would not be doing battle to erase French or European cultures. It would simply be trying to make itself at home among them. And, as French writer Jean-

François Revel pointed out, culture circulates. Any effort to attach one nationality to such a living, breathing, and continually transforming entity is inherently misguided. The Euro Disney Resort, described by one journalist as "an extraordinary triumph of commerce over ideology," would prove itself to be much more than this.[114]

WHEN YOU WISH UPON A STOCK

Amid continuing controversies over the European development, Disney executives began to prepare for the official launch of stock. Because the Walt Disney Company controlled 49 percent of Euro Disney SCA (the public holding company that owned the theme park), 51 percent of all shares could be sold to investors. But the French government, which had restricted Disney's ownership interest in the park to less than half, was concerned that American investors might buy up the remaining stock quickly, locking Europeans (and especially the French) out of the profits to be earned. As a result, it required that shares be offered first to residents of the European community, who would then be permitted to sell them to American investors after a period of ninety days. The Walt Disney Company agreed to these terms, and on September 12, 1989, it unveiled plans in its pathfinder prospectus to make 51 percent of the stock—more than 85.88 million shares—available for purchase in the European markets.[115]

Half of this stock was to be offered to French investors on the Paris Bourse, and half would be split between London and Brussels for distribution around the rest of Europe at 72 francs (about $11.30) per share.[116] According to Gary Wilson, chief financial officer of the California-based Walt Disney Company, the issue would represent "the first public offering of shares in all EC countries simultaneously."[117] To build excitement, the Walt Disney Company undertook a ten-nation road show tour of Europe for financial analysts and news media; it ran advertisements in nearly forty European newspapers; and it produced a huge television ad

43

campaign that aired on several networks. On October 8, 1989, the Walt Disney Company released a prospectus containing detailed financial information as well as a full measure of Disney hype. Images of Mickey, Minnie, and castles were splashed across the front and back covers, and elaborate descriptions of rides featuring cowboys, pirates, and fairy-tale characters were included within.[118]

In both London and Paris, the launch of the $1.2 billion "Mickey Mouse share flotation" was marked by a grand ceremony. At the Broadgate complex in London, the offering turned into a celebration. Appearances by Minnie, Goofy, and Donald brought roars of applause from the crowds. But the scene was quite different at the Paris Bourse. As Michael Eisner took the stage to launch the sale of Euro Disney stock, he noticed that something was awry. The Disney characters who had arrived with him were not alone. Ten people in the audience, lurking behind dime-store Mickey Mouse masks, glared up at him. They were young members of the Communist Party who had come to protest the concessions of more than $6 billion made by the French government. They waved signs that read "Mickey, Go Home" and "We do not want to be Euro Disneyland's Indians" in a determined effort to disrupt the ceremony and draw attention to their cause.[119]

Their efforts were successful. Chanting and screaming, the demonstrators hurled eggs, flour, and tomato sauce at Eisner and other Disney officials, sending them scurrying behind nearby pillars. The protesters also circulated leaflets that carried a message from the group's leader, Communist Youth general secretary Jacques Perreux, who objected to the 41 billion francs of public money being spent on park-related infrastructure rather than on schools, suburban ghettos, and training programs for the unemployed.[120] Eisner expressed surprise, noting that it was "the first time I have ever been on that side of a demonstration. I grew up in the Vietnam era of protests."[121] He also stressed that the tens of thousands of new jobs to be created by

44

Euro Disney would benefit France and all of Europe. While many present observed that the protest seemed to be aimed more at French government officials than at the Walt Disney Company, it was not they who ended up with egg—or globs of flour and ketchup—on their faces.

Because news of this colorful disturbance was picked up and circulated by journalists around the world, people everywhere were reminded of France's supposedly united opposition to the park, both in print and on television. International media reports rarely acknowledged the much greater levels of popular support for Euro Disney in France and Europe. Marc Fumaroli, a professor at the Collège de France, argued that positive coverage was unnecessary, as all media attention—good or bad—ultimately served to promote the theme park. He warned demonstrators to be wise. "The temptation is alive," he commented, "to shout against Euro Disneyland. Let's admit that it's a little late. It would have been necessary to mobilize before the deal was concluded. The big notables of the left and right who built this 'cultural affair' and who preached its virtues didn't meet any resistance when it was necessary. The more one shouts now, the more one raises the decibels of publicity for Disney, the more one serves it."[122]

Despite opposing factions, European investment activity revealed true levels of enthusiasm for—and confidence in—the success of Disney's newest venture. Approximately 86 million shares sold. And on October 11, 1989, just six days after the stock launch, the public offer throughout Europe was oversubscribed by at least eleven times. It seemed that everyone wanted to cash in on the inevitable success of the new Disney park. Share allocations were announced ten days later, and official trading began in London, Paris, and Brussels on November 6, 1989. Traders attributed the "unprecedented demand" for this stock to Disney's massive publicity program, which left would-be investors literally clamoring for shares.[123]

45

THE SPREAD OF DISNEY FEVER

Surprisingly, enthusiasm for the Euro Disney Resort was not contained to Western Europe. Countries on the other side of the iron curtain were also hit hard by waves of Disney fever. In July 1988, following a ten-day visit to the United States, Hungary's prime minister Karoly Grosz made a formal bid to host Eastern Europe's first Disney park. Like officials representing Spain, Portugal, and Britain years earlier, he campaigned hard for the deal, touting Hungary's rapidly expanding tourist industry as well as its history of leading the Eastern bloc in introducing economic reforms. He even leveraged the fact that his country had been the first to welcome McDonald's to Eastern Europe (the first outlet opened in April 1988) as proof of Hungary's commitment to American enterprises.[124]

But proposals for an Eastern European Disney theme park, as well as ideas for the one under construction outside of Paris, had to be seriously reconsidered with the fall of the Berlin Wall. This event, which not only united West and East Germany, but also opened up Eastern Europe, marked the beginning of another stage of this region's involvement with Euro Disney. Dave Kehr, a reporter for the *Chicago Tribune*, commented on the dramatically changing nature of political landscapes in Europe:

> If the Berlin Wall was the perfect symbol of the old Europe—divided, defeated, depressed—Euro Disneyland promises to embody the new, go-go Europe of the 1990s. . . . As the Berlin Wall crumbles, taking the discredited Communist system down with it, so does Sleeping Beauty's Castle rise: the cartoon emblem of triumphant capitalism, American style.[125]

John Forsgren, Euro Disney's chief financial officer, forecasted major consequences for the developing theme park, including as many as two million additional visitors each year from the newly liberated Eastern bloc.

Even these updated projections were beginning to seem conservative. According to *Amusement Business Magazine,* Disney parks in America attracted an average of 41 million people per year. If Western Europeans visited Euro Disneyland at the same rate, the park's annual attendance could surpass 60 million—a calculation that failed to factor in the populations of Eastern Europe. In light of this whopping figure, nearly six times larger than Disney projections, company officials began to fear that the size of the proposed theme park (which had been designed to handle a maximum daily capacity of 50,000) would not be adequate. Disney executive Gary Wilson commented on the problem: "A groundswell is developing among analysts that Euro Disneyland's vision for the future is projected too conservatively."[126] Perhaps they hadn't thought big enough.

Accordingly, Disney officials decided to make some adjustments. They raised investment in the park by a full 9.4 percent and announced plans to build a number of new attractions so that at least 15 percent more visitors might be accommodated.[127] They agreed to accelerate the 1996 opening date of a second "gate" or theme park (the Disney-MGM Studios Europe, modeled after the one in Florida) to 1995 or possibly even 1994, depending on how soon infrastructure projects could be completed.[128] Finally, Disney officials drew up plans for emergency radio and Métro announcements to warn people away on days that the park was filled to capacity. When Robert Fitzpatrick said, "My biggest fear is that we will be too successful," he was not being facetious.[129]

All in all, the process of laying the foundation for a new Disney theme park in Europe was a long and arduous one, filled with strings of victories, defeats, and surprises for all parties concerned. Its establishment was complicated further by the fact that it represented many different things to many different people throughout negotiations. Farmers, timber workers, and hunters viewed the Euro Disney Resort as an infringement upon their land. Local residents saw it as a noise- and trouble-making venture that would disrupt the simplicity of village life. Small

47

amusement park operators regarded it as a monstrous opponent that would drive them out of business. And Left Bank intellectuals adopted it as a symbol of American vulgarity that would rot France's cultural heritage and turn its people into mindless, mouse-eared consumers of U.S. entertainment.

Such views, which received regular press coverage, contributed to the perception that all of France stood united in opposition to the Euro Disney Resort. But, as previously indicated, some 86 percent of those polled expressed enthusiasm for the new Disney park. Government officials saw jobs and increased revenues from tourism. Young graduates saw opportunities for professional advancement in a quality leisure and hospitality organization. Investors saw mountains of profits. And children saw fanciful images of Sleeping Beauty's castle, Pirates of the Caribbean, and Mickey Mouse brought to life in a three-dimensional world of family fun.

Disney executives, for their part, saw a priceless opportunity to tap into a new financial frontier—the global marketplace—and lay the foundation for continued growth in the new millennium. The words of Robert Fitzpatrick expressed the true level of importance that he and his colleagues attached to the Euro Disney project. "Europe," he commented, "is going to be as important as the United States to the Walt Disney Company."[130] With financial arrangements for Phase I of the Euro Disney Resort locked into place, Disney executives focused their energies on an even more challenging creative task: designing the world's newest Magic Kingdom.

2 Designing the Euro Disney Resort

One day in 1989, as negotiations for the Euro Disney Resort proceeded in France, Michael Eisner placed a call to his personal assistant, Arthur Levitt III. The Disney chairman was at home, ill. But somehow he had learned that a group of America's most celebrated architects (including Michael Graves and Robert A. M. Stern, among others) would be dining together that evening at an exclusive restaurant in Venice, California. Eisner instructed Levitt to contact the party and persuade them to move their meal to Walt Disney Imagineering headquarters in Glendale. The architects promptly agreed to the invitation. Later that evening, as waiters from a local Chinese restaurant served a full-course meal, the architects brainstormed how the Euro Disney Resort might be laid out. Discussions for the project turned out to be so engrossing that they stayed late into the night, debating the merits and flaws of different plans.[1]

Of course, designing Europe's second-greatest construction project (Euro Disney was surpassed only by the continuing work on the Eurotunnel beneath the English Channel) required more than architectural insight. Decisions regarding the kinds of attractions to be built and the ways in which they might be reinvented to suit diverse multinational audiences would demand creativity, cultural savvy, and a good deal of guesswork. After all, nobody at the Walt Disney Company (or anywhere else, for that matter) had ever created an entertainment and hotel agglomerate of such magnitude—especially on foreign soil. Tokyo Disneyland, the next nearest thing, was puny in comparison to the French project. And Walt Disney World in Florida had taken many years to evolve into a gargantuan spread.

Disney Imagineers had their work cut out for them. Not only did they face the challenge of bringing the massive project to life, they also had to determine the relative roles of American and European themes in the new development. That meant revisiting and redesigning familiar attractions as well as creating new ones from scratch. Observation, research, sketches, and modeling were all part of the creative process as Imagineers struggled to realize a single, coherent vision (that they hoped would appeal to Europeans) in a collaborative environment. But the Euro Disney Resort, described by Michael Eisner as "the most exciting Disney park in the world," was actually the product of many visions, past and present.[2] Every ride, every building, and every performance space echoed the ideas—and ideals—of its many creators, who wished to honor Walt Disney's dream for an all-new French Disney park.

FRENCH ACCENTS, AMERICAN-STYLE

From the very beginning of negotiations with the Walt Disney Company, French officials insisted that visitors to the new park could not enter an entirely American world. Unlike Tokyo Disneyland, which had been designed at the urging of Japanese authorities to reproduce the main features of Disney's U.S. parks, the Euro Disney Resort was expected to be strikingly original. It was to have its own continental flavor and identity. Magazine editor Léon Mercadet has suggested that the French government made this demand in the name of cultural protectionism and preservation: "The French feel threatened because the cultural landscapes in France are changing too fast. They sense France is becoming part of the American Empire. After decades of cultural penetration, we know culture is ruled by economies, and we in France have learned to be suspicious of whatever comes from America."[3]

That Euro Disney was stirring to life in the midst of Europe's efforts to reorganize itself into a single common market did not make matters easy. Europe was a place divided by national borders. The unification, which promised to grant new power to a collection of hitherto battling nation-states, also represented the breakdown of centuries-old notions of national identity.

French officials were sensitive to the turmoil that this ongoing transformation might cause. They also wanted to protect their huge financial investment in the new theme park. Recognizing that a dazzling display of Americana might be misconstrued (especially by cultural critics, who would take pleasure in blasting the park as another example of creeping cultural imperialism), Jean-René Bernard, France's chief negotiator with the Walt Disney Company, made it his mission to ensure that Euro Disney respected "European and French culture."[4]

Tony Baxter, senior vice president of creative development at Walt Disney Imagineering, was eager to oblige. "We're building a resort next to one of the most sophisticated, cultured cities in the world, and we're going to be competing with the great art and architecture of Europe," he explained. "We have to do something unique."[5] Baxter and his team believed that a park custom-tailored to European tastes (whatever those were) would help them to sidestep a common problem faced by many new international business ventures—something Professor Levitt of Harvard has called the N.I.H. (Not Invented Here) Syndrome.[6]

Redesigning the Disney theme park also would be a reward in and of itself. The Imagineers would have a rare chance to improve upon—and not merely duplicate—earlier models. They could take some real creative risks. Almost instantly, they began churning out fresh ideas for restaurants, rides, shops, and performance spaces. The sky was the limit as teams produced new ideas and revived old ones that had been suggested for previous parks but never built. The Euro Disney Resort would be much more than a recycled American park transplanted in Europe: it would be a whole new concept in leisure entertainment created specifically for Europe by a whole new generation of Disney Imagineers.

But part of the appeal of existing Disney theme parks, they realized, was rooted in their embodiment and ultimate expression of the American Dream. Why else would people the world over, especially Europeans, make pilgrimages to Disney parks in the United States year after year? Why else had Tokyo Disneyland, the most intensely "American" Disney park of all, attracted record crowds in Japan? To eliminate all traces of America from Euro Disney would be to do away with Main Street, U.S.A., and Frontierland, two favorite thematic areas from Disney's other parks; it would require that hot dogs, hamburgers, and chocolate chip cookies be stricken from the menus of park eateries; and most drastically, it would mean replacing Mickey Mouse and all his animated friends with the likes of more cerebral French comic book characters such as Tin-Tin. In short, exorcising "America" from the new theme park would be like cutting the "Disney" out of Euro Disney.

Fortunately for the Walt Disney Company, French government officials were not suggesting anything so drastic. They recognized the importance—as well as the popular appeal—of American culture in Europe and understood that its representation would play a crucial role in the future success of the theme park. They simply wanted the Euro Disney Resort to be a place where diverse audiences might also celebrate the richness and beauty of European cultures. The challenge facing Imagineers was to strike a very precise balance between attractions representing the New and Old Worlds. Focusing too much on the former risked alienating significant numbers of would-be patrons; concentrating too much on the latter risked boring (or worse yet, insulting) them with the redundancy of bringing Europe to Europe. The Imagineers aimed to create an environment that would seem different enough to be exciting, yet not so unfamiliar as to be disquieting—a place that would charm and amuse people of all ages in the diverse multinational community of Europe.[7]

MAIN STREET, U.S.A.

Perhaps nowhere was the task of reinventing the Disney park for European audiences more difficult than on its central thoroughfare, Main Street, U.S.A. In fact, the very thought of placing an idealized American streetscape in France sent up a number of red flags in the minds of planners, who feared how such a design might be misinterpreted by xenophobes. But after looking at other Parisian parks—and exploring the possibility of refashioning the newest Main Street into a multinational promenade, like Tokyo Disneyland's World Bazaar—the Imagineers came to two major conclusions. First, because the region had nothing similar to a Gilded Age American-style townscape, such a place promised to be unique and charming against the backdrop of Paris. Second, the Imagineers surmised that even the most skeptical of Europeans would be able to enjoy the optimism and energy of small-town America without feeling unduly threatened. So Eisner directed that the nationalistic character of Main Street, U.S.A., should not be compromised in any way: it was to remain ultra-American to capture the lively spirit (as opposed to the politics) of the United States.[8]

But this didn't mean that Disney Imagineers would simply duplicate what had already been done. To give the new Main Street its own special touch, they first considered the question of when America had become most interesting to Europe. Senior Main Street designer Eddie Sotto recalled that planners immediately hit upon the Jazz Age as a period of vitality whose energy had reached across the Atlantic. Artists fleshed out the concept by making sketches of a Roaring Twenties streetscape populated with speakeasies, Keystone cops, and women in flapper dresses. But such renderings, which represented a dramatic clock-forward revamping of the 1890s-themed Main Streets at existing Disney parks, were ultimately turned down. Eisner, who had initially supported the Prohibition Era plan, felt in the end that the reworked Main Street—with its gangster tone—would be too sinister. It needed to be less urban and more child-friendly, he decided, with a spirit of innocence more suited to families. So Imagineers returned to the familiar Victorian style of the Gay Nineties Main Streets at other Disney parks and consulted images of America in French and British books to gain insights into historical and artistic perceptions of the United States.[9]

Disney Imagineers grappled with other questions as well: What kind of conceptual story should this particular Main Street tell? How might it best be told? As architectural historian Richard Francaviglia has pointed out in his comparative study of Disney streetscapes, the story line for the original Main Street, U.S.A., in California revolved around an America in transition: cars were beginning to replace horse-drawn carriages, electricity had just come onto the scene, and people were gingerly stepping into the promise of the twentieth century.[10]

Euro Disneyland's Main Street, U.S.A., would capture this same transitional moment. But Imagineers went out of their way to inject an extra dose of Americana and contemporary energy. They positioned big retro-looking billboards on top of the buildings (a feature not to be found at any other Disney park) to capitalize on European perceptions of American commercial life. They paved Main Street with red New York–style brickwork (instead of the plain asphalt used at other Magic Kingdoms) to lend sound and texture to an otherwise drab black surface. At one point, they even planned to string phony power lines on either side of the road to emphasize the chaotic transformation of a small midwestern town.[11] Their purpose was simple: to heighten the entertainment value of this themed region for Europeans seeking a taste of turn-of-the-century American dynamism.

Baxter admitted that in-house designers made special efforts to detail the newest Main Street. "The French demanded more depth and sophistication," he noted. "They regard America as on the shallow side." For this reason, Imagineers stuffed empty spaces with props, decorated blank walls with paintings and shelves, and accented walkways with elaborate tilework. "Euro

Disney is so extravagantly detailed," one reporter would later remark, "that in many ways it makes Disney's parks in Florida and
California look like penny arcades." The complex layering,
copied line by line from historic pattern books, ensured that there
would be no dead spaces. The last thing they wanted was to create what Baxter described as a "no-man's land with no meaning."[12] But Imagineers were also careful not to go to the opposite
extreme and overclutter. As advertising mogul John O'Toole once
wisely observed, "creativity is not something that's applied like
frosting."[13]

In an effort to engage the senses and imaginations of future
park guests, Disney Imagineers worked to create what some call
a "museum-like interface." They used materials like real wood
and bricks for the storefronts, real stitched canvas for upper-story
window awnings, and real flickering gas lamps to light the sidewalks of Main Street after sunset. The rich sense of detail and
craftsmanship was unlike the canned, plastic look of strip malls
in the outside world—or the simplicity of the fiberglass structures on Main Street, U.S.A., at Walt Disney World in Florida. The
unique, made-by-hand quality was utterly believable and visually entertaining. And like its counterparts in America and Japan,
Euro Disneyland's Main Street was planned to charm the eye at
any distance, from close-up to long-shot, and to unfold as a series
of carefully controlled visual surprises.[14]

To better understand how Euro Disneyland's Main Street,
U.S.A., would be experienced from the perspective of a park
guest, Imagineers constructed tiny scale models. Working in
three dimensions freed them to look beyond detail so that they
could consider how people might actually move through and experience the spaces. They even separated the two sides of the
Main Street model and positioned each half at eye-level so that
planners could "walk through" the miniaturized townscape in
either direction. Imagineer Eddie Sotto noted that this exercise
yielded an interesting observation: that most American visitors
to Disney parks stick to the right side of Main Street, U.S.A., as

they move toward the center of the park. This response, designers believed, was most likely conditioned by the habit of driving on the right-hand side of the road.

At Euro Disneyland, however, pedestrian traffic would probably not proceed in a single orderly flow, given that people from different sides of the English Channel drive on different sides of the road. To produce an experience that would be equally satisfying for everybody, while encouraging guests to visit every "address" on Main Street, Disney Imagineers organized the thoroughfare according to the gender identity of its shops. In other words, they "checkered" each side with an alternating sequence of male- and female-themed places. So Casey's Corner, a hot-dog restaurant with a strong baseball theme, was located directly across from the Gibson Girl Ice Cream Parlour, a decidedly feminine eatery with ruffled drapes. Some places along Main Street, U.S.A., such as the Emporium, were designed to be genderless. In other words, Imagineers envisioned the space as a human pinball machine, with an array of shops that would draw people in and then ricochet them off to the other side. An even better analogy, perhaps, would be to a living pool table, on which planners sought to evenly distribute the stripes and solids, or masculine- and feminine-themed, shops and restaurants.[15]

In any case, Main Street, U.S.A., was not designed to be a bowling alley with "gutters" on either side that visitors would try to avoid "rolling" into. Imagineers sought to make the required passage into—and out of—Euro Disneyland come alive with an energy that would appeal to Europeans, specifically. Even more important in the often frigid climate of northern France, they sought to make it glow with the homespun warmth of turn-of-the-century America. The heaters they installed, not to mention the covered "Liberty" and "Discovery" arcades running parallel to Main Street on both sides, were efforts (albeit futile ones) to keep guests dry and toasty in the worst of conditions.[16] Euro Disney president Robert Fitzpatrick expressed his hope that the park would one day come to be seen as the warmest place in all of France: "We hope it will be so people wake up on a rainy day in Paris, look out their window and say 'Gee, it's a miserable day, let's go to Euro Disneyland.'"[17]

Such trademark optimism, mingled with the desire to give Europeans "what they want," reveals the degree to which Euro Disney planners simply had to hope for the best. It was impossible to know which parts of Main Street, U.S.A., would charm continental visitors most and least, which themes should be expanded upon, and which should be eliminated altogether. Research guided their inquiry to a degree. But ultimately, the Imagineers had to make a leap of faith to predict—and interpret—the specific expectations of diverse European audiences in three-dimensional form. The Main Street they designed for France thus articulated the projected needs and desires of future visitors as much as any particular vision of U.S. history.

FRONTIERLAND

Another themed region designed to satisfy European appetites for American culture, Frontierland, was positioned at the far left end of Main Street, U.S.A. Disney Imagineers originally referred to it as "Westernland," as its counterpart at Tokyo Disneyland is called. But they revived the name "Frontierland" upon learning that it had meaning for continental audiences.[18] Market research conducted throughout France and Europe proved to be a critical tool in making such decisions. Not only did it reveal a strong association between the United States and the "Wild West," it also indicated high levels of public enthusiasm for this particular slice of American life (along with New York, and, of course, Disneyland).[19]

But European—especially French—intrigue with the American West was nothing new, as journalist René Gast has affirmed. "Cowboys," he noted, "are as much a part of our past as the chevaliers de la Table Ronde."[20] And this had been true since the early years of cinema, circa 1910. Hollywood Westerns like *My*

Darling Clementine (1946), *High Noon* (1952), and a flood of others had fueled this interest over the years, capturing the imagination of continental audiences with tales of handsome heroes and despicable villains on the open range. So popular were these New World frontier dramas that many French found further pleasure in acting them out. As observed by historian Robert Athearn, the Western House store (near the Arc de Triomphe), with its huge supply of cowboy hats and boots, has never lacked for local customers. And a fabricated "western" village in the Paris area inviting would-be cowboys to participate in what Athearn has called "that internationally favorite saga known as The Conquest of the West" has also met with amazing success.[21] Disney planners concluded that the majority of future park guests (unlike the French intellectuals, who agonized over the "Americanism" of Euro Disneyland) were eager to wear cowboy hats, chow down on barbecue food, and take part in country hoedowns, just like the ones shown in Hollywood Westerns.

As a result, the Imagineers enlarged Frontierland, making it the biggest section of Euro Disneyland. They moved it nearer to the Main Gate entrance (the location of Adventureland at each of the other Disney parks) to build coherence with the American motif of Main Street, U.S.A. And they fine-tuned all of its familiar attractions to make them correspond with Western-skewed continental perceptions of the United States. The Rivers of America ride at other Disney parks, for instance, became Rivers of the Far West; the Frontierland Shootin' Gallery was redubbed the Rustler Roundup Shootin' Gallery; and the Diamond Horseshoe became the Lucky Nugget Saloon. The fun nomenclature evoked movie images of the Wild West and invited people of all linguistic backgrounds to participate in Euro Disneyland's fantasy of American frontier life through the simple act of pronunciation.[22]

But such name changes represented just part of the push to create a newly styled American home on the range in the middle of Europe. As noted by historian Michael Steiner, regional settings were also adjusted. Designers replaced traditional Frontier-

land scenes—from mountains to the lush Mississippi valley—
with the red-toned desert colors of the Great Southwest.[23] Tony
Baxter explained the reasoning behind this decision:

> [W]e noticed the intrigue that the American Southwest had
> for the French and for other Europeans. The Grand Canyon or
> Monument Valley, the images that have become familiar
> through John Wayne westerns are symbolic for Europeans of
> the entire American West, even if we feel that in reality these
> regions are as varied and diverse as Europe is diverse. That is
> why we created . . . a stunning red environment that is as
> much in contrast with Marne-la-Vallée here as the greenery of
> our Disneyland river is with the dry Southern California cli-
> mate. Our aim is to give people a fresh, startling impression.[24]

By bringing the arid southwestern landscapes of "Marlboro Man
country" to life in France, Disney Imagineers offered a glimpse, a
taste, and a feel of American exoticism to European visitors. "It's
truly the legends of cowboys and Indians that rule this land," one
opening-day guest would later remark. "It's just the kind of place
where John Wayne–loving Europeans can get a dose of what they
must think is America."[25]

Disney Imagineers also re-themed many Frontierland attractions to reflect Europe's special interest in Native American and
Mexican-American cultures.[26] The Pueblo Trading Post and the
Indian Canoes (known as the Frontier Trading Post and Davy
Crockett's Explorer Canoes, respectively, at Disney's U.S. parks)
stand out as two examples of how planners represented the experiences of America's indigenous peoples on European soil—
and water. The Fuente del Oro Restaurante, an adobe-style
cantina serving southwestern cuisine, was another unique addition to Europe's Frontierland. Given the popularity of Tex-Mex
restaurants all over Paris in the late 1980s, Imagineers felt sure
that theirs, too, would be a hit. But they wanted it to be more than
just another eatery with spicy traditional dishes. So they created

59

a fiesta-like atmosphere with piñatas, sombreros, strolling mariachi bands, and an ancient Mayan fountain to give European visitors the flavor of life "south of the border." The festive spirit, they hoped, would be every bit as appealing as the cuisine.

The strong Western American character of Frontierland also included some distinct European touches. But Imagineers were careful to make them subtle. After all, research indicated that would-be park guests wanted a "real" Wild West experience, like that at Disney's other parks—not one that they perceived to be watered down with continental niceties. "They want the real thing," affirmed one lawyer in Paris working on the Euro Disney project. "They want what the Americans get."[27] The Lucky Nugget Saloon would pay homage to Europe in a nightly vaudeville show starring a Miss Lil' and her French boyfriend, Pierre Paradis. With a cast of high-kicking cancan dancers, it would suggest that European cultures had a real presence in the Wild West—and contributed to the making of America.

Another Frontierland attraction that Disney Imagineers redesigned for Europe was the Big Thunder Mountain Railroad. Like its counterparts in the United States and Japan, this ride was intended to transport passengers back to the days of the American Gold Rush in a runaway mine train adventure filled with falling rocks, teetering buttes, and audio-animatronic wildlife. But unlike the other Big Thunder Mountains, which were added to the Disneyland-scapes years after the parks had been built, Europe's did not need to be relegated to one of the open spaces on the periphery. Imagineers had a blank slate in France. So they positioned the wildly popular ride smack in the middle of Frontierland, where it could serve as a powerful visual magnet.[28] More dramatically, the Imagineers surrounded it with water, making the island peak accessible only to those brave enough to endure a roller-coaster ride that pulled passengers—"Chunnel style"—underneath the Rivers of the Far West.

Perhaps the most extensively redesigned attraction in Frontierland, however, was Phantom Manor. Unlike the Haunted

Mansions in California, Florida, and Japan (located in New Orleans Square, Liberty Square, and Fantasyland, respectively),
Euro Disney's spook house was reconceptualized to be part of a
Western mining town. For this reason, Imagineers decided not to
duplicate the familiar southern-plantation-style architecture of
its California cousin. They also decided not to repeat Walt Disney's own "happy haunting ground" theme from other park
sites, with "999 happy ghosts, ghouls, and goblins" lurking behind the walls of an otherwise well-tended home.[29] To convey
the creepy nature of this attraction to multilingual audiences,
Imagineers designed Phantom Manor's exterior to appear old
and dilapidated. Even more important, they drew upon a pastiche of powerful movie images, namely *Psycho* (1960), to create a
frightening landmark that would communicate its contents to diverse populations without so much as a word.[30]

Disney Imagineers similarly retooled the interior of Phantom Manor. As at other Disney parks, they used the "stretching"
elevators that transport guests to the basement level, as well as
the automated, two-person "doom buggies." But in France, the
Imagineers wanted to offer visitors something more than a nocturnal voyage through spooky (yet separate) spaces filled with
special effects. So they designed the ride to function as a living
narrative, with characters and a scary plot that would unfold in
a linear progression. The tale they created, about a ghostly frontier bride in the American West, had no specific Hollywood ref-
erent (unlike other Disney "dark rides"). But it was purely
cinematic, through and through.[31] The doom buggies that trans-
ported guests into the story—visually and physically—were designed to function like movie cameras by twisting, turning, and
directing the gaze of passengers from scene to scene. Their high
backs and sight-restricting sides, not to mention the metal lap
bars that held guests firmly in their seats, guided the experience
further by erasing from view anything that might spoil the illusion, while imparting their own curious mixture of imprison-
ment and protection.[32] The passenger-turned-participant would

be projected into the screen of a 3-D film to see—and live—the tale as it unfolded in time and space.

In all, the Frontierland that Disney Imagineers designed for France was new and strangely sophisticated. Combining elements of New and Old Worlds, it resonated with themes that were at once past and present, ultra-American and worldly. Jean-Marie Gerbeaux, Euro Disney's French spokesman, explained the intent of park planners in designing this special land. "We are bringing a naive, simple view of America," he commented, "reflecting the idea of America that Europeans have."[33] But in trying to identify and accommodate intangible perceptions of the United States, Imagineers also revealed their own unquestionably American notions of Europe. That is why Frontierland ultimately wound up casting such a huge shadow over much of the Disney development in France. As Steiner would later observe, its presence permeates the entire park: "From Big Thunder Mountain, the Grand Canyon Diorama, the steamboat ride 'round Monument Valley, and the forests of saguaro cacti inside the park to the flashy necklace of postmodern western-themed hotels flanking it, Euro Disneyland reeks of the imagined West."[34]

ADVENTURELAND

Located clockwise around the park from Frontierland is Adventureland. Disney Imagineers, it has been noted, swapped the positions of these two realms to anticipate the huge crowds that had expressed a hankerin' to visit the Wild West. As a result, Adventureland was squeezed into a much more compact space than its rootin'-tootin' neighbor: it became the smallest "slice" of the Euro Disneyland pie, with the fewest attractions. But Imagineers did not simply make the new Adventureland into a stripped-down version of its predecessors in California, Florida, and Japan. They designed it to be an original interpretation of a familiar Disney environment that would please and entertain a whole new clientele.

The single greatest change Imagineers made to this domain in Europe was to tighten its conceptual theme. Instead of copying the lush, leafy jungles of other Adventurelands, which recalled a blend of places (ranging from the Pacific and Southeast Asia to the Amazon rain forest), they designed a place that would reflect a new geographical mix—and a new vision of paradise. "Here," observed Tony Baxter, "we found that there was a strong tie to the romance of the Baghdad storybook setting."[35] As noted by Edward Said, this "tie" could be traced back to early days of French Imperialism under Napoleon.[36] "The Orient was almost a European invention," he noted, "and had been since antiquity a place of romance, exotic beings, haunting memories and landscapes, remarkable experiences." Said underlined its importance to the European psyche:

> The Orient is not only adjacent to Europe; it is also the place of Europe's greatest and richest and oldest colonies, the source of its civilizations and languages, its cultural contestant, and one of its deepest and most recurring images of the Other. In addition, the Orient has helped to define Europe (or the West) as its contrasting image, idea, personality, experience.[37]

The paintings of French artist Eugène Delacroix, inspired by an 1832 trip to Algeria and Morocco, express the European fascination with what Said terms "Orientalism."[38] And the 1938 film *Algiers*, which follows the tale of French jewel thief Pepe le Moko (played by Charles Boyer), brings to life the mystique of the Casbah—a world "where blazing desert meets the blue Mediterranean, and modern Europe jostles ancient Africa."[39]

In France, Disney Imagineers went to great lengths to emphasize the special intrigue of this region. They swept back the thick canopies of other Adventurelands and replaced them with the arid landscapes of French North Africa; for safari-style huts made of bamboo they substituted the thick stone walls and onion

63

domes of desert architecture; and they revamped the look of cast member costumes, trading khaki explorer outfits and pith helmets for brightly colored turbans, veils, and the billowing fashions of not-too-faraway "foreign" lands.[40] "We took our cue from Moroccan and North African styles," Baxter noted, "but then we layered on pure Hollywood."[41]

Nowhere was the spirit of Mediterranean exoticism captured more tangibly than in the Adventureland Bazaar, a collection of specialty shops featuring decorative items from the far reaches of the world. Disney Imagineers designed this area, positioned at the hub entrance to Adventureland, to capitalize on French pictorial impressions of the East.[42] Baxter explained the importance of achieving absolute authenticity in the winding alleyways and canvas tenting that they "imagineered":

> I think the suspension of disbelief . . . is directly related to how well the illusion is created in the background. You come in and you are the participant. For awhile, you step into the realm of the Arabian Nights, or you journey to an island of pirates. If the environment isn't a complete space of illusion or theater, then people are more inclined not to participate in the performance. That doesn't mean you have to sing or dance, but you can explore, you can use your imagination, you can believe in the environment. If we paid less attention to details you would find people standing back and observing as they would a window display, or a painting. . . . It's not that we're trying to re-create architecture so much as create an absolutely disarming backdrop, so that people's guard is let down and they actually live these experiences.[43]

By building settings that would compel visitors to suspend their disbelief, Imagineers wanted to nudge them to step into the screen, as it were, and experience the frenzy of an ancient marketplace selling genie lamps, flying carpets, and handmade baskets. Traders, veiled dancers, and snake charmers would add to the illusion and invite guests to explore the exotic worlds of *Ali Baba* (1943), the *Thousand and One Nights* (1945), or *Aladdin* (1992).

The decision to make such dramatic changes to the theme of Adventureland in Europe naturally prompted a rethinking of its other would-be attractions. Some, which had been favorites at other Disney parks, did not fit in with the new Arabian-style motif. Others simply wouldn't fit into the modest space allotted for this particular Adventureland. For both of these reasons, not to mention the brutal winter climate of northern France, the Jungle Cruise was not rebuilt in Europe. Anthropologist Stephen Fjellman, who described the attraction as "the core of Adventureland" at Walt Disney World in Florida, was not overstating its importance to the Disney landscape.[44] Without the Jungle Cruise, Imagineers were forced to look for a different nucleus. They decided, in the end, to locate La Cabane des Robinson (the Swiss Family Robinson Treehouse) at the center of Adventureland on an actual island, unlike its counterparts in the United States and Japan. The tall mossy branches of this concrete banyan tree, ornamented with more than 800,000 vinyl leaves, were designed to reach into the sky (much like the stony peak of Big Thunder Mountain next door) and serve as a centerpiece for Adventureland guests—as well as a visual magnet for those who had not yet ventured inside.

Another favorite Disney attraction, which fell outside the new geographical theme but fit into an overarching motif of French colonialism, was Pirates of the Caribbean. Like its counterparts in America and Japan, this nocturnal cruise through a small West Indies island town was designed to feature the rollicking exploits of a band of buccaneers. Disney Imagineers, however, took special pains to make this audio-animatronic show even better for Europe. Some changes, such as the French and Spanish voices audible in certain scenes, were added to acknowledge the presence of Europeans in the attraction, both as performers and as spectators. Others—such as the pirate swinging from an overhead mast, collapsing support beams, and state-of-the-art dueling swordsmen—represented an effort to make the

65

ride more realistic, more entertaining, and more dramatic. Pirates of the Caribbean, a ride that was completely redesigned for Euro Disneyland, expressed the new, upgraded look and feel of France's Adventureland, as well as the conviction of Disney Imagineers that past successes can always be improved upon.

In sum, the Adventureland Disney Imagineers created for Europe was a compelling mix of old and new, with an identity all its own. The exotic theme and the redesigned attractions made it a unique place where, in Baxter's words, "fantasies of paradise can be fulfilled, of living in a tree or climbing the rocks and looking for buried treasure chests."[45] But Imagineers did not wipe out all hints of its predecessors at Euro Disneyland. Skull Rock, carved into the stony side of Adventure Isle just like at the original Disneyland, would gape at tourists in France, inviting them to experience the mystery of Never Land. The Explorer Club, a restaurant located in a thick jungle setting, would treat diners to an audio-animatronic show put on by the enchanted Tiki birds (who have their own attraction at other Disney parks). And La Girafe Curieuse, a shop specializing in safari clothing and accessories, would bring to life the dream of journeying into the tropics of central Africa. By building on previous successes and daring to take new creative risks, Disney Imagineers struggled to create a place that would charm and surprise, entertain and inspire, thrill and reassure.

FANTASYLAND

Positioned on the other side of Adventureland was Fantasyland, the traditional heart of the Disney theme park, which brings animated film classics to life in three-dimensional form. With its proud castle standing at the park's center, this area has been billed as "the happiest land of all."[46] But the idea of bringing Fantasyland to Europe took on special urgency in the minds of Imagineers, who recognized that most of Disney's animated features had been inspired by continental folk and fairy tales. Their challenge was not simply to rebuild a Fantasyland that had worked in the United States or Japan, but to reinterpret it so that multinational audiences would not view the space as an Americanized bastardization of their own sacred stories. In many ways, their success or failure in this politically charged task would be crucial to the definition of Euro Disneyland's overall character.

Without hesitation, the Imagineers agreed to acknowledge—and celebrate—the Old World heritage behind Disney's animated storybook films. Europe's Fantasyland would represent a continental homecoming, of sorts, for centuries-old storybook characters who had simply been given cinematic "makeovers" by an American artist named Walt Disney. Euro Disney president Robert Fitzpatrick explained the guiding philosophy: "Europe isn't North America. It seemed appropriate and politically astute to understand that Pinocchio was an Italian boy, Peter Pan used to fly out of London, and Cinderella was a French girl. We've tried to emphasize the European roots of these stories."[47] One way in which they did so was through language. The woodcarver's shop in which Pinocchio came to life was named "La Bottega di Geppetto" in honor of Carlo Collodi's Italian tale; Peter Pan's Flight retained its English name because its author, J. M. Barrie, was British; and Cinderella's restaurant was dubbed "L'Auberge de Cendrillon" as a tribute to French writer Charles Perrault. Living storybook characters would also support the multinational flavor of Disney's Fantasyland-scape by speaking in the tongues of their mother countries, whether on-stage or during personal autograph sessions with guests.

Because linguistic diversity was intended to be endearing—and not confusing—to tourists from Europe and around the world, Disney Imagineers took pains to minimize the need for translations of every street sign, banner, and restaurant menu. In the spirit of Disney's earliest films, the silent ones, they designed Fantasyland to rely upon dramatic visual symbols rather than written words to communicate park features and rules. Themed sculpture, plantings, and a host of pictograms featuring Mickey

67

Mouse and his friends made up Euro Disneyland's visual vocabulary, identifying rides, restaurants, shops, and shows. Together, these familiar movie icons would help to underscore the fact that Fantasyland was one step removed from continental reality, existing in an imaginary realm of experience that was at once timeless, placeless, and, in many ways, voiceless. The visual signs would invite guests to suspend their linguistic differences momentarily and learn a new lingua franca: the cartoon language of Disney symbolism.

Perhaps nowhere was this visual Esperanto "spoken" more fluently than in It's a Small World, an enchanted boat ride showcasing the diversity of human cultures. As at other Disney parks, the Imagineers designed this attraction to feature hundreds of singing, dancing, audio-animatronic dolls. But they took special care at Euro Disneyland to make this ride meaningful for multinational audiences. By selecting eye-grabbing symbols (such as leprechauns, pots o' gold, and shamrocks for Ireland) the Imagineers aimed to transcend language barriers with lively visual displays that would "speak" to everyone—and charm guests from the areas depicted. The Imagineers also expanded the scope of American scenes in this ride to give European passengers a glimpse of life in different regions of the United States. Tableaux with freckle-faced boys playing football, diverse groups of youngsters frolicking on a farm with barnyard animals, and dressed-up children dancing in a chorus line before a glittering "Hollywood" sign brought to life many popular images of the land of plenty. That many such scenes consciously reaffirmed European stereotypes about the United States and other areas of the world is important. It demonstrates the lengths to which Imagineers went to meet the projected expectations of the new clientele, rather than express any sort of overarching historical vision.

Disney Imagineers also used themed architecture to communicate with visitors on unspoken and unwritten levels. The Old Mill, a tea shop housed within the base of a revolving Dutch windmill, recalled Disney's 1937 animated short of the same name while evoking images of a tulip-filled countryside in Holland. The gingerbread styling of Au Chalet de la Marionnette suggested the quaint beauty of an Alpine village, with its shingled roof, leaded glass windows, and finials carved in the shapes of characters from *Pinocchio* (1940). The Pizzeria Bella Notte, a brick building tilted to one side like the Leaning Tower of Pisa, re-created the charm of a meal for two at an Italian restaurant straight out of *Lady and the Tramp* (1955). And Alice's Curious Labyrinth, a 5,000-square-foot hedge maze arranged to resemble the grinning form of Lewis Carroll's Cheshire Cat, recalled Disney's 1951 animated film as well as the meandering pathways of an English garden.[48] Individually and collectively, such fanciful structures were designed to emphasize the European roots of Disney's animated films. More importantly, they were intended to confirm the out-and-out reality of cinematic fantasy while celebrating the fantasy of cinematic reality.

Nowhere was this liquid interchange between two and three dimensions brought to life more powerfully than at Le Château de la Belle au Bois Dormant (Sleeping Beauty's castle). With its delicately fluted towers, chiseled stonework, and rose-toned walls leafed in lacy gold patterns, this fantasy palace was designed to command attention by giving material form to images seen in Disney comics and films. It was also intended to evoke one of the most stirring sights shown on television: the dramatic view of a storybook castle at night, showered in fireworks and pixie dust by an animated Tinker Bell. By inflating cartoon and live-action imagery to full-bodied form, the Imagineers created a prominent landmark for Fantasyland and all of Euro Disneyland, one that promised to capture the spirit of a place where fairy-tale dreams could come true.

Designing the newest fantasy palace, however, was no simple task—especially since this one was to be located in a countryful (and continentful!) of the originals that had inspired Disney's earlier make-believe castles. For this reason, the Imagineers were reluctant to seek exact models in the European countryside, reasoning that a copycat version of a landmark château would make a feeble heart for their new theme park. This, commented Marty Sklar of Walt Disney Imagineering, would be like "bringing coals to Newcastle."[49] They were equally opposed to the idea of duplicating one of their previous creations (the Cinderella palace at Tokyo Disneyland, for instance, is a replica of Florida's Walt Disney World castle) in France, since there it was almost certain to be viewed as an imitation of a "foreign" imitation. Eager to turn out more than a cookie-cutter product this time, Disney Imagineers sought to create an original fantasy castle that would impress even European audiences accustomed to seeing such structures. Only such a palace—a new palace—could communicate the new approach, the new feel, and the new identity of this Disney theme park in the tourist heart of Europe.

But the decision to design something new, innovative, and different to suit the special needs of a European setting limited the extent to which Imagineers could draw upon past successes. So they started from scratch. Early renderings of futuristic castles that appeared ready to blast off into space reveal exactly how far members of Disney's design team went to "imagineer" a new fantasy château.[50] Planning gained greater momentum when Chinese-American architect I. M. Pei, designer of the controversial glass pyramids in the courtyard of the Louvre, suggested that the Disney team consider an illuminated manuscript once owned by the Duc de Bérry, the third son of John II the Good, King of France.[51] Les Très Riches Heures, a fourteenth-century French masterpiece of miniature illustration best known for its pictures of quasi-imaginary palaces, served as a major inspiration for the newest Disney castle, as did Mont St. Michel, the famous French island-church that spirals delicately out of the water during high tide.[52]

The question of which storybook character to "theme" the palace after was resolved by studying imagery from Disney's animated films. Hoping to honor a French fairy-tale princess, the Imagineers were immediately drawn to the cinematic story of

70

Sleeping Beauty (1959). But they were inspired less by the castle as it appeared in the film than by the striking angularity of shapes and forms created by stylist Eyvind Earle, working in a popular version of the cubist idiom.[53] "The styling and background for that movie," noted Baxter, "was very reminiscent of French tapestry and Renaissance art. In fact, the Unicorn tapestries hanging in the Cluny Museum were used in referencing the movie."[54] Disney Imagineers drew upon this distinctive look, with its strong visual edge, in an effort to define France's newest fantasy palace. Thus the castle they designed was remarkably different from the edifice featured in the movie—and from Sleeping Beauty's more modest, Bavarian-style home rooted in the Disneyland-scape of California. But it brought to life the artistic style of the animated classic, capturing its tone of abstract beauty and mystery with warm colors, drastically razored trees, and an eighty-nine-foot audio-animatronic dragon hidden in a darkened dungeon below, hissing and lunging at those who dared to enter.

Disney Imagineers created another important space just outside the palace walls: le Théâtre du Château, a large outdoor theater modeled after the garden arenas of eighteenth-century French nobility. They positioned an enormous mechanical storybook center-stage as its chief attraction. During performances, the book would open, page by page, to reveal pop-up scenery. Characters such as Sleeping Beauty, Snow White, and Cinderella (as well as their respective princes) would step out of the giant tome, paying homage to their literary roots, and re-create scenes from Disney's animated films in a visual and musical show that transcended language barriers. The sight of an enchanted storybook opening up before the backdrop of a fantasy castle was designed to send chills up the spines of guests and remind them that in Fantasyland, all good things were not only possible, but inevitable.

In all, Europe's Fantasyland was designed to be an impressive combination of Old and New Worlds, artifice and reality. Dominated by the imposing presence of Le Château de la Belle au Bois Dormant, it was in many ways the heart of Euro Disneyland. 71

But it was also the most difficult to imagineer. By honoring the European roots of Disney's cinematic tales, designers created a place where storybook characters would be seen not as Hollywood celebrities, but as hometown kids who had made good on the American Dream—and returned, in all their glory. Belle, Alice, Mary Poppins, and all the rest were consciously cast as symbols of a united Europe at home in France. Fantasyland, a place where differences of language, culture, and nationality could be set aside in the name of fun, mirrored the aspirations of a transforming Europe engaged in the struggle to define itself.

DISCOVERYLAND

The final themed region Imagineers created for Euro Disneyland was Discoveryland, a place intended to connect Europeans with the proud tradition of looking forward in time. Unlike the Space Age–style Tomorrowlands built at other Disney parks, which quickly became outdated, Europe's Discoveryland was located in a different temporal dimension altogether. Imagineers had grown painfully aware, over the years, that building and maintaining a futuristic landscape were, in fact, two very different things. The ever-advancing nature of time, which transforms "today" into "yesterday," they realized, can and will do the same thing to "tomorrow." As Walt Disney had pointed out years earlier at his first theme park, "[t]he only problem with anything of tomorrow is that at the pace we're going right now, tomorrow could catch up with us before we got it built"—and it frequently did in the Tomorrowlands of years past.[55]

To remedy this limitation in France, thereby avoiding a duplication of what many felt was the "Achilles' heel" of previous Disney theme parks, the Imagineers did something daring: they drew upon a rich heritage of historical thought and re-themed Discoveryland to reflect *past* visions of the future—most notably those held by European luminaries, such as Jules Verne, H. G. Wells, and Leonardo da Vinci. According to Imagineer Tim Delaney, the new temporal and geographical orientation of Discoveryland was intended to do three things: create an atmosphere of timeless beauty that would not be so quickly outdated; pay special tribute to the contributions of European visionaries, whose dreams of the future have shaped and enriched the present; and reassure visitors with the promise of an even brighter tomorrow.[56] Discoveryland would distinguish itself from the stark, milky-white "concretelands" in America and Japan by featuring creative architecture, warm earthtone colors, and a mix of new attractions.[57] Like a fine French wine, planners hoped, it would have meaning and relevance for new generations, year after year—and get even better with age.

As part of the overall plan to reposition Discoveryland, Imagineers located at its center a brand-new attraction: Orbitron. Crafted out of polished bronze spheres of different sizes that whirl around and around high in the sky, it was designed to offer voyages through an animated galaxy of planets and constellations. But Imagineers envisioned Orbitron as much more than a ride: they viewed it as a compelling piece of kinetic sculpture and as a dramatic visual magnet for Discoveryland.[58] Like Big Thunder Mountain, La Cabane des Robinson, and Le Château de la Belle au Bois Dormant in other sections of the park, the towering, motile presence of Orbitron was intended to draw people inward to explore the future of years past. Details, such as the side fins and rear nozzles of the spaceships, reinforced the retro look of Discoveryland by recalling the space-age styling in Buck Rogers and Flash Gordon films of the 1930s.[59]

Imagineers built upon the motif of time travel in Discoveryland with Le Visionarium, an art deco–style building which featured a 360-degree "Circle-Vision" screen to envelop its audience. Although the idea for this attraction was hardly groundbreaking (a similar theater first appeared at California's Disneyland in June 1967), Disney planners energized the presentation by adding computer-generated special effects and audio-animatronic emcees. They even developed a new story line.[60] The movie, entitled

73

From Time to Time, replaced the *American Journeys* film shown at the other three Disney parks: it traced the cultural development of Europe over thousands of miles and centuries. Panoramic scenes of Mont St. Michel, Vienna's Imperial Palace, and Moscow's Red Square aimed to transport viewers into the screen—and into the future of the past. Headsets offering translations of the narration in a variety of tongues, as well as a smattering of European celebrities on screen (actors Gérard Depardieu, Michel Piccoli, and Franco Nero played the parts of H. G. Wells, Jules Verne, and Leonardo da Vinci, respectively) further added to the distinctly continental identity of Discoveryland in a film that had been designed to celebrate "the people, heritage, and breathtaking beauty of France and Europe."[61]

Disney Imagineers decided to reinforce the theme of European futurism in two new restaurants, which they located on either side of Le Visionarium: Le Café des Visionnaires and Le Café Hyperion. The former, designed with a highly contemporary decor of bronze, copper, and shaded granite, like Orbitron, featured a panoramic fresco depicting famous scenes from Europe's great works of science fiction (much as the "Black Ship" display at Tokyo Disneyland celebrates the heritage of Japan). The Imagineers were even more dramatic in their treatment of Le Café Hyperion. Its exterior, marked by the protruding presence of a thirty-meter zeppelin docked in a loading bay before takeoff, drew inspiration from Tony Baxter's design for a never-built thematic area at California's Disneyland called Discovery Bay.[62] Café Hyperion was intended to celebrate the romance and excitement of one of mankind's oldest dreams: a voyage through time. The interior was themed like the departure area for such a trip, with an overhead timetable display of menu items and condiment stations built upon stacks of luggage. Imagineers enhanced the travel decor further by creating a vast, darkened eating area that looks out onto Videopolis, a hi-tech performance area. Both Le Café des Visionnaires and Le Café Hyperion were designed to function as fanciful time machines, inviting would-

be passengers inside to savor a voyage of the visual—and gas-
tronomic—variety.

In many ways, Discoveryland was a suitable summary statement for Euro Disneyland, embodying the best of old and new in
a special place filled with new frontiers, new adventures, new
fantasies, and new discoveries. By positioning guests in the past,
as opposed to the present (like the pre-renovated Tomorrowlands
of other Disney parks), the Imagineers created a world that
melded more seamlessly with the nostalgia of neighboring lands.
More important still, they created a world of endless possibility—
located light-years before "today"—that celebrated a sense of
nostalgia for the future.[63] If advertising mogul John O'Toole's
maxim that "creativity in the arts is doing the unexpected suc-
cessfully" is true, the Disney Imagineers surely succeeded in their
task.[64] By bringing into being a place of yesterday and tomorrow
at once, they helped to enrich the present with surprising—and
reassuring—visions of times past and times to come.

THE HOTEL DISTRICT

Located outside the gates of the theme park was the second half
of the Euro Disney landscape: the hotel district, which would feature on opening day some 5,200 hotel rooms, Festival Disney (a
restaurant and nightclub area loosely modeled after Walt Disney
World's Pleasure Island), and an eighteen-hole golf course complete with mouse-eared sandtraps.[65] When planning this area,
Disney executives agreed to think big for several reasons. First,
they hoped to discourage parasitic hotel/motel operators from
setting up shop around Euro Disney as they had at both California's Disneyland and Florida's Walt Disney World. Second, they
believed it was the most efficient way to develop the property.
"We could wait until the second gate opens to build more
rooms," noted Disney's chief financial officer Gary Wilson, "but
by then it would be much more expensive and disruptive. Better
to do them all up front."[66] Finally, Disney executives wanted to

make a symbolic gesture to the people of Europe: the Euro Disney Resort was not just another park built for one-day visits, but a full-fledged vacation destination that was taking permanent root in the continental landscape.

The Disney Imagineers, however, were less involved in the design of the hotel district than the theme park. As part of Disney CEO Michael Eisner's overall push to come up with new resort treatments that echoed and moved beyond the parks, he commissioned a team of high-profile architects to take charge of this operation in France. Euro Disney president Robert Fitzpatrick shared Eisner's sentiment that the hotel district would require its own identity. "Disney is an entertainment company," he commented, "it's about pleasure and fun. You want to do something compatible but different from the theme park to carry the theme outside the walls."[67]

For this reason, Disney executives (in collaboration with consulting architects Frank Gehry, Michael Graves, Robert A. M. Stern, Stanley Tigerman, and Robert Venturi) decided early on that the hotel district should have an all-American theme.[68] After all, they reasoned, it made little sense to offer lodging in quaint French-style flats or magnificent fantasy châteaux when the real things were less than an hour away by train or car. Stern, who designed two hotels for the Euro Disney Resort, said it best:

> [T]he hotel district had to be seen as being totally different from Paris or any other European city. . . . You had to design buildings that were heavily themed in the Disney way about America. This is a resort that you reach on the subway from Paris in thirty-five minutes. You have to come out of the subway and have a completely different view of the world. Disney can't pretend to be French, it's an American idea that has become international, but it should maintain its identity, otherwise it would be like a bad French restaurant in Kansas City.[69]

Each Euro Disney hotel, executives decided, should re-create the ambience of a particular region or city in the United States. Each one would also tell a unique story with its design, simple enough for everyone to grasp and compelling enough to hold everyone's interest. Disney officials felt certain that such a vacation resort would be irresistible to tourists from all over Europe (and all over the world) who craved a taste of America. "The most exciting thing about Euro Disney," noted Daniel Coccoli, vice president of resort hotel operations in France, "is that guests will be able to walk from the park to a hotel that allows them to continue the fantasy, instead of going back to a hotel that interrupts that fantasy."[70] The Euro Disney hotel district promised to provide an unbeatable alternative to staying in Paris, which, Michael Eisner was happy to point out, "is an adult attraction."[71]

Selecting who would design the Euro Disney hotels, however, proved difficult. After Disney executives had fleshed out the concept of the hotel district and refined the size of each land parcel, they invited fifteen world-famous architects to participate in a competition, or charette. Each was to submit an entry for one of six hotel sites, and each site would have two or three architects competing for the job. The Hotel New York, for instance, was a contest between Michael Graves and Arata Isozaki; the Hotel Cheyenne, between Robert Stern and Jean-Paul Viguier; and the Hotel Santa Fe, between Antoine Predock and Stanley Tigerman. "We tried to be international," noted Wing Chao, senior vice president of the Walt Disney Design and Development Company, "with Americans competing against other nationalities for each site. Each one had three weeks to come up with a first concept."[72]

Disney executives, led by Michael Eisner, Robert Fitzpatrick, Peter Rummell, and Wing Chao, scrutinized each project. They even invited the architects to comment on and criticize the work of their colleagues. In the end, they eliminated a few proposals that were not practical from a budgetary or design standpoint. But the competition was far from over. Disney executives invited two additional architects, Christian de Portzamparc and Aldo

77

Rossi (both European), to look at plans for the developing Euro Disney Resort and throw their hats in the ring. They also asked Antoine Grumbach, who was doing a lake-edge study of the hotel district, to submit a concept design.[73]

But despite concerted efforts to include European architects—and others, such as Hans Hollein, Rem Koolhaas, Jean Nouvel, and Bernard Tschumi—in the design process, most of their proposals proved to be too avant-garde for Disney's tastes. Nouvel's "Hotel of Rational Thought," an abstraction in steel and glass, exemplified the stark intellectual style of some continental bids.[74] "I think we could be candid," Stern observed, "and say that many European architects are very uncomfortable with the idea of building themed architecture, unless the theme is technology or modernity. In my view, and this is not the company's view, European architecture is often uncomfortable with the theme of the past or with regional imagery."[75] Many European designers also were unfamiliar with what Peter Rummell, president of the Walt Disney Design and Development Company, meant when he expressed his desire to fill the hotel district with "Entertainment Architecture."[76]

As a result, the collection of architects Disney executives ultimately hired was mainly American. Michael Graves, Robert A. M. Stern, and Frank Gehry, who had been involved in early plans for the Euro Disney Resort, would lead the effort: Graves would design the Hotel New York; Stern would do the Newport Bay Club and the Hotel Cheyenne; and Gehry would be responsible for Festival Disney, the district's main entertainment center. Architect Antoine Predock was later signed to do the Hotel Santa Fe.[77] Rossi's plan for a New Orleans Hotel was also accepted by the Disney team, but he backed out because of too many threatened changes to his design. Grumbach's plan for a Wright-esque mountain retreat nestled in a forest setting, the Sequoia Lodge, was also selected: it ended up being the only Euro Disney hotel designed by a European architect.[78]

One vacation residence at the Euro Disney Resort, however, was planned to stand apart from all others, conceptually and geographically: the Hotel Disneyland. Described by architectural critic Suzanne Stephens as "a high-Victorian-style confection with rabbit-eye pink wood siding and lobster-red turreted and mansarded roofs," it was the first hotel at any of the Disney theme parks to be located at the Main Gate entrance to the park.[79] It was also the only hotel that Disney Imagineers designed, because it would be part of the theme park experience, serving as a roof for the guest ticket booths and as a powerful visual backdrop for Main Street, U.S.A.[80] The architectural firm of Wimberly, Allison, Tong and Goo of Newport Beach, California, collaborated on the Hotel Disneyland and helped the Imagineers to combine functional necessity with a fanciful building in the style of San Diego's Hotel Del Coronado (which had also inspired the Grand Floridian Beach Resort at Walt Disney World).[81] Together, the two teams brought into being a nineteenth-century American railroad hotel (the Euro Disneyland Railroad Station was located behind it, inside the park, while the RER and TGV lines that serve Paris and all of Europe were just outside the park's gates) that captured the spirit of refinement befitting a luxurious five-star palace.

The hotels by other architects were clustered around an artificial lake and river on the far side of Festival Disney. Stuffed with a variety of overhead signs and billboards, this pedestrian arcade was intended to create a whirlwind of excitement for America by evoking the atmosphere of Route 66.[82] Restaurants such as the Los Angeles Bar and Grill, Key West Seafood, Carnegie's (New York–style) Deli, and Annette's Diner (which featured 1960s sportscars out front to reinforce Festival Disney's identification with the American road) offered glimpses—and tastes—of the American experience. Shops, including the Disney Store and Hollywood Pictures, were installed to showcase a range of souvenir memorabilia from different regions of the United States. And performances, such as a re-created dinner-theater version of Buffalo Bill's Wild West Show (which captivated European audiences in Paris more than a century ago) offered entertainment starring cowboys, Indians, trick horses, buffalo, a runaway stagecoach, and a sharpshooter named Annie Oakley.[83]

In all, Festival Disney aimed to connect the different themes of the resort hotels in a pastiche of regional imagery—and experiences—that would entertain and encourage visitors to dream about the United States. It was designed to be a postmodern extravaganza that both exaggerated and juxtaposed the different architectural styles, color schemes, and kitsch of American cultures from coast to coast.

The Hotel New York, a 575-room four-star hotel located just beyond Festival Disney, was meant to capture the urban vitality and beauty of the Big Apple in its heyday. Multicolored towers recalled different parts of Manhattan, from brownstones to skyscrapers, while feeding fantasies of romance and glamour.[84] A Rockefeller Center–style ice-skating rink (used as a fountain in warm weather) and a Rainbow Room restaurant also evoked 1930s New York. Tourist iconography, including wallpaper covered with red apples and baseballs—not to mention the skyscraper-shaped lamps in guest rooms—replaced real world ugliness with a sense of American whimsy that Graves believed "can be deciphered by an 8-year-old as well as a 68-year-old."[85]

Adjacent to the Hotel New York was the Sequoia Lodge, a 1,011-room, seven-story mountain retreat that Michael Eisner called "the most romantic and quintessentially American of all our hotels."[86] French architect Antoine Grumbach, who holidayed in the American West, designed it to echo the adventure of Yellowstone, Yosemite, or any one of America's national parks. More specifically, the Sequoia referenced the Prairie-style architecture of Frank Lloyd Wright, whose horizontal designs have come to define the look of existing hotels in the Rockies. Solid stone construction and hewn redwood siding complemented the hotel's ambience inside and out. Sloping green roofs added another note of color, emphasizing the forested landscapes below, which would include more than two thousand newly planted trees (among them four hundred young sequoias imported from the United States). And a century-old tree growing in the lobby brought the great outdoors inside, investing it with the raw charm of a chalet in the middle of God's country.[87]

The Newport Bay Club, an enormous three-star hotel located next door to the Sequoia Lodge and opposite the Hotel New York, echoed the stick style of New England. Designed by Robert A. M. Stern, who earlier created the Yacht and Beach Club hotels at Walt Disney World in Florida, it recalled turn-of-the-century East Coast estates with its pale yellow siding, dormers, striped awnings, and shingled gable roofs. A lighthouse and a seventy-yard observation deck filled with rocking chairs reinforced the summer seaside theme, as did the anchors and paddleboat steering wheels that accented the interior decor. The Newport, which Disneyites proudly billed as the largest hotel in all of Europe (with 1,100 rooms), would also be disparaged by architectural critics for its very size, with published descriptions referring to it as "a fat lady in a tutu" that looks "monstrously overblown."[88]

Downriver (the "Rio Grande," to be precise) from the New York, the Sequoia and the Newport were two other vacation residences, both of which celebrated the spirit of the American West: the Hotel Cheyenne and the Hotel Santa Fe. The former was designed by Stern as a simulated Wild West town, like those used in the making of famous Hollywood Westerns: its 1,000 two-star guest rooms were tucked behind two-story, false-fronted frame buildings, labeled with names such as the Bunk House, the Blacksmith's, and the Wyatt Earp Saloon. And in the main lodge, the Chuckwagon Cafe displayed branding irons and lariats, wagon wheels, bleached cattle skulls, antler chandeliers, Western movie posters, studded-leather armchairs, and bar stools topped with horse saddles. With its wooden sidewalks and dusty streets leading suggestively onto High Noon Square, the Hotel Cheyenne was planned as a mini–theme park in and of itself, so that guests could explore—and experience—every corner of the cinematic layout.

81

The Hotel Santa Fe, by Antoine Predock, built on the frontier theme with a highly poeticized version of the Southwest and its mosaic of cultures. Like its neighbor across the river, it too had a "motel feel," with guest rooms widely dispersed into a number of separate buildings. Earthtone colors accented by turquoise dominated this landscape, along with terraced architecture meant to resemble Indian pueblos in the hot and arid climate of New Mexico. But the Hotel Santa Fe was not intended to be simply a themed cultural village. Predock drew inspiration from Wim Wenders's film *Paris, Texas,* and created a place that would suggest the weirdness of pop culture and the desert.[89] "I wanted to get at the intensities of the West that depart from nostalgia," he commented. "Otherwise it becomes an airport-gift-shop mentality."[90] For this reason, strange things—a neon road runner, a volcano, a crashed spaceship, and an auto graveyard—were positioned outside among the mesas and buttes. But the pièce de résistance of Predock's plan was the large drive-in movie screen atop the reception building. Though he lost the battle to leave it poignantly blank (it instead features the frozen image of Clint Eastwood's face in *A Fistful of Dollars*), he succeeded in capturing the complexity and quirkiness of the American Southwest.[91]

Created by a showcase of the biggest names in contemporary postmodern architecture, the Euro Disney hotel district was designed to be new, both thematically and architecturally. Each vacation residence was intended to make an individual statement and complement the others to capture many different aspects of the American experience. But not all agreed, in the final analysis, that this goal was ever achieved. "It's as if Disney commissioned five different screenplays," one critic noted, "and mushed them together to satisfy market tastes."[92] Still another described them as being "ungainly and uncomfortable with each other."[93] Given the decision to engage outside architects instead of Disney's in-house Imagineers, it should come as little surprise that different artistic visions and personalities bubbled to the surface. Such diversity and complexity have added to the overall richness of the Euro Disney experience.

To their credit, Disney planners recognized from the start that designing a theme park and designing a hotel district were two fundamentally different tasks. The Disney theme park, which had traditionally sought to transport guests to new worlds of cinematic wonder, was an environment of constant motion, with guests circulating through an array of rides, restaurants, shops, and shows. All experiences were designed to be of limited duration and to cohere with one another, like the parts of a film, in order to encourage the willing suspension of disbelief. The hotel district, on the other hand, needed to be a place that would hold up under extended scrutiny. As observed by architectural critic Suzanne Stephens, "hotels aren't meant to be experienced for only two hours and at a comfortable distance."[94] They are seen close-up—and not through the rose-colored glasses that guests put on (with their mouse ears) at the Main Gate entrance to the Magic Kingdom.

Each half of the Euro Disney Resort was designed to surprise and delight with a kaleidoscope of striking architecture, activities, and artistry. Each half was also intended to thrust guests into the plotline—conceptually and physically—of a familiar Disney story. But as planners were quick to discover, creating such a place in the multinational community of Europe was a serious challenge. The plethora of choices before them at every stage of development was staggering. "What we're doing is an entertainment experience," commented Tony Baxter, of the Disney park in California. "We feel we have created prototypes in terms of experiential design. What we sometimes talk about is eliminating contradictions that are a part of our daily life. By eliminating those contradictions, people can get on with the business of enjoying the show. That experience is not the same as seeing a fine piece of art, but on the other hand Disneyland has made many peoples' lives happier."[95] The Euro Disney Resort, which had called on the creative talents of Imagineers and outside architects, aimed to do

83

the very same thing in the diverse, multinational community of Europe. As design efforts led to actual construction in Marne-la-Vallée, Disney executives focused their attention on the next pressing matter: promoting the world's newest Magic Kingdom.

3   Marketing a New Magic Kingdom

For years, April 1992 had been a distant goal for Euro Disney planners. But the day they had long awaited was suddenly upon them—and they made the most of it in a dramatic TV special. Swooping camera angles of Sleeping Beauty's palace captured the architectural splendor of France's newest landmark. Ticker-tape parades with pumpkin dancers and the famous Disney characters spanned the length of Main Street, U.S.A. Crowds strained against velvet ropes waiting to hop on the nearest Disney ride. And waves of celebrities strolled past photographers on a red carpet walk toward the Magic Kingdom. Taking in all of the Hollywood heavyweights who had turned out for the event, CBS correspondent Pat O'Brien commented: "Stars, stars, and more stars. But I'm sure that by the end of the evening you'll agree . . . that the 'l'Étoile du Jour' of this place is the park itself."[1]

But how could this be? April 12, 1992, the publicized opening date of the Euro Disney Resort, was still a full day away. Had Disney executives decided at the last minute to bump up the much anticipated "Grand Ouverture" by twenty-four hours? Had the gloved hands on their Mickey Mouse watches misled them into believing it was actually the twelfth? Was there something just a little bit strange going on here? No, no, and . . . well, yes. The inaugural celebration, which was beamed live into the homes of more than 60 million Europeans (and countless Americans) one day early, was really just a preview—a two-hour "infomercial"—of the new theme park and hotel complex. But it was

85

teeming with so many celebrities and so much fun that, to many, it did not even seem like an ad. Television critic Kathleen O'Steen gushed over the $10 million media event and described it as "an entertaining mix of variety entertainment [that] gave perspective to the magnitude of the project."[2] Her double emphasis of the program's "entertainment" value suggested that Disney had succeeded in elevating the act of promotion to an art form.

It seemed that the Walt Disney Company had scored yet another public relations victory by exploiting the very medium used to capture the grand opening of Disney's flagship park in California nearly forty years before: television. But the small screen was only one part of the marketing mix this time around. Film, radio, newspapers, magazines, posters, and corporate sponsors all helped to spread "Disney fever" across the Continent. Executives in charge of tailoring a media campaign for Europe, however, had not had the luxury of promoting their most recent product in its best possible light. Given the barrage of scathing—and often purely speculative—reports from a hostile press in Europe and the United States, they were forced to devise an aggressive plan that would function both offensively and defensively. Walt Disney's own words, "You can dream, create, design and build the most wonderful place in the world . . . but it takes people to make the dream a reality," seemed to support this two-pronged promotional strategy for Euro Disney by suggesting the importance of comprehensive marketing.[3]

PAINTING THE TOWN DISNEY

For more than half a century before Euro Disneyland was built, Disney films and products had been a staple in European life. Comic books, T-shirts, and school supplies stamped with the smiling face of Mickey Mouse were a part of everyday experience. Nonetheless, the prelaunch media blitz—said to cost some $220 million—took France and all of Europe by storm.[4] It was a gargantuan affair that called upon the talents of outside advertising

agencies, public relations specialists, and Disney's many entertainment divisions (film, television, home video, consumer products) over a period of several years in an effort to blanket the
Continent with enthusiasm for the new theme park. In the words
of one Paris analyst, the Euro Disney publicity campaign represented "an object lesson in synergy, control, great dealmaking
and a fair amount of secrecy."[5] It also gave people across Europe
a clear picture of what doing business Disney-style really meant.

The Walt Disney Company could scarcely have afforded to
be half-hearted in its promotional efforts. Just years before, three
brand-new $150 million amusement parks in France had fallen
flat—and two of them had been forced into bankruptcy.[6] Tides of
negative publicity for the Euro Disney Resort did not help matters. So Disney execs put together a comprehensive media campaign designed to snuff out arguments that went no further than
objecting to the idea of an "American" theme park in Europe. By
giving potential guests a taste of Euro Disney's ambience and
showing them that it would fit comfortably into the European
landscape, they sought to appeal to the child in everyone. Company officials justified the astronomical budget for media and
community relations as a mandatory investment in the long-term
success of the project.

Two events set the wheels in motion: the grand opening of
Europe's first Disney Store in England and the unveiling of "Espace Euro Disneyland," a preview center for curiosity seekers in
France. The Disney Store, which opened on London's Regent
Street on November 3, 1990, was a natural continuation of previous successes. Given that the original store in California's Glendale Galleria had spawned seventy-seven others in three short
years, Disney executives gambled that they could crack open the
European retail market and generate excitement for Euro Disney
in one fell swoop. Donna Moore, vice president of Disney Stores,
expressed confidence that the new outlet (with its four thousand
different items of merchandise) would work wonders. "I don't
think we need worry about over-exposure providing the quality

is there," she commented. "And because the store itself is so entertaining, I think it will just enhance the Disney experience for everyone."[7] The throngs who showed up on its opening day confirmed her instincts.

"Espace Euro Disneyland," which threw open its doors one month later on December 6, 1990, was also as much an exercise in public relations as it was a commercial venture. Located near the park site amid the construction, it offered visitors a taste of coming attractions. Its design was pure Disney: a sixty-five-foot wizard's hat positioned above the entrance capitalized on imagery from the "Sorcerer's Apprentice" sequence in *Fantasia* (1940). Drawings and tiny scale models of the park's attractions filled the interior areas. And on the terrace was a Texas-style chili counter and a souvenir shop selling Disney character merchandise. John Winder, Euro Disney's vice president for marketing, noted that "we were getting so many letters and telephone calls, that we simply had to open up."[8] Thousands visited each week for a sneak preview of the new park, paying two dollars each for an entry ticket—and most left with armfuls of souvenirs. Special sales receipts thanked them with a French-printed message: "Welcome to the magic style of Walt Disney."[9]

But this pair of ventures was only the beginning. Before long, the handiwork of Euro Disney marketers (who had offices in Paris, London, Frankfurt, and Amsterdam) was visible everywhere. Articles about the new theme park were printed in magazines and newspapers across the Continent. Mickey, Donald, and other Disney characters made appearances at hospitals and other public places. Catalogs of Europe's largest mail-order companies (such as La Redoute and the Quelle Group) were stuffed with some twenty pages of promotional merchandise. Special Euro Disney tags were attached to the wares of Disney licensees. A large walk-through facade of Le Château de la Belle au Bois Dormant (Sleeping Beauty's castle) made its way from city to city on a tour of Europe called "En Route pour la Magie." Four hundred French children were invited to a birthday party for Mickey

Mouse. And dozens of local officials were flown to Walt Disney World in Florida so that they might see for themselves how the new enterprise might function in Europe.[10]

Other branches of the Walt Disney Company also pitched in to help promote the Euro Disney Resort. In its many children's magazines, Disney Publishing portrayed the soon-to-be-open theme park as a wonderland. Buena Vista Home Video, the distribution arm for Disney films, attached a five-minute promotional trailer for Euro Disney at the end of *The Little Mermaid*, *The Rescuers Down Under*, and other supporting film titles. Dennis Hightower of Disney Consumer Products, Europe/Middle East, reported that his division would deliver an additional $40 to 45 million of "equivalent media value" in exposure for the theme park and expected it to be seen by some 162 million—"people we might not have reached otherwise," he noted. One entertainment analyst predicted that the synergy-based campaign would have a major impact: "The public may not know or care about Buena Vista or Disney Consumer Products, but they certainly know and care about a theme park of this size."[11]

Perhaps the most powerful piece of the Euro Disney media campaign, however, was television. In addition to the enormously popular European Disney Channel (and Sky Movies, a satellite-based broadcast system that beamed Disney programming into one million homes in England and Ireland), TV spots designed by WPP Group's Ogilvy & Mather began airing in the United Kingdom, Holland, Belgium, Germany, and France as early as January 1992. Members of the Euro Disney marketing team had set up extensive agreements with some of Europe's biggest commercial TV stations, which allowed them to air weekly Disney shows for children. Each program was packed with images of Euro Disney's coming attractions. One episode of the *Disney Club*, a Sunday morning favorite throughout Europe, was even broadcast from the soon-to-be-open park. The three hosts went behind the scenes, tried on cast-member costumes, and even announced a contest that would award a trip for four to Euro Disneyland. At the end of the segment, one of them sighed: "I wish I could have stayed longer."[12]

Étienne de Villiers, president for television at Buena Vista International, rejected all hints that the *Disney Club* was merely an advertisement for the Euro Disney Resort. "We feel very sensitive about the amount of promotion we do on the show," he noted, "because if you do too much, people start to feel exploited." He added that focus group research had shown the theme park segments to be among the most popular of all. In any case, European television stations didn't treat the *Disney Club* as a paid commercial. Because they were so desperate for quality children's programs, they offered Disney top dollar for the right to broadcast them. The *Disney Club* and other shows that hyped the Euro Disney Resort were a source of clear profit for the Walt Disney Company.[13]

SPONSORING THE DREAM

Television, however, was not the only source of free publicity for the Euro Disney Resort. Corporate sponsorship agreements also proved to be lucrative, just as they had in the 1950s when Disneyland was opening in California. In return for an investment in the theme park, Euro Disney executives agreed to display the logos of sponsors (or "participants," as they are called in Disney lingo) on its rides. They also allowed Disney characters to be featured in the ads of corporate partners.[14] Before long, Euro Disney had signed twelve official participants: Renault, Banque Nationale de Paris, Europcar, Kodak, Nestlé, Coca-Cola, Philips, Esso, France Telecom, American Express, IBM, and Mattel—each of which had agreed to help out with prelaunch advertising. No arm twisting was required. Participants benefited from the prestige of the Disney name while Euro Disney received funding for its attractions and visibility in the campaigns of many family-oriented European businesses.

The French carmaker Renault was the first Euro Disney participant to come on board and celebrated the new partnership by dedicating its huge showcase window on the Champs-Élysées to Mickey Mouse.[15] It also poured a lot of francs into a print ad campaign that united the two businesses before European audiences. One spread pictured a family of the future piloting a bubble-domed aircraft to the Euro Disney Resort. The caption read: "In 2328, Thanks to Renault, you'll arrive at Euro Disney aboard the latest 'Reinastella.' Having taken the Skyway A-4, turned left at the following cumulus-nimbus, swooped down towards the stratus-cirrus cluster on the right on anticyclone 'Minnie,' you will land gently at the foot of Sleeping Beauty's castle. In the meantime, from April 12, 1992, you can visit Euro Disney aboard your Renault Espace." Adventure. Fantasy. Futurism. New frontiers. The advertisement celebrated the imaginative spirit of Renault and the Euro Disney Resort. Even more important, it encouraged people to visit the park, where a prototype of the Reinastella, "the only car in the world capable of reading your mind," would be on display at Le Visionarium in Discoveryland. The closing message cemented the partnership between Renault and Euro Disney. "As you're well aware, today, Renault takes you to a world of dreams," it read. "But tomorrow the dreams may well become reality. . . ."

Perhaps the most avid Euro Disney promoter during the pre-opening campaign was Swiss food giant Nestlé, which had secured exclusive use of Disney's image in the food sector.[16] It viewed the partnership as a huge marketing opportunity and hyped the park in ads for all of its products, from cheese to chocolate. In Holland, Nestlé launched what it claims was the largest single promotion in the country's history. By installing ten different product display cases—each of which enticed shoppers to enter a contest for a Euro Disney family vacation—in some 2,500 stores, Nestlé achieved high visibility in the places where 90 percent of all Dutch groceries were sold. It financed 250 such getaways and awarded a host of lesser Disney prizes (such as Mickey Mouse mugs, pins, and footballs) to the runners-up, to publicly reinforce the partnership. In the words of one Nestlé spokesman, the company engaged in "a massive effort all over Europe in every market, to get the Disney idea across to consumers."[17]

But corporate participants were not the only ones to promote the Euro Disney Resort. Major sell-through accounts, such as Woolworth's in the United Kingdom, also helped the marketing effort by developing Euro Disney holiday giveaways. McDonald's agreed to launch an $8 million Euro Disney campaign in 1,388 fast-food outlets across Europe shortly after the grand opening. P & O European Ferries Ltd. signed a four-year agreement that would enable it to feature Euro Disney displays on its nearly seventy sailings per day between Britain and continental Europe.[18] Even small players participated, like Travel Europe, an eleven-vehicle bus company in northern England, which invested in two new coaches (at a cost of nearly $500,000) and distributed 100,000 copies of a twelve-page flyer for special Euro Disney tours. All over Europe, businesses climbed on board. "It's one of the smartest deals I've seen," noted Emmanuelle Fradet-Vananty of the specialist French publication *Communication CB News*. "Euro Disney really knows how to get people to pay."[19]

Thanks to the extensive network of tie-ins that members of the sales and marketing team had engineered, promotional messages for Euro Disney seemed to be coming from every direction. "Good fun, good food, go well together: Nestlé." "Coca-Cola welcomes the Euro Disney Resort to Europe." "Get closer to the magic with Europcar." "American Express. The Official Card of Euro Disney." "Sounds, Images and Lights by Philips at Euro Disney: Philips, It's Already Tomorrow." "Mattel: We Know Just How to Make Children Happy." "Esso: It's Magic." Images of parades, castles, costumed workers, and golf courses with mouse-eared sand traps complemented such slogans with powerful visual appeal in flyers, newspapers, magazines, and wall-size Métro posters all over Paris. Margo Vignola, an analyst with Salomon Brothers, was impressed by the scope of the media plan. "I don't think it can miss," she stated. "They are masters of marketing.

When the place opens, it will be perfect. And they know how to make people smile—even the French."[20]

But while Euro Disney's omnipresence dazzled many and helped to heighten anticipation for the new theme park, some industry insiders complained that the high-powered marketing campaign was simply too aggressive. "I was in France 18 months ago," recalled California-based theme park analyst Ray Braun. "There were billboards all over Nice and Cannes that said, 'Come to Euro Disney, opening in two years,' sponsored by Renault. That kind of cross-marketing in advance is unheard of. Europe has never seen anything like that, on that scale."[21] Braun was right. Media publicity and community relations programs were a rarity in Europe, especially France. "It's certainly a different way of working than I've come across before," admitted Andy Fairburn, sales and marketing manager of Sally Holidays in Britain. "But it doesn't leave a bad taste in the mouth because they are so professional."[22]

THE CASTING CALL

In addition to layering France and all of Europe with messages about the Euro Disney Resort, the company also had to prepare operationally for the grand opening. The task before the Euro Disney team was monumental. Not only did they have to find, select, and train 12,000 employees for 1,200 different positions (thereby making Euro Disney the largest single source of jobs in all of Europe), they also had to meet the special hiring requirements of France.[23] Writer Judson Gooding has described the goal as "one of the more demanding personnel challenges of this decade," adding that "it is somewhat like telling an army general to recruit, train, prepare, and equip an entire army division, and bring it into combat readiness, in a few months' time."[24] But even Gooding understated the magnitude of the task, for the directors of Euro Disney were not just aiming to assemble and train an otherwise homogenous staff. They were trying to forge a diverse

93

multinational team that would mirror the expected proportions of visiting guests: 45 percent French, 30 percent other European, and 15 percent from outside of Europe.[25]

To accomplish this, planners opened an on-site casting center at Disney University in September 1991. Their goal was to "enlist" some 10,000 employees within six months while maintaining selective applicant-to-hire ratios. A team of sixty interviewers was assembled to screen potential "cast members" at the rate of 750 per day, six days per week; only about 70 persons each day (or fewer than 10 percent of all applicants) would be offered positions, or "roles," in the Disney "show."[26] Euro Disney could afford to be choosy. In one month, more than 9,000 resumes came in, half of them unsolicited.

The flood of professional interest in Euro Disney can be attributed, at least in part, to a sudden economic downswing in Europe that hit France particularly hard. The idea of earning approximately $6.50 per hour—a full 15 percent more than France's minimum wage at the time—was not unappealing to the majority of would-be cast members facing the prospect of unemployment.[27] And the further promise of tips on top of this already competitive pay rate made the Euro Disney jobs seem downright lucrative in what would turn out to be a period of crippling recession.

But recruiters, charged with hiring la crème de la crème, were not content to wade through existing applications alone. They kicked their outreach plan into high gear by booking meetings with hotel, technical, and restaurant schools, as well as local French chambers of commerce. They introduced a system of employee referrals. They oversaw the "It's Time To Come Home" campaign, directed at European citizens who had worked in the hospitality industry in North America (including former Disney cast members who had staffed the World Showcase at Epcot Center). And finally, they ran newspaper advertisements in Los Angeles, San Francisco, Dallas, Chicago, Montreal, New York, and Orlando—which produced more than 2,600 applications in just a few weeks. By early 1992, nearly 8,000 positions had been filled. Disney scouts combed Europe in the remaining months before April, visiting twenty-eight cities in all twelve European Economic Community countries (except Greece) in the hopes of rounding out their cast with a bit more international flavor.[28]

But hiring was only step one of the process. Step two, training, was even more formidable. Not only did the directors of Euro Disney face the challenge of overcoming language and culture barriers, they also had to communicate their vision of what the Euro Disney Resort would be to a diverse crew. This was no small task, considering that new cast members had come from at least thirty-five different nations.[29] Most had never even been to a Disney theme park. One executive stressed that the new venture would be unlike anything Europe had ever seen. "One of the key differences at Euro Disney is that we are neither in the hotel nor in the parks business alone," he explained, "but that two businesses complement each other to potentially create Europe's most desired and complete vacation destination resort."[30] The concept of a "vacation destination," where visitors could go to get away from it all without ever having to leave the property, was new for most Europeans. So training was designed to provide a broad overview of the project and give new recruits a sense of Euro Disney's unique mission and service philosophy.[31]

A two-day program called "Traditions" introduced cast members to "Disney culture" using films, worksheets, and team-building exercises. According to David Kanally, director of France's Disney University, one group of French students spent twenty minutes debating the meaning of "efficiency." "That wouldn't happen in Orlando," he noted. But Euro Disney president Robert Fitzpatrick saw no immediate cause for alarm. "The French question everything," he observed. "We're seeing Cartesian skepticism meeting American can-do-ism."[32] A collection of reference guides distributed to each cast member reinforced the message that Euro Disney would be a place unlike any other. "La Magie C'est Vous!" ("The Magic Is You!") provided an overview of the many units of the Disney organization and situated Euro Disney at the end of a long line of creative innovations. "Le Guide du Cast Member," explained the importance of each person's "role in the show." And "La Courtoisie Selon Disney" ("Courtesy Disney Style") offered guidelines on how to communicate (verbally and nonverbally) to provide unmatchable levels of guest service.

One handbook, however, touched off a minor controversy with applicants, French labor unions, and the press. Entitled "The Euro Disney Look," it set out a series of detailed guidelines regarding personal appearance. Thorolf Degelmann, Euro Disney's Austrian-born vice president of personnel, who had helped to staff Tokyo Disneyland, explained:

> We have appearance standards that are a condition of being hired. For men, it means no facial hair, a conservative haircut with no hair over the ears or the collar, no earrings, no exposed tattoos, and no jeans. For women, no extremes in dying hair or in makeup, and no long fingernails. We want a conservative, professional look; we want our employees to be warm, outgoing, and sincere. We don't want guests to be distracted by oddities or mannerisms of the cast members.[33]

France's second-largest labor union, the Confédération Français Démocratique du Travail, attacked Euro Disney for imposing repressive rules of appearance and behavior on its employees. Union spokeswoman Isabelle Perrin-Boucher led the charge, arguing that they infringed upon individual freedom—even though French labor legislation allows employers to establish certain rules of dress. "It's true some firms impose a number of criteria," she admitted. "But Disney is going much too far. They impose a regulation length for women's nails and have banned lipstick and eye makeup. Women's heels must be between 2 centimeters and 10 centimeters (0.8 and 4 inches) high. Skirts must be 8 centimeters (3.2 inches) above the knee—no more, no less."[34]

Perrin-Boucher's words, which encouraged people to imagine Euro Disney as an oppressive place patrolled by millimeter-measuring "grooming guards," caught the attention of the international press, who reported on the "Mauschwitz scandal" with zeal.[35] Despite the inaccuracies of her statement, the story was circulated—and followed—by people around the world who were intrigued by the idea of Disney's clean-cut wholesomeness sparking a storm in France.[36] What went largely unreported was why Euro Disney officials were insisting upon such rigid grooming and dress codes. As explained in the "Euro Disney Look" manual, it was less about forcing American values upon Europe than bringing Disney magic to life, just as they had in California, Florida, and Japan:

Euro Disney is a show . . . an immense, three-dimensional show in which our guests are the audience . . . and in which our cast members are the actors. . . . The Euro Disney Look is designed to ensure that there are no extremes in appearance that might contradict the carefully planned setting and ambience of an on-stage area. In fact, the entire show is the "star" with each cast member playing a supporting role.[37]

According to Euro Disney spokesman Nicolas de Schonen, resistance to the "Euro Disney Look" was a sign that many in Europe did not grasp the nature of a Disney resort. "They have difficulty imagining that everything will have a theme," he noted, "and that half the employees will need to wear costumes in keeping with that theme. We are a show business company. Disneyland is a 3-D film in which there are actors playing roles. Employees—or cast members, as we call them—must conform with our grooming policy."[38] Charles Ridgway, the park's publicity director, agreed: "We try to train into our people an attitude that they're part of a show. They dress the part, they act the part, they live the part."[39]

But strict rules also served another purpose: they helped to create a common culture among members of a diverse staff,   97 many of whom were transplants to France. All cast members, regardless of age, linguistic ability, or rank, would be held to the same set of high standards. And they could take pride in maintaining—even showcasing—them. Daniel Coccoli, vice president of resort hotel operations for Euro Disney, noted the importance of such well-defined expectations, especially in the multinational community of Europe:

> With everyone coming from different backgrounds and cultures, our set of rules is essential. Otherwise, we won't make it. As a matter of fact, the employees are very happy with the standards we've set forth. They know exactly what they have to do, what they're being judged on and what we're asking of them. As far as the French are concerned, I believe they understand and appreciate this.[40]

Coccoli's assessment that all French cast members appreciated the rigid guidelines was wildly optimistic, to be sure. Many openly resented them. But the sense of order that they helped to generate did offer a solid foundation upon which the venture could build as 12,000 fresh cast members came together to discover—and ultimately, create—the meaning of an all-new Disney resort. The labor leaders, unsuccessful in their bid to relax Euro Disney's rules, got their first taste of a company whose fierce protection of its own corporate culture rivaled that of France.[41]

THE GRAND OPENING SPECIAL

On April 11, 1992, training manuals were put down, costumes were put on, and cast members buzzed with anticipation. It was time to show the world that the Euro Disney Resort was more than just hype. The two-hour grand opening TV special, put together by American producer Don Mischer and Buena Vista Productions, was to be beamed live to twenty-two countries on four continents and show on five different networks in Europe alone, including TF-1 in France, RAI in Italy, TV-1 in Spain, and ARD in Germany. Thousands had been invited to attend the event, too: journalists, media analysts, travel agents, tour operators, suppliers, and just about anybody who could affect the future of the park.[42] Euro Disney execs kept their fingers crossed, hoping that the live TV special would be "the entertainment event of the decade" and not a repeat of the disastrous Disneyland opening, nearly forty years before.[43]

In the end, their anxiety proved to be unfounded. Aside from the atrocious pronunciation of occasional French words by the program's hosts, "Madame Melanie Griffith and Monsieur Don Johnson," as they were introduced, the show went off without a hitch. Splashy overviews of Frontierland, Adventureland, Fantasyland, Discoveryland, and Main Street, U.S.A., offered viewers a taste of the many rides, restaurants, shops, and shows; a tour of the hotel district provided a look at the six American-themed vacation residences and Festival Disney; and footage of the model shop at Walt Disney Imagineering took viewers behind the scenes to peek at the design process in action. A cavalcade of celebrities—including José Carreras, Cher, Gloria Estefan and the Miami Sound Machine, the Gipsy Kings, Angela Lansbury, the Four Tops, the Temptations, Tina Turner, and France's silver medal–winning ice skaters Isabelle and Paul Duchesnay—added to the excitement with colorful performances. And many others, such as Jean-Claude Van Damme, Jane Seymour, Michael J. Fox, Peter Gabriel, Candace Bergen, and Eddie Murphy, also helped to ring in the birth of Europe's new Magic Kingdom.[44]

The mix of celebrities was diverse by design. It reflected the multinational character of the Euro Disney enterprise and suggested to viewers everywhere that Disney art, in all its many forms, was not simply an American product, but a transnational experience—something that could be shared and enjoyed by everyone. The Euro Disney Resort, like most names on the star-studded guest list (and Mickey Mouse, himself), was to be an international symbol of goodwill. Michael Eisner, sporting a character tie, reinforced this message at the dedication ceremony for Le Château de la Belle au Bois Dormant:

> The founder of our company once said: "What I want more than anything else is for Disneyland to be a place where grown-ups and children can experience together the wonders of life, of adventure, and come out feeling the better for it." Well, Walt's dream is also our dream for Euro Disney. And so, with young voices from all over Europe, we dedicate Le Château de la Belle au Bois Dormant to both the young and the young-at-heart. To those who believe when you wish upon a star, your dreams come true.[45]

A choir of children from all over Europe singing "When You Wish Upon a Star" before Le Château de la Belle au Bois Dormant drove the idea home. When star-shaped fireworks exploded above the illuminated palace at the end of the song, a visibly moved Melanie Griffith gasped, "It's just like a fairy tale!" Indeed it was.

But the grand opening special was much more than a fairy tale. It was a promotional media event that celebrated the spirit of different times, places, peoples, and cultures. In the words of special correspondent Pat O'Brien, it showed that the new resort was "uniting the world under the name of Disney."[46] The mariachi bands in Frontierland had come all the way from Mexico. The African Tam-Tams in Adventureland had traveled from Zaire. The fairy-tale characters in Fantasyland had stepped out of the pages of European storybooks. The herds of buffalo in Buffalo Bill's Wild West show had come—via 747, Johnson noted—from the United States. Even the custom-made steam locomotives circling the park had been crafted in Wales. By importing back into France all of the colonialist gesturing that America had learned from the Old World, Euro Disney executives demonstrated their desire—and their capacity—to create a place of multinational beauty and richness, a land filled with familiar reassurances and new discoveries, a spot where all people might feel at home.

In the interest of forging an all-new identity for the Euro Disney Resort, producer Don Mischer and his team had taken conscious steps to capitalize on the excitement of an Old World–New World partnership. A film clip of Roy Disney on location in the small village of Isigny-sur-Mer (from which the Disney name was derived) dramatized his family connection with France, which dated back more than nine hundred years. A collage of Disney movies dubbed in continental languages demonstrated that Mickey Mouse and his friends were indeed citizens of Europe, "known and loved in every corner of the globe," according to host Don Johnson. A tour of Discoveryland by a fake Jules Verne (played by actor Michel Vallete) was conducted in French, with English subtitles, to stress the European roots of this "land." And a segment highlighting a ceremony at the Hotel Disneyland, taped earlier that day, showed a flurry of cheerleaders and band members dressed in red, white, and blue—reminding viewers that France and America share the same national colors.

As the program continued, anticipation for the big event— the grand opening of the Euro Disney Resort—mounted. Periodic check-in reports with Pat O'Brien, stationed in the park, offered a running countdown of the time left. An illuminated clock with the minutes remaining heightened the sense of expectation, much like that of a New Year's celebration. Black-and-white clips of emcee "Ronnie Reagan" at the grand opening of Disneyland in 1955 reinforced the event's importance by providing a window to the past and suggesting that April 12, 1992, would also be a day that people would gaze back upon. "We are about to witness an event that will be remembered for many years to come," noted Johnson. Madame Griffith had made the same point earlier in the program. "I mean, this is a big event here," she observed. "After all, it's only the fourth time in history that a Magic Kingdom has come to life, and tonight's grand opening is being broadcast live on five different networks to more than 60 million Europeans in five languages. I mean, that's big!"[47]

THE REAL OPENING DAY

Disney executives must have been thrilled when the reviews came in. Michael Williams reported in *Variety* that "the verdict was an almost universal thumbs up."[48] Writer Kathleen O'Steen concurred, noting, "Spec hosts Don Johnson and Melanie Griffith looked and acted jet lagged. But the entertaining and informative program had enough fireworks and hoopla to make every child want to start saving pennies toward airfare to France."[49] Even high-powered French types expressed approval. Pierre Flabbée of brokerage Coureoux Bouvet described the event as "[a] total success. It corresponded exactly to my expectations."[50] Christophe Cherblane of Cholet Dupont said, "What struck me was the absence of what you could call the 'French weaknesses,' such as litter. This park compares very well with Disney's operations in the United States."[51] And Jean-Jacques Limage of DLP James Capel in Paris dryly admitted, "I was suitably impressed."[52]

The financial picture was also promising. In anticipation of the grand opening, the share price of Walt Disney Company stock had been climbing for weeks—and Wall Street experts predicted that it would go even higher. Stockpicker Jessica Reif of Oppenheimer and Company observed that Disney shares had outperformed the market again and again after a major gate opening. Prior to the unveiling of the Disney-MGM Studios in 1989, for example, Disney's share price had climbed 33 percent, and it soared a further 44 percent in the following six months. Even with the 1982 debut of Epcot Center—which was late, over budget, and the target of bad press—Disney shares had outperformed the market in the first six months: they rose 34 percent in price while the market increased just 26 percent. Analyst Margo Vignola of Salomon Brothers projected that in 1992 Euro Disney

102

would add $.27 per share to Walt Disney Company stock and that by 1994 its contribution could rise to $.96 per share. She also predicted that attendance at Euro Disney would exceed the stated goal of 11 million guests in its first year by as many as 3 to 4 million.[53]

But not all was champagne and roses that first day. Two terrorist bombs set off the night before damaged electricity pylons and almost blacked out the park. Villagers from nearby Meaux demonstrated against the noise that would be caused by Euro Disney's nightly fireworks. And a twenty-four-hour rail strike protesting security and staffing problems shut down the suburban RER line connecting Paris and Marne-la-Vallée. French police forces braced themselves for a possible onslaught of traffic heading toward the park and feared that the 11,383-space parking lot might be backed up with as many as 90,000 cars.[54] The big crowds, however, stayed away. Deterred by reports that some 500,000 might be swarming to get into a park built to accomodate one-tenth that number, much of Europe decided to wait.[55] One Euro Disney spokesman breathed a sigh of relief that attendance had leveled off at about 20,000. "We avoided the nightmare and are very happy," he commented. "In addition, it's probably the first time that Disney has opened one of its parks and had all the rides functioning on day one."[56]

France's minister of culture, Jack Lang, who had described the park just days before as "an enclave of the American leisure industry in France," snubbed the event, explaining that he was too busy to attend.[57] So did French president François Mitterand, claiming, "It's just not my cup of tea."[58] But the first wave of visitors, less tormented by the threat of American cultural imperialism, wouldn't have missed it for anything. One French couple, Gilbert and Patricia Le Clercq, pulled their two kids out of bed at 4:00 A.M. in order to surprise them with a trip to Euro Disney. Their fourteen-year-old daughter, Severine, adored the place. "It's wonderful," she said. "I love watching the Disney cartoons."[59] Other children were equally thrilled. As reported in *Le*

Parisien, an eleven-year-old visitor named Vincent exclaimed, "I loved everything. There was nothing I didn't like. I'll never forget the haunted mansion." Thirteen-year-old Cyndie added, "I've asked my parents if we can come back. We just didn't have enough time to see everything."[60] The same French press that had been the voice of criticism recorded such rave reviews, lending credence to the front-page headline of the *New York Times* on April 13, 1992: "Only the French Elite Scorn Mickey's Debut."

The word was out: Euro Disney was a hit. A London newspaper reported that a group of German visitors had all "had a great time."[61] One family from northern Europe exclaimed how nice it was to finally have a Disney park in their corner of the world because trips to California or Florida had always been prohibitively expensive.[62] And a letter from an elderly French woman simply burst with praise: "I would greatly appreciate it if you could send my deepest thanks [to Snow White] for her sensitivity, from a grandmother who was reduced to tears just by seeing her. Thank you and bravo again for giving us these lifelike characters who welcome us into the cartoons in the marvelous world of Disney."[63] Fitzpatrick capitalized on the tide of goodwill, declaring that the Euro Disney Resort was "the most wonderful park we have ever created."[64]

By most accounts, the visitors who came to the Euro Disney Resort in its inaugural days found everything they had hoped for: lots of fun rides, good food, souvenirs, and photo opportunities with Mickey Mouse and his friends. Others grumbled about the long lines and high prices. A trip to Euro Disney, admittedly, was not inexpensive, especially considering that Europe's smaller middle class had less discretionary income to spend than their American counterparts. With single-day adult passes selling for $41 and children's passes going for $27 (at April 1992 exchange rates), visitors were paying dearly to experience Disney magic in Europe. Hotel rates, ranging from $130 to $410 per night, made a trip seem more costly still—even though all rooms were equipped to sleep four, rather than two, like most European hotels.[65] "The prices that we set for admission, hotel rooms, food, and merchandise were ambitious," Michael Eisner would later reflect, "but especially so given the poor state of the economy."[66]

In addition to pricing issues were concerns that Euro Disney just wasn't the same as Disneyland or Walt Disney World.[67] One American visitor lamented the multinational flavor of the Euro Disney Resort:

> The park has kind of a strange feel to it. They haven't yet figured out whether it is going to be an American park, a French park, or a European park. This is in the atmosphere of the park itself, and it is compounded by the behavior of visitors from various parts of Europe, which can be quite different. Little things like the attitudes of different nationalities with respect to disposing of trash are very noticeable. And differences in waiting-line behavior is striking. For instance, Scandinavians appear quite content to wait for rides, whereas some of the southern Europeans seem to have made an Olympic event out of getting to the ticket-taker first.[68]

Puzzled remarks such as this were made frequently by American visitors—especially those familiar with Disney's stateside parks, who couldn't help but project their homegrown expectations of Euro Disney onto continental soil. But their observations ultimately highlighted the awkwardness of European responses to the new theme park—and each other—more than any specific design or thematic flaws in Euro Disney itself.

Concerns about Euro Disney's ability to accommodate diversity were also picked up on by the popular press. Reporting on the grand opening, one newspaper queried, "Can an American theme park in Europe please all ages and nationalities? And in what country, if any, is this fantasy never-never-land which started with a Hollywood mouse? It is not, except in the most literal sense, France."[69] But that was precisely the point. Imagineers had worked hard to create a place that was radically different from the surrounding French countryside. In the words of Natalie Lewis, a Euro Disney cast member who was interviewed by Pat O'Brien as part of the grand opening special, "when you leave the park and you realize you are in France, it's a big shock. But if you are in this park, there is no way of telling that you are in France. . . . It's very neat."[70] Lewis was right. Everything about the park—the architecture, the topiaries, the music—was other-worldly. And because it was surrounded by miles and miles of vacant French countryside, there was nothing to interrupt the illusion.

Poor service was another factor mentioned by the press in early reviews of the resort. Cast members taken on to work at Euro Disney "are, mostly, nice enough," wrote one British journalist. "'Mostly,' because even on opening weekend some clearly couldn't care less. . . . My overwhelming impression of the . . . employees was that they were out of their depth."[71] An American tourist expressed a similar point of view: "Most of the workers are simply not aiming to please, even though they are thrilled to have jobs in the rotten economy. They are playing a different game than their American counterparts. They are acting like real people instead of 'Disney' people. Unfortunately, you get the feeling that the whole thing is not yet under control."[72] To be sure, it wasn't. All the training in the world could hardly have ironed out every difficulty before the huge theme park and hotel complex became operational. And problems were magnified by the curious expectation that European cast members would internalize the Disney service philosophy overnight. As one journalist noted, "The Disney style of service is one with which Americans have grown up. There are several styles of service (or lack of it) in Europe, unbridled enthusiasm is not a marked feature of them."[73] The words of another reporter put the problem in proper context: "Even at its worst the service at Euro Disney was better than the best I encountered in Paris."[74]

That is not to say, however, that poor service did not exist at Euro Disney. Some employees delighted in refusing, in subtle—or not so subtle—ways, to become "Disneyfied." One French cast member bragged about exacting revenge on "demanding" guests by cutting off their heads in the group photographs he was asked to take. Others, stationed outside attractions as "greeters," capitalized on the confused expectations of visitors by charging an entrance fee of 20 francs (approximately $4) before admitting them. (All Disney theme park attractions are free with the purchase of a Main Gate admission passport.) But perhaps the most disturbing offenses were committed by select cast members outfitted as the famous Disney characters. While the great majority of these roles were filled by people dedicated to upholding Disney ideals, some took vindictive pleasure in subverting the Disney mythology by staring down hopeful children and denying them autographs.

SUMMERTIME BLUES

Such startling on-the-job behavior, however, was not unique to France, or Europe. Similar instances of employee rebellion at the other Disney parks in California, Florida, and Japan can be recited ad nauseum—especially during the turmoil of an opening year, before proper disciplinary mechanisms are in place. Things finally came to a head at Euro Disney in May 1992 when the *Hollywood Reporter* printed an explosive story, revealing that some three thousand disgruntled cast members (25 percent of the total workforce) had walked off the job, never to come back, supposedly because of low pay and poor working conditions. People around Europe—and the world—gasped. The plot was thickening. Was Mickey Mouse really an American oppressor, as the intelligentsia had warned? Fitzpatrick said no. In an interview with Richard Turner of the *Wall Street Journal*, he admitted that cast members had worked under "tough conditions" during the grand opening but shrugged off the story: "It's pure fiction, a good script."[75] In reality, only one thousand had left, slightly less than half of them voluntarily. The others, he said, "we asked to leave," adding that "we've separated those who really wanted to do the job from those who thought it was a joyride."[76]

Fitzpatrick dismissed another claim by the *Hollywood Reporter* as well: that theme park attendance was dwindling. He conceded that there had been fewer visitors from the Paris area than expected but declined to discuss it any further, citing the longtime policy of the Walt Disney Company not to issue any statistics until year-end. Unfortunately the damage had already been done. The erroneous article—and others that highlighted Fitzpatrick's fierce denial of its claims—only called attention to the fact that things were amiss chez Mickey. On May 27, 1992, when Turner's article appeared, the market reacted swiftly: Euro Disney's already fading stock began a dramatic tumble and fell from 1277 pence to 1250 on the London market; it closed two days later at 1213 pence.[77]

In an effort to halt the downward spiral and squash rumors that the Euro Disney Resort would shortly be sounding the death knell, Fitzpatrick broke with Disney tradition: he issued a report in the first week of June, stating that more than 1.5 million guests had visited Euro Disneyland in its first seven weeks.[78] While this figure when annualized would bring Euro Disney within striking distance of its first-year goal of 11 million, some analysts came to a more unhappy conclusion. "Given that attendance will almost certainly be well below 30,000 [per day] in the winter months," noted one, "Euro Disney really should be up at around 40,000 visits [per day] at the moment. These are disappointing results."[79] But Fitzpatrick cautioned against speculation. "After only seven weeks of experience," he wrote in his report, "it would be impossible to extrapolate meaningfully from these results or draw any conclusions regarding attendance for either the calendar or the fiscal year."[80]

Fitzpatrick also announced that special measures were being taken to ensure success in the long term. The Disney-MGM Studios Europe, a $2.3 billion park that had been slated to open next to Euro Disneyland in 1995, was being temporarily shelved.[81] Prices at the budget hotels were being slashed from 750 francs ($150) to 550 francs ($110) to encourage lengthier stays over daytrips. And efforts to increase the percentage of French guests (the bedrock of repeat business, expected to account for half the park's attendance) were being made.[82] Fitzpatrick warned that the ride ahead might be bumpy as things fell into place: "In the light of operating uncertainties, there obviously can be no assurance as to whether the group will achieve profitability during this fiscal year."[83] Following the report, shares of Walt Disney Company stock dropped 5 percent in New York. Euro Disney stock also plummeted. Having started the week trading at 120 francs ($22.2) on the Paris Bourse, it closed at 109.5 francs ($20.2) on June 5.[84]

Matters were not helped by a much publicized blockade of the Euro Disney Resort. On June 28, some five hundred French farmers, protesting proposed cuts in European Community farm subsidies, drove three hundred tractors across the main car entrance and roads leading to the park before dawn. They had decided to launch their demonstration at Euro Disney because it was seen by many as a symbol of America within France—and the United States supported the proposed cuts at that time. Leaders of the National Federation of Agricultural Unions also knew that if they put Mickey Mouse at the center of their protest, reporters would flock to cover the story. For Euro Disney, such a display could not have come at a worse time. Added to the negative publicity value of news items that portrayed the park as a "Tragic Kingdom" was the anger of guests that day: many were forced to abandon their cars and buses a mile from the park and trudge in— through crowds and teams of riot police—on foot. Others, disgusted by all the turmoil, simply turned around and went home.[85]

On July 23, 1992, company officials announced that the Euro Disney Resort would incur a net loss in its first fiscal year, ending September 30. The message didn't come as a complete surprise.[86] John Forsgren, Euro Disney's chief financial officer, explained: "We were geared up for a very high level of operations. It has been very strong, but not as strong as we geared up for."[87] He also expressed his belief that the market had "overreacted a bit emotionally to preliminary information" and added that "by objective standards the park is very successful."[88] Between April 12 and July 22, the report stated, a total of 3.6 million

109

guests had come to Euro Disneyland—a number greater than that of other Disney parks in comparable start-up periods. One insider pointed out that this put Euro Disney a full "30 percent above the number of entries that Tokyo achieved during its first three months of operation," and added that "this is a long-term project that should be judged over three years."[89]

But most weren't willing to wait. Shareholders wanted to know right away if they should bail out. Paribas Capital Markets Group, which estimated attendance to be 15 percent below projected levels and spending (on food and merchandise) to be 10 percent shy of expectations as well, predicted that the Euro Disney Resort would lose 300 million francs (or $60 million) in the current fiscal year. It capped off the dismal forecast with a recommendation to sell Euro Disney stock. Investors paid attention. Euro Disney shares dropped 2.75 percent on the French Bourse following the announcement, bringing the stock value down a total of 31 percent since the grand opening.[90]

Euro Disney executives reassured one another that getting off to a rocky start was not cause for alarm in the theme park business. Universal Studios–Florida had had a disastrous opening in June 1990, with technical difficulties galore. But it had managed to recover from its initial setbacks and become successful.[91] The Euro Disney Resort, they knew, could do the same. Still, the bad press was a severe blow to Disney pride. Even more disturbing was the apparent enthusiasm with which the public had followed reports of its struggles. That people, both inside and outside Hollywood, seemed happy to see Disney's latest theme park falter was not a good sign. The situation called for serious attention if Mickey's reputation in Europe was going to be saved.

NEW PROMOTIONS

In an effort to undo damage to Euro Disney's image and increase its chances for financial success in the coming winter months, company executives took the bull by the horns and devised an ambitious plan. One set of goals focused on increasing the quality of the guest experience at the Euro Disney Resort: operations would be streamlined, cast member training would be stepped up, and time spent in queues would be reduced. As Sanjay Varma, executive vice president of resort hotels and Festival Disney, later noted, "How we assess our performance in the future [is tied to] how we get rid of the lines."[92] A second set of goals centered on marketing the theme park to bring in as many people as possible before the weather turned cold. Given that 65 to 70 percent of guests at Disney's stateside parks came during the period from April to September, it was crucial to capitalize on the remaining days of sunshine.[93] Anything could happen in winter.

To jump-start the new program, serious measures were taken. A new ad blitz blanketed France with posters that proclaimed "California is only 20 miles from Paris." In-house marketing strategists, known as the "Dream Team," swept France, visiting companies, local authorities, and tour operators to increase awareness of the Euro Disney Resort.[94] Such efforts seemed to do the trick. In August, the traditional time for summer vacations in Europe, crowds at Euro Disney were huge—and hotel occupancy was 100 percent.[95] Company executives, it seemed, had been right in contending that French families were merely postponing their visits to the new park. But they knew attendance would drop off as colder weather approached.[96] So they decided to close the 1,100-room Newport Bay Club hotel for the coming low season (October through most of April). Insiders explained the move by pointing out that the Newport was designed as a "summer theme" hotel.[97] The real reason, however, was that Euro Disney executives were making good on their promise to run a tight ship: it made little sense to keep open the largest hotel in Europe when there was no sign that it would be filled.[98]

Another Euro Disney promotion was announced in the first week of September 1992. Effective October 1, Robert Fitzpatrick would assume the newly created position of chairman. Frenchman Philippe Bourguignon, who had joined Euro Disney in 1988

111

as senior vice president of real estate development, would become president.[99] And Steve Burke, who had developed the Disney Stores from an idea into a hugely successful operation in the United States, would hop the pond to serve as executive vice president, theme park. While some skeptics viewed the shuffle as a "kick upstairs" for Fitzpatrick, he denied that it was a reaction to operational difficulties. Nonetheless, the market reacted favorably to the news, and Euro Disney share prices—which had dropped to 75 francs from an all-time high of 165.2 francs in March 1992—closed on September 3 at 81.9 francs.[100]

On September 4, 1992, the six-millionth guest pushed through the turnstiles to enter Euro Disneyland. Company officials, who had invited TV crews to capture the event, were delighted that the special visitor was French, because only 1.6 million guests at that point had been from France.[101] Fitzpatrick and Bourguignon presented her and her family with a bouquet of flowers at a ceremony in Town Square, and Mickey Mouse personally welcomed them to the Magic Kingdom. Upon returning home, her family sent a letter: "We would like to thank you personally for putting your heart into welcoming us and for helping us to realize a dream that will remain engraved in our memories. Your enthusiasm was infectious. . . . The geographic location of your Park made it possible for us to discover this unique universe. The warm welcome we received from cast members is the extra something that makes this American dream come true. Every time we visit your exceptional Park in Marne-la-Vallée, it will be with as much pleasure as the first time."[102]

The swell of special events continued in an effort to generate still more positive publicity for the Euro Disney Resort. On September 7, Fitzpatrick, Bourguignon, and Michel Giraud (president of the Île-de-France Regional Council) welcomed five thousand children to the park who had been unable to go away for summer vacation. Sabine Marcon, the 1991–1992 Euro Disney Ambassador, introduced Mickey Mouse to Curro, the Expo '92 mascot, outside the Euro Disney Pavilion at the World's Fair in

Seville, Spain. Two new forty-second commercials to be shown on all French TV channels (and in movie theaters) beginning September 23 were produced under the creative guidance of Jacques Benoit. And two big-screen heroes in France, Kevin Costner and Clint Eastwood, made special appearances in the park.[103]

On October 12, 1992, six months to the day after the grand opening, French prime minister Pierre Beregovoy bestowed an award upon Disney chairman Michael Eisner for his contributions to the people of France: the honorary title of Chevalier de la Légion d'Honneur. Walt Disney himself had received the award fifty-seven years earlier, in 1935, before being promoted to Officier in 1953. "In bestowing upon you the insignia of the Chevalier de la Légion d'Honneur," Beregovoy stated, "I am affirming the continued goodwill of the government that was first expressed in 1987 when the title was accorded at the signing of the convention for the creation of Euro Disney in France." He added that "the Park has already hosted 7 million visitors—the results speak for themselves. The projected economic advantages are being felt." Eisner accepted the honor on behalf of those who had contributed to the realization of the project. "[W]e have definitely made the best choice by settling in Marne-la-Vallée in the heart of Europe," he declared. "The opening of Euro Disney on April 12 has had a positive impact on French tourism and we are proud to participate in reinforcing France's predominant position in this industry."[104]

This message was affirmed on October 29, 1992, at a meeting attended by Christian Cardon, the interministerial delegate, and representatives of governmental departments, the Île-de-France Region, the Seine-et-Marne Department, SAN (new town agency), and EPAFRANCE (public developer). The Euro Disney people were there to present a report: "The Impact of Euro Disney on the Economy and Tourism after Six Months in Operation." By early October 1992, they revealed, nearly 7 million people had visited the park: 36 percent had been French and the remaining 64 percent (including 16 percent British, 14 percent German, and 8 percent Benelux) came from other parts. Most foreign visitors had indicated that Euro Disney was their first reason for visiting France: officials estimated that they had spent some 2.5 billion francs in the resort and another 4.3 billion outside the complex. In addition, Euro Disney had created and filled 12,596 positions (not including the 5,100 construction and public works jobs between March 1990 and March 1992). Euro Disney had even invested in housing for its cast members, in a region that suffered an acute housing shortage, by building 1,800 new units.[105]

Mickey Mouse was beginning to seem a little less monstrous. To reinforce this sentiment, Euro Disney executives invited some 1,500 VIPs from the political arena, the art world, and the entertainment industry in France to bring their families to the park for a special advance screening of *La Belle et La Bête (Beauty and the Beast)*. The film, which was inspired by a French tale and sprinkled with Gallic references, was not scheduled to open in the rest of France until two days later, on October 21. Afterward, they were given a backstage preview of the new parade float, which featured a two-story robotic Beast, and were greeted by the film's lead characters.[106] The grand opening of France's first Disney Store (the 188th outlet worldwide) on November 11 at Velizy II, a shopping mall sixteen kilometers west of Paris, helped to generate additional excitement for Euro Disney.[107]

But it was Euro Disney's comprehensive media plan that had the most powerful impact on Europeans. Designed to span France, Spain, Italy, Germany, Belgium, the Netherlands, and the United Kingdom, it covered Europe with enticing messages of price breaks (for students and groups) and special convention facilities that would bolster attendance up to and through the long-anticipated winter months.[108] The campaign hit France especially hard: it included frequent television commercials; tie-in promotions with *La Belle et La Bête* at 234 movie theaters; magazine advertisements in *Télé 7 Jours, Paris Match, Le Figaro, L'Express,* and *Geo;* radio announcements on NRJ, Europe 2, Cheric FM, Nostalgie, Sky Rock, RFM, and FUN; and plugs in children's magazines,

114

such as *Le Journal de Mickey*. In Paris, the Euro Disney message was inescapable. Ads appeared in *France Soir, Officiel des Spectacles, Pariscope, 7 à Paris;* they took to the screens of sixty area movie theaters; they decorated the walls of Charles de Gaulle and Orly airports; and they were positioned in 210 different Métro stations across the city.[109]

As a result, Europeans became more and more familiar with the Euro Disney Resort throughout the fall of 1992. Visitors to the park were giving it high approval ratings, too. But the recession tightened its grip on Europe (especially France) and the real estate market caved in, destroying all hope of profits from the sale of land.[110] Euro Disney executives knew that they would have to take decisive action to reverse the trend.

HAVE A MICKEY, MICKEY CHRISTMAS!

On the weekend of November 21, 1992, just two days after reporting its results for the fiscal year ending September 30, the Euro Disney Resort hosted a gala press event to launch its first Christmas season.[111] Nothing was left to chance. Overnight, the theme park and hotel district were transformed into a vast winter wonderland filled with candy canes and hot cocoa. Towering Christmas trees appeared in Town Square and in each of the hotels. Garlands and gingerbread houses decorated shop windows. Cast members everywhere sported fluffy red Santa caps. Snow White and the Seven Dwarfs sang carols before Le Château de la Belle au Bois Dormant. "Le Noël de Mickey," a new stage show, premiered in Fantasyland. Disney characters skating at the Rockefeller Center ice rink outside the Hotel New York invited all guests to celebrate the winter season. And a team of Lapland reindeer pulled the Father Christmas float down Main Street during the "Parade de Noël."[112] But the highlight of the holiday festivities was "la Cérémonie d'Illumination," during which a child was selected to light the Christmas tree in Town Square: with the simple push of a button, millions of colored lights flickered to life.[113]   115

Images of the event were circulated everywhere. But because only two million of the park's seven million guests during the first year had been French, Euro Disney planners concentrated their promotional efforts within France's borders.[114] Flyers advertised the magic of a Euro Disney Christmas: "Vous rappelez-vous l'émerveillement de votre premier Noël? Venez le revivre avec nous" ("Do you remember the amazement of your first Christmas? Come relive it with us"). "Pour séjourner à Euro Disney, pas besoin d'écrire au Père Noël, un coup de téléphone suffit" ("To vacation at Euro Disney, there's no need to write to Santa Claus, a phone call will do the trick"). "Noël à Euro Disney: Vos Nuits Seront Aussi Belles que Vos Jours" ("Christmas at Euro Disney: Your Nights Will Be As Beautiful As Your Days"). Glossy photos showing warm stone fireplaces, room service, luxurious pools, ice skating, and meals with Disney characters promised a one-of-a-kind Christmas holiday at once-in-a-lifetime rates.

Euro Disney planners undertook an aggressive campaign of community relations, too. On November 26, 1992, they invited twenty centenarians from the Paris area for a greeting by Mickey Mouse and a guided tour of Euro Disneyland.[115] Club Bénévole, a group of cast members dedicated to granting the wishes of terminally ill children, stepped up its efforts during the holiday season by selling UNICEF greeting cards and conducting a clothing drive for needy Yugoslavians.[116] And Roy Disney made a splash on the covers of several Spanish newspapers in December by competing in a transatlantic sailing race that retraced the route Columbus took to the New World in 1492: La Ruta del Descubrimiento. Though a damaged rudder forced him and his two sons to pull out of the race just before arriving in Miami, his vessel (which he had christened "Euro Disneyland") served him well, enabling him to stay in second or third position for much of the race.[117]

It seemed that possibly the tide had begun to turn for the Euro Disney Resort. To be sure, predictions of low attendance during the holiday season were not far from the mark. But the slow period enabled Euro Disney executives and cast members to do something that had not been possible since the grand opening, eight months before: catch their breath, take stock of their operation, and regroup for the coming spring season. Philippe Bourguignon noted how important the off-season would be for staff development:

> For thousands of cast members, Euro Disney is not the same as it was before opening. Before April 12, everyone was attracted to a concrete project that involved design, construction and completion with one unifying challenge: to open. This helped create a solid team spirit. Our objective today is less concrete. It has become more subjective. Now we must create our own identity and a goal that goes beyond our day-to-day challenges.[118]

Training sessions encouraged cast members to think about how systems and service might be improved. A cross-utilization program called "Show Time," which sent them to work in different roles throughout the theme park and hotel district, encouraged a broader view of Euro Disney.[119] And after-hours holiday parties in the park invited cast members to take pride in their place of employment and bask in the Euro Disney experience—as honored guests. Such programs had a positive impact on staff morale. "When I first arrived," noted one cast member, "I have to say it really felt like the army, everyone had to stay in his place. Now we feel there is an opening, we are being listened to."[120]

On January 15, 1993, Robert Fitzpatrick announced his intention to step down as chairman in order to start an international consulting firm in Paris. He would turn over the job of heading the company to Philippe Bourguignon as of April 12, 1993, the resort's one-year anniversary. "Six years ago Michael Eisner asked me to oversee the creation and opening of the Euro Disney Resort and to put into place a solid European management team," he wrote in a memo to cast members. "This has been accomplished and I am immensely proud of all that we have been able to achieve together and of the quality of the men and women who comprise the cast of Euro Disney. Bringing new projects into being is what I do best. The task of managing and developing the project in the years to come will be the job of the competent teams that are already in place working alongside Philippe." He assured everyone of his continued involvement in the venture, both as a board member of Euro Disney S.A. and as a consultant to the Walt Disney Company.[121]

The news came as a surprise to many. But others, who had viewed his promotion in September as the beginning of a transition to European management, expected the move.[122] It would be up to Philippe Bourguignon to put a French face on the Euro Disney Resort. One week after Fitzpatrick's announcement, on January 21, the two men took a big step in that direction by signing an agreement with Bernard Attali, president of the Air France Group. It united the most extensive air network in Europe (more than thirty million passengers per year) with what had become Europe's most visited vacation destination. The two companies would produce joint promotions and organize package tours to reach—and develop—new markets. The agreement, which was to be put into place progressively, included France, Belgium, Holland, Luxembourg, Austria, Switzerland, Spain, and Portugal and would later be extended to include Great Britain, Ireland, Germany, and Italy.[123] The Euro Disney Resort would be the talk of Europe with its new fleet of flying billboards, capable of hyping the theme park to air travelers at thirty thousand feet.

Mickey's World Tour, a promotional show for members of the travel industry, was also kicked off on January 21 at the Hotel New York. Organizers had arranged for visits to sixteen European cities over the course of three months. Each presentation included displays for Euro Disney participants and local tour operators, a multimedia program featuring the many attractions of the Euro Disney Resort (plus Disneyland and Walt Disney World), and a high-powered musical performance with Disney characters and dancers. The tour offered travel agents ideas for selling and promoting Disney theme parks year-round.[124]

In the meantime, a new radio campaign featuring 33 percent price reductions for Île de France residents was also launched to promote winter theme-park attendance by Paris-area families. Its delivery (in French) was nearly as colorful as the many images of Euro Disney that had been plastered all over the City of Lights:

> Watch out! You are going to hear something very rare for this time of year: WAAOOOUH!!! It's the happy scream you, dear neighbours of the Paris area, will shout when you discover the magical present that Euro Disney is giving you, in January, to celebrate the new year: Very small prices: 100FF for children under 12 years old and 150FF for adults!! And at Euro Disney in January, it is also Beauty and the Beast on stage, ice skating with Mickey and Donald Duck, and of course, all the fantastic trips through time and space. . . . And now, it's your turn to go: WAAOOOOUH!!! This offer is limited to Île de France residents only, upon showing a residence verification.[125]

Steve Burke noted that seasonal pricing structures were "something our other parks don't have but which are the rule rather than the exception in Europe."[126] In June 1993, Euro Disney would also introduce "Star Nights" (reduced-price tickets for evening entry, 5:00 P.M.–11:00 P.M.). If such special offers succeeded in bringing new guests to the park just once, Euro Disney execs believed, people would like what they saw and want to return.[127]

JOYEUX ANNIVERSAIRE, EURO DISNEY!

On April 12, 1993, Euro Disney executives and cast members came together to celebrate an important milestone: the first anniversary of the Euro Disney Resort. Many outsiders had thought—and   119 hoped—that Euro Disney would never live to see such a day. To be sure, it had been a tumultuous year, "as full of ups and downs," writer Michael Williams noted, "as the theme park's Big Thunder Mountain rollercoaster ride."[128] Protests by French labor unions, farmer blockades, a hostile press, a $35 million loss in fiscal 1992, and the resignation of Euro Disney's American chairman had all contributed to the sense of doom. But cast members never let it grip them. That they had managed to conquer such setbacks and survive their first year made the victory that much sweeter.

To celebrate the accomplishment, park engineers transformed the forty-three-meter Château de la Belle au Bois Dormant into a giant birthday cake, using inflatable plastic forms. Towers and columns became colorful candy sticks. Rockwork was hidden behind rows of enormous strawberries and layers of frosting. Dozens of cherries and mirabelles, gobbed in what appeared to be whipped cream, climbed all the way to the highest peak. The "Château Gâteau," as it was soon nicknamed, looked good enough to eat.[129] It was the tasty centerpiece of a celebration that took its theme from *Alice in Wonderland* (1951), in which the Mad Hatter pointed out that everyone had 364 "Unbirthdays" each year.

A steady stream of celebrities added to the spirit of festivity. But, as Burke was quick to point out, big-name stars from the grand opening TV special like Cher and Tina Turner would not be there. "We'll be having a few European names to the park," he told one reporter, "but I'm not sure how much they'll mean to your American readers."[130] The guest list included a wide variety of names: Hervé Christiani (French singer, songwriter); Yves Duteil (mayor of Precy-sur-Marne); Jeroen Krabbe (Dutch actor); Franco Pippo (Italian TV star); Lizzy Power (English actress); Henri Salvador (French singer); Pierre Tchernia (France's Mr. Cinema, famous TV host); Paul Young (British singer, songwriter); and Disney characters galore.[131] But Burke was right in his assessment. As the stars moved down Main Street in a procession of vintage convertible cars, waving to park guests, one French cast member remarked that the event should have been called "La Parade des Célèbres Inconnus" (the Parade of Unknown Celebrities).

At the Château Gâteau, Roy Disney and Mickey Mouse congratulated cast members on a wonderful first year. Robert Fitzpatrick passed the torch to the company's new chairman, Philippe Bourguignon. Marsupilami, a spotted yellow character whose rights had recently been purchased from Belgian artist Franquin, was welcomed to the Euro Disney family with a round of hugs and high-fives.[132] And a daylight fireworks display filled the sky with sprays of glittering pixie dust. Cast members completed the ceremony by serving up slices of a real Unbirthday cake to park visitors.

In all, more than 250 members of the media attended the event. More than three hundred articles were written about it throughout Europe and the world. Fifty newspapers and magazines published the official event photo of the Château Gâteau with fireworks overhead. In France alone, the Euro Disney Unbirthday celebration received more than ninety minutes of television news coverage—a remarkable feat, given that a typical news report averages between one and two minutes in length.[133] Twenty babies born on the morning of April 12, 1992 (the same day as the Euro Disney Resort) were invited to the park by the public relations department: they were honored as Mickey's "godchildren" so that they would forever be associated with the European vacation destination.[134]

The Euro Disney Resort had turned an important corner in surviving its first year. As Roy Disney noted at the anniversary party, "The Park has integrated into Europe in a big way. . . . French culture stands unruffled. More and more, it's the children that show their parents how to use the Park; there is something for everyone."[135] Easter weekend drew more than sixty thousand visitors from all over Europe—and even the skeptics were impressed. Michel Sivade, a Frenchman from Briançon, confessed that he had expected the worst. "Actually it was much better," he admitted, "very clean and well organised."[136]

121

Slowly but surely, Euro Disney's image was improving. Word of mouth, a better understanding of the product, and an appreciation of the price-value rating had all played a part in this shift. But it was the media who had made the most dramatic turnaround. European newspapers, magazines, and television were reporting more objectively and limiting their criticism to the length of lines, the prices of souvenirs, and the continuing financial struggles of the park. A number of headline stories even betrayed a note of enthusiasm for the Euro Disney operation after its one-year anniversary. "Disney in Fashion," proclaimed *Le Monde*. "Cowboys Discover Socialized Economy," announced *Libération*. And *L'Express* ran a piece entitled "Mickey Mouse Learns to Speak French." But a feature in *L'Événement du Jeudi* magazine took perhaps the most aggressive stance. "Euro Disney's detractors are far more grotesque than any little Mickeys, their greatest bane," it noted. "A visit once a year with the family is infinitely less offensive than the hours that our children spend watching violent trash on TV. . . . Going to Euro Disney doesn't keep anyone from spending three days a week for the rest of the year at Beaubourg." The article concluded with one final assurance: "Euro Disney, Walt Disney World, Disneyland: of course your children won't become instantly fat and stupid!"[137]

In many ways, being in the spotlight of the international press was a mixed blessing for the Euro Disney Resort. The marketing team had done a masterful job of making people aware of—and interested in—the new vacation destination. But high visibility drew attention to the many controversies that swirled around it during opening year. In no time at all, its every action had proved to be newsworthy.[138] Jean-Marie Gerbeaux, vice president of communications, reflected on the difficulties of the start-up operation. "At the beginning of the project," he noted, "we had our nose to the grindstone; our sole objective being to build and to open. We did not have enough time to develop relations, to explain what we were doing. In addition to all of this, our introduction to the stock market in 1989 forced us into advertising our product too early. We were very visible, like a well-established and fully-operational company that has been around for fifty years."[139]

Europe's poor financial climate only made matters worse: "If you had to say why the park isn't profitable," noted Burke, "you'd have to put it down to lower-than-expected occupancy of our hotels, financial charges that are higher than we expected and the general real estate situation" in which development had been thwarted by a decline in property values.[140] Other factors, such as competition from the Olympic Games and the World's Fair in Spain, had also undoubtedly taken a toll. Euro Disney spokesman Paul Charoy offered one final explanation. "The biggest problem we had was that it was our first year," he concluded. "We had no element of comparison on which to base events or projections."[141]

The Euro Disney Resort had charged headlong into uncharted territory: the seductive—and seemingly lucrative—world of global corporatism. That it encountered serious difficulties during opening year is ultimately less incriminating than telling. In fact, such fumbling and fixing would reveal Euro Disney (and the Walt Disney Company as a whole) to be anything but the monstrous, monolithic force feared by critics. It was, rather, a complex corporate entity struggling to be responsive to an ever-changing (and ever-perplexing) multinational landscape riddled with surprises. Steve Burke's assurance, that "where we can, we are making changes to combat the difficulties," reflected both the vulnerability and the shared determination of Euro Disney officials to somehow make a lasting home for this new Magic Kingdom on the Continent.[142]

On April 12, 1993, the Euro Disney Resort took a big step toward achieving this goal. Its eleven-millionth guest would arrive just days later, making Euro Disney "the single most frequented tourist destination in France"—ahead of such famed attractions as Le Centre Pompidou, the Louvre, and the Eiffel Tower.[143] This accomplishment suggested the wisdom of an insight by Polygram

CEO Alain Lévy, part of a new generation of managers entering Europe's entertainment industry, which *Variety* reporter Peter Bart has termed the "Euroyank." "My approach has always been to give things time," Lévy noted. "You don't measure a company or an executive by its initial year. You build with patient determination. That is the way we have done it in the music business and you can see the results."[144] Euro Disney executives would count on the truth of these words as they forged ahead, for they knew that there would be many new struggles—and opportunities to shine—as they put down roots in the European community.

4 Rescuing the Euro Disney Resort

July 8, 1993, marked a dark day for the Euro Disney Resort. Not only did company officials announce losses of around 500 million francs ($87 million) for the period of April 1 to June 30, they also predicted losses for the following three months, or fourth quarter, which covered the peak summer vacation season. Many factors had contributed to the bleak forecast: an economic downturn in Western Europe; a depressed real estate market; low visitor spending on food and merchandise; waning hotel occupancy; as well as high charges for interest, leasing, and depreciation, all resulting from the large initial investment in the park. "As a consequence of these difficulties," the public statement read, "the Company, together with the Walt Disney Company, the Company's major shareholder, is engaged in a thorough review of its financial structure and its development strategy." Philippe Bourguignon, the new president–directeur général of Euro Disney, tried to offset the news with a note of reassurance: "It seems reasonable to us to be prudent for the short term even if we and the Walt Disney Company remain confident in the long term."[1]

But not everyone shared Bourguignon's optimism. A three-month $87 million loss was more than most people (or businesses) could comprehend. And predictions of still more red ink, even after the park's high season, filled investors with terror. If Euro Disney was willing to go public with such dismal information, many feared, the really bad news—the stuff that hadn't been mentioned—was even worse. Rebecca Winnington-Ingram, an entertainment analyst at Morgan Stanley in London, suggested that Euro Disney's stated losses were just the beginning of its financial difficulties. "My assessment is that Euro Disney will lose 1.9 billion francs ($333 million) in fiscal 1993," she noted. "Practically the only way I can see things improving is if Walt Disney refinances Euro Disney so that the heavy interest payments and debt are drastically reduced."[2]

The Euro Disney Resort's early financial perils were serious indeed. But company officials, planners, and investors were determined not to let the huge vacation destination they had so painstakingly built go up in smoke. They introduced new strategies—from attractions and seasonal price structures to fresh marketing campaigns—to help reinvent the enterprise so that it might fit more comfortably within European landscapes. Their efforts were boosted by a highly publicized financial "rescue package," made possible by the Walt Disney Company, a consortium of some sixty banks, and Euro Disney's own knight in shining armor: Prince Al-Waleed Bin Talal Bin Abdulaziz Al Saud of Saudi Arabia. The size and diversity of this group suggested to the world that the Euro Disney Resort was not just the European branch of an American firm, but a whole new company, a multinational venture that many different parties had an interest in saving. Their shared commitment to keeping Euro Disney afloat in the short term reflected a desire to preserve Mickey's place on the Continent—and rake in huge dividends when the newest Magic Kingdom inevitably paid off.

THE PRESSURES OF FAILURE

The July announcement came as a shock to people around Europe. That the Euro Disney Resort had celebrated its first "Unbirthday" in grand style and welcomed its eleven-millionth guest just months before seemed to indicate that it was on the road to recovery. But many who had wished for Euro Disney's failure refused to admit surprise when the financial news broke. Conservative movie critic Michael Medved was beside himself with delight. "Euro Disney was the most carefully and comprehensively marketed venture this century," he chirped, "with suppliers of every leisure-related product—from cross-Channel ferries to crisps—lured into tie-in deals by the marketing-mad Disney organisation. And why didn't it work? Simple: because people didn't want it."[3]

Medved, who presumed to speak about the Euro Disney Resort as if it had already closed, was only one of many critics who felt this way. Nigel Reed, a leisure industry analyst with French bank Paribas, agreed that the Walt Disney Company was guilty of expecting instant success on the Continent. "The Americans didn't assess European tastes sufficiently," he remarked.[4] The November 1993 report of an outside consulting firm echoed these sentiments: "It seems the transposition to France of Florida structures, procedures and modes of organization . . . has created perverse effects."[5]

The "Euro Disney crisis," as many called it, was more than a financial problem. It was a blow to the pride of Disney executives in the United States, most notably Michael Eisner, who had built an ailing Walt Disney Company into a $22 billion empire. Under his leadership, Mickey and Company had churned out strings of hit movies, breathed new life into TV programming, made a splash in the music business with Hollywood Records, and opened hundreds of Disney Stores in U.S. malls. Brand-new theme parks, hotels, and professional sports teams had added to the list of accomplishments, enriching shareholders while restoring the pizazz of the Disney name within American culture.[6] "We had a generation of executives who had never been around failure," admitted Eisner. "We had this momentum that never seemed to end. We were climbing this ladder that seemed to have no top. Even I got kind of used to it and comfortable with it."[7]

But the spirit of invincibility that had guided the Walt Disney Company for so long vanished when it became clear that the Euro Disney Resort was less than a money-magnet. Executives scrambled to figure out what might turn things around. Their winning streak was on the line, to say nothing of the company's earnings and reputation. If Euro Disney could not be pulled out of what seemed to be an accelerating nosedive, the Walt Disney Company would forever be haunted by the reminder that it wasn't always able to write its own happy endings. What's more, the park's failure would serve as a lasting symbol of Eisner's arrogance for insisting that Mickey Mouse and his Magic Kingdom could be installed anywhere he chose. The closing of Euro Disney would be a public disgrace.

As Disney executives sized up the situation, they saw that the deck was not stacked in their favor. The economic prospects in Europe were dismal: British, Italian, and Spanish currencies were greatly devalued, increasing the cost of a vacation in France by as much as 25 percent. The recession had pushed companies all over Europe to tighten their belts, making people fear for their jobs.[8] Negative publicity surrounding the resort had encouraged everyone to envision the place as a hellhole surrounded by violent protesters. And Phase II of the Euro Disney development, which included the Disney-MGM Studios and an additional 13,000 hotel rooms, had been officially put on hold. Despite projections that the second gate, with its movie-making theme, would draw some eight million sorely needed visitors in its first year of operation, Euro Disney officials thought it best to wait. It made little sense, they reasoned, to rush into another major investment (some $3 billion had been budgeted to complete Phase II) given the unexpected struggles of Phase I.[9] The last thing they needed was to compound an already desperate situation with more financial problems.

Bourguignon apologized that plans for the new park had stalled. "I regret that the current economic environment does not allow us to proceed to an immediate signing of the [Second] Detailed Program," he noted, "especially since this program was developed with the excellent and close cooperation of the French Public Parties."[10] But this did not mean that Phase II was being abandoned altogether. As one insider observed, "1996 is a target date [for opening the second park]—we're not ruling out the possibility that it could be moved."[11]

"PLUSSING" EURO DISNEYLAND

While the level, timing, and nature of the investments for the Disney-MGM Studios Europe were being discussed, Euro Disney executives began making other improvements to the property. They added six new attractions in 1993 to both revitalize the experience for new and returning visitors and increase the park's capacity. But this was no scaled-back development scheme designed to take the place of a second park. Disney officials had mapped out a twenty-five-year plan for Euro Disney—including a steady stream of new rides, office complexes, residential housing units, time-shares, hotel rooms, campsites, retail shopping space, and a water recreation area—long before ground was ever broken in France, to guide the new development through the year 2017.[12] Dick Nunis, chairman of Walt Disney Attractions, observed that the process of "plussing" was hardly new to Disney Imagineers. "It was true when Walt was alive and it's true today," he noted, "that our executives are always dreaming past their lifetimes."[13]

On March 20, 1993, just prior to the park's one-year anniversary, the first of the new attractions was unveiled: La Galérie de la Belle au Bois Dormant. Located on the mezzanine level of Sleeping Beauty's château, this "walk-through" exhibit traced the tale of Princess Aurora (Sleeping Beauty) in a series of hand-woven tapestries, stained-glass windows, and illuminated storybooks placed on pedestals. Tree-shaped columns, sculpture fountains, "snoring" suits of armor, and the spinning wheel upon which Sleeping Beauty pricked her finger added to the atmosphere of medieval times.[14] A balcony overlooking Fantasyland concluded the experience, enabling guests to survey the Magic Kingdom from above, like a character in the 1959 animated film.

129

La Galérie was an important addition to Euro Disneyland: it made Sleeping Beauty's castle into an attraction in and of itself. Unlike the other Disney palaces in California, Florida, and Japan, in which only special sections (housing a series of miniature dioramas, a restaurant, and a Mystery Tour, respectively), were open to the public, the Euro Disney château was fully accessible.

Legends of the Wild West, a new Frontierland attraction, was added in June. Located in Fort Comstock, it invited guests to explore a nineteenth-century American pioneer outpost. An "Old West" jail, cavalry quarters, and life-size figures of actors Fess Parker and Buddy Ebsen (as Davy Crockett and George Russel) offered passage to new worlds of cinematic adventure. And a Native American village—complete with teepees, handmade artifacts, and Cherokee actors in ceremonial garb—demonstrated that the western frontier had been a place rich with many cultures.[15] The archaeological or "museum" quality of the Native American exhibits stood in stark contrast to the more make-believe feel of the Davy Crockett movie displays. Recognizing that the people of France, in their passion for Hollywood Westerns, had learned a great deal about American Indians, the Imagineers sought to create an experience that would both entertain and resonate with historical authenticity.

Two other attractions were unveiled in the month of June: Les Pirouettes du Vieux Moulin (the Old Mill Ferris Wheel) in Fantasyland and L'Astroport in Discoveryland. The former, grafted onto the existing Old Mill food counter, was themed after the 1937 animated short and designed especially for young children. Eight swinging water buckets lifted passengers on a slow rotation that allowed a special aerial view of Fantasyland before dipping them down to skim the surface of the pond below.[16] And L'Astroport, developed jointly by Disney Imagineers and IBM computer specialists, was added as a special "post-show" attraction to Star Tours (the George Lucas simulator ride based on *Star Wars*). Featuring a selection of interactive, futuristic experiences from space navigation games to PhotoMorph (which allowed people to transform their own appearance on a giant computer screen), it set out to launch guests headlong into the twenty-first century and beyond.[17]

On July 30, 1993, Le Temple du Péril debuted in Adventureland. Inspired by *Raiders of the Lost Ark* (as well as the Indiana Jones Stunt Spectacular at the Disney-MGM Studios in Florida), it carried guests seated in ore carts on what Euro Disney spokesman Paul Charoy described as a "thrilling high-speed chase through an archaeological dig in a dense rain forest."[18] Larger-than-life cobra statues, crumbling walls, and thick jungle landscaping set the scene for this fast-paced tour. But it was the gravity-defying loop at the end of the ride that distinguished Le Temple du Péril from every other attraction at Euro Disneyland. Never before had a Disney ride—at any of its theme parks— dared to turn passengers upside down. Imagineers had long prided themselves on their ability to entertain without resorting to standard amusement park fare. But Euro Disney executives, who broke with tradition to buy the prefabricated Intamin coaster from an outside manufacturer, recognized the need for a splashy new ride that would attract attention. They justified the purchase as a cost-saving measure in times of financial uncertainty and promised that the new ride would help take some of the capacity pressure off the park's most popular attraction, the Big Thunder Mountain Railroad.[19]

The final theme park addition slated for 1993 was Le Pays des Contes de Fées (Storybook Land) in Fantasyland.[20] Offering rides aboard Le Petit Train du Cirque (the Casey Jr. Circus Train) or in flat-bottomed boats, it recalled the charm of the original Storybook Land at Disney's flagship park in California with miniature tableaux. But the Euro Disney attraction differed from its predecessor in one important way: it paid homage to the artists who inspired Walt Disney to create animated films. The result was a landscape of geographically structured tales. Stories such as the Grimm Brothers' "Snow White," "Hansel and Gretel," and "Rapunzel" were grouped together to capture the spirit of the

131

Black Forest in tiny landscaped settings. Scenes from the "Little Mermaid" paid tribute to Denmark, the home of Hans Christian Andersen. England's "Sword in the Stone" and France's "Beauty and the Beast" completed the experience. Le Pays des Contes de Fées also included some new and distinctly American touches, such as the Emerald City from *The Wizard of Oz*, whose gleaming castle and yellow brick road captured the eye—and the imagination—with their glowing Technicolor presence.[21]

In all, "plussing" Euro Disneyland was an important strategic move. "The reason we're adding the new attractions is twofold," explained one park official. "First, we want something new so those who have already been here want to come back, and secondly, we need to increase our capacity. Our lines are too long on very busy days."[22] But there was another reason as well. As noted by Jeff Summers, an analyst at debt broker Klesch and Company in London, "There aren't enough attractions to get people to spend the night."[23] The Euro Disney Resort would invest more than $12 million in new rides and attractions over the next two seasons to remedy this situation. Together, they would help to expand the park's capacity a full 20 percent by the end of 1994.[24] More important still, each of these attractions was brand new—not to be found at any other Disney park. Europeans could take pride in the fact that their Magic Kingdom was unique. And people who had visited a Disney park in California, Florida, or Japan might be tempted to pay a visit to the Euro Disney Resort to see the many ways in which it differed from them.

PUTTING ON A EUROPEAN FACE

In addition to the new attractions, Euro Disney executives made other important changes to their struggling enterprise. They dropped hotel and admission prices in the off-season; reconceptualized many of the shops and eateries on-site; and introduced new park festivities to celebrate such European holidays as Bastille Day (France) and Oktoberfest (Germany). Reviewing the many changes that had been made, Euro Disney vice president Malcolm Ross remarked: "We've adapted this park for European tastes."[25] But their job was far from complete. In an address to Euro Disney management on August 19, 1993, Philippe Bourguignon declared that a spirit of innovation and adaptability would be crucial to the future success of the Euro Disney Resort. "The answer to our problems can only come from inside the company," he stated. "We cannot just blame the economy or simply hope to improve our financial structure if we do not demonstrate our ability to improve our performance. . . . We are entering a difficult period both individually and collectively. We must fight aggressively and adapt quickly. Our future lies in our hands, nobody else's."[26]

The reduction of park-entry and room rates in the off-season helped the Euro Disney Resort to take a big step in that direction.[27] But it was also a risky move. Disney executives in America had long feared that tampering with hotel and ticket fees would undercut the full-price market. The special demands of a European setting, however, made seasonal variations seem advisable—especially given that competing hotels and parks in the Paris area had made a practice of doing so. As noted by Steve Burke, Europeans expected price differentiation. "A bigger risk," he argued, "was not offering seasonal prices if the market demands them. Our job now is to figure out what the market wants and provide it, rather than being ideological about what's done in the U.S."[28]

In this spirit, planners revamped many of the park's restaurants. "In France," noted Euro Disney executive Jim Cora, "we thought we would have to adapt to European eating habits by creating table-service restaurants. We quickly learned that European guests prefer counter-service."[29] At least, they preferred it at midday within the unique setting of Euro Disneyland, where rides, shows, and shops all competed for their time and attention. In addition, the gourmet-style meals served up in places like Walt's (on Main Street, U.S.A.) or the Explorer's Club (in Adventureland)

133

were not cheap. One British guest was horrified by the price of food inside the park. "One imagines it will be perfect," he commented. "Who imagines . . . 4 quid ($6) hamburgers?"[30] One reporter agreed, noting, "Big Macs colonized the world because they were cheap, not fancy."[31]

But that didn't mean Euro Disney guests wanted Egg Mc-Muffins for breakfast. The French, planners discovered, were less than charmed by the light croissants and coffee featured on morning menus. They wanted full sit-down breakfasts—not "continental" ones, as witnessed by the long lines snaking out of hotel restaurants at daybreak. To meet this unforeseen demand, hotel managers beefed up morning room service and invited guests to place their breakfast orders before turning in for the night.[32]

Planners also reworked menu selections throughout the Euro Disney Resort. Initially, international cuisine had been featured to cater to the diverse tastes of European visitors. But guests quickly made their preferences known by mobbing the places that served American-style food. Hot dogs, cheeseburgers, chili, and barbecued ribs were the meals of choice, namely because European dishes were commonplace to most Euro Disney guests.[33] Eisner admitted that he and his team of executives had learned an important lesson. "We know that Americans don't want us to open a French restaurant in New York or Los Angeles that serves a double patty cheeseburger," he noted, "and that the French don't want us to come over there and do crepes, and the Germans don't want us to serve knackwurst and sauerkraut. They want us to do what we do."[34] Euro Disney guests—like their counterparts at Tokyo Disneyland—literally wanted a taste of America.

This was not to suggest, however, that European visitors were willing to suspend all of their eating habits the moment they pushed through the entrance turnstiles to Euro Disneyland. Many tried to bring picnic lunches into the park—a practice common on family outings in Europe, but forbidden chez Disney. (Such guests were asked to check their baskets at the Main Gate storage facility and later directed to a picnic area outside the Hotel New York when they came back to retrieve their food.) Many more tried to order wine with their meals at the park's eateries—only to learn that Euro Disneyland, like its counterparts in the United States and Japan, was strictly a "dry" facility.

The decision to serve, or not to serve, alcoholic beverages had been an ongoing source of debate among Disney executives long before the Euro Disney Resort ever opened. In fact, Eisner admitted that it was perhaps the most discussed topic of all. Wine was, they knew, a part of French tradition and daily eating habits. But Walt had banned alcohol from Disneyland in 1955 for a very important reason: to create a safe family haven free of drunken, boisterous behavior. In the end, Eisner and his team decided to pass on the projected $11 million in annual profits and not to make any special exceptions for France. Wine and other spirits would be made available in each of the hotels and at Festival Disney (the entertainment complex located across from the park's Main Gate entrance), but not inside the theme park itself. In April 1992, Eisner promised that the policy would stick: "We will not change this decision."[35]

In June 1993, however, the alcohol ban was dropped. Wine began flowing inside the park, but only at table-service restaurants. One writer described the move as "nothing short of corporate revolution."[36] But it was really just a business decision, part of the ongoing plan to put a European face on what many still perceived to be an all-American enterprise. By bowing to cultural reality, the Euro Disney Resort demonstrated its respect for French (and European) dining habits while helping to showcase the country's reputation for excellence in wine making. And, as Euro Disney executives well knew, there was money to be made in serving more than mere "mocktails."

In addition to Euro Disney's eateries, many gift shops throughout the theme park and hotel complex were also overhauled, beginning with merchandise selections. Park planners had initially filled stores with pricey upscale goods, much as they had in Japan. High-quality clothing items, jewelry, and Disney

135

character memorabilia were intended to demonstrate that Euro Disney would not be in the business of peddling tourist junk. But the cost of such souvenirs proved to be too expensive for many families in a recession. One French guest proclaimed, "I refuse to pay 49 francs (roughly $9) for a little Mickey Mouse statue."[37] But price wasn't the only factor responsible for low sales. According to Euro Disney spokesman Jacques-Henri Eyraud, guests were less than impressed with the muted colors and tasteful discretion of the merchandise that had been designed especially for them. Most, he said, "wanted the big bright Mickey or Goofy on their T-shirt."[38]

So, to clean out the stores in order to fill them up again with the screaming colors of more moderately priced souvenirs sold at Disney's U.S. parks, Euro Disney slashed prices on items from Frontierland to Discoveryland. Signs reading "Soldes" ("Clearance") appeared in shop windows throughout the park, and red-lined price tags dangled from souvenirs. A British reporter for *New Statesman and Society* remarked on the irony of seeing a flurry of mark-down sales inside the Magic Kingdom. "The theme park," he noted, "is beginning to resemble one of those discount shopping centres on the edge of towns, at which 'everything must go' in an end-of-line sale."[39] The suggestion was clear: Euro Disney was desperate. It would come as a surprise to no one, therefore, if the theme park closed down for the winter, as media reports were starting to predict—or for good.

But Philippe Bourguignon was committed to preventing this and took special measures to ensure that Euro Disney's workforce, as well as its guests, were satisfied. On June 23, 1993, he appointed Michel Perchet of Club Méditerranné to the newly created post of vice president, cast members.[40] At last, employees would have representation in all key decisions affecting them. Bourguignon also helped to end labor disputes by shifting American working practices toward a more French approach: the new Euro Disney administration recognized standard French job classifications, set a maximum working week, and annualized hourly work schedules.[41] On August 19, 1993, Bourguignon appointed Steve Burke executive vice president of the Euro Disney Resort. This move, which put Burke in charge of the theme park, the hotels, and Festival Disney, streamlined the corporate hierarchy by making a single person responsible for areas once overseen by several vice presidents. It also humanized Euro Disney by encouraging insiders and outsiders alike to think of the company as being directed by a partnership of two rather than an endless stream of nameless, faceless "suits."[42]

Bourguignon and Burke defended the many changes being made at the Euro Disney Resort as simple adaptations to the market, not acts of desperation. "The changes we're making today," noted Bourguignon, "stem from a natural evolution as we shift from running a construction project to actually welcoming guests." "Our priority," added Burke, "was getting the park up and running by April, 1992. That left no room for innovation. But we always knew that afterwards we would have to make adjustments." The problems Euro Disney had faced thus far, they argued, were not cultural, but simply the growing pains of any new enterprise in difficult economic times. Nonetheless, the two executives agreed that their greatest challenge would be to strike a precise balance between Old and New Worlds, to ensure that the park "went native" without losing the American feel that was its main draw. "Euro Disney is forging its own identity, a unique blend of Disney tradition reflecting European expectations," Bourguignon asserted. "One of our highest priorities will be to continue our effort to adapt to our European environment."[43]

TROUBLE IN TOON TOWN

Despite the changes made to Euro Disney in the wake of its first anniversary, the financial picture was not quick to improve. Paribas analyst Nigel Reed revealed that attendance had risen 8 percent in the first quarter of the new year, but turnover had fallen 10 percent and spending had dropped 17 percent.[44] The price cuts—on hotel stays, restaurant meals, and souvenirs—that brought people in were undermining profit margins. An article in the cast member newsletter entitled "Tourisme: Une Année Difficile" offered reassurance to employees. "While the results may be disappointing," it read, "there is no reason to be apocalyptic." After all, it noted, the hotel occupancy rate had increased by ten percentage points in one year to reach 68.5 percent, results well above those recorded by the hotel industry in Île-de-France. The ratio of French visitors had also risen: one out of two theme park guests was French, and some 30 percent came from nearby towns, proving that local populations—the bedrock of repeat business—were finally starting to visit Euro Disneyland.[45]

But attendance, guest spending, and hotel occupancy were still below expectations after eighteen months in operation. The week of October 11, Euro Disney shares traded just above its 1993 low on the European market.[46] In an effort to offer relief to the financially burdened enterprise, the Walt Disney Company stepped in to help finance the park's capital expansion and working capital requirements: it made $175 million in emergency funds available to help tide Euro Disney over until spring 1994.[47] It also deferred the collection of management fees (fixed at 3 percent of total revenue) until fiscal 1994 and agreed to accept payment then only if the Euro Disney Resort was showing a profit. Analyst Rebecca Winnington-Ingram felt that this scenario was unlikely. "Unless something radical happens," she noted, "I don't expect the park to make money for the next two or three years."[48] Analyst Reed concurred, noting that the parent company (whose management fee was scheduled to double to 6 percent of the turnover in 1996) should prepare itself for disappointment. "Whatever changes they make to the park itself," he commented, "its real problem lies in a financial structure set up for the benefit of the Walt Disney Company, not for European shareholders."[49]

At the end of October 1993, the Euro Disney Resort revealed its plans to eliminate 950 administrative jobs (8.6 percent of the total workforce) to ease a growing cash-flow problem.[50] An announcement on November 10, 1993, that Euro Disney had lost a whopping 5.3 billion francs ($960 million) for the fiscal year ended September 30, confirmed that the situation was grave. To many, it seemed that Euro Disney was beginning its final slippery slide downward. One reporter made an ominous prediction: "Unless it can solve its problems soon, Euro Disney could end up on the scrap-heap."[51]

Euro Disney's balance sheet confounded analysts everywhere. Even the project's harshest critics hadn't dared to predict losses greater than $300 million for the period.[52] Their estimates, it turns out, were not far from the mark: Euro Disney's actual net loss for the fiscal year amounted to 1.7 billion francs ($308 million). But executives had tacked on a one-time write-off charge of 3.6 billion francs ($652 million), which represented the start-up costs for the resort. Clearly, this was a financial maneuver: Euro Disney had previously planned to amortize these payments over a period of up to twenty years. By taking a big hit all at once, the new management team could start over with a clean slate, disassociate themselves from the dismal performance of their predecessors, and protect shareholders in the long term. The move also afforded Euro Disney executives some extra leverage in their dealings with French bankers. If they could show that the worst was behind them, the bankers might be more generous in refinancing a lingering debt of some 21 billion francs ($3.46 billion).[53]

Of course, this would not be easy. The *London Independent* had, just weeks before, branded Euro Disney "America's cultural Vietnam."[54] It was hemorrhaging as much as $1 million each day according to some reports—and there was no end in sight.[55] Even the U.S.-based Walt Disney Company seemed to have lost its magic touch. Its films—which fueled the entire Disney operation, from merchandise to theme park attractions—had fallen off the charts. Ticket sales at Disney's U.S. parks were in a slump too, thanks in part to the murder of several German tourists in Florida. And rising competition from other theme parks, like

139

Universal Studios, was squeezing Disney's place in the market. Analyst Emanuel Gérard gave voice to what many on Wall Street were thinking: "Disney is having a lousy year."[56]

Despite its huge financial struggles at home and in Europe, the Walt Disney Company forged ahead and in November 1993, announced its plans to build a new three-thousand-acre theme park in Haymarket, Virginia. Disney's America, as the $650 million project was to be called, would bring to life Walt Disney's vision for a park based on U.S. history. It would feature nine themed areas representing everything from seventeenth-century Native American life to the family farm experience of the 1930s and 1940s. It would also include a golf course and a single 150-room hotel. Planners had learned from the Euro Disney Resort— with its 5,200 underoccupied rooms—that shooting for the stars could backfire. Better to start small and expand according to demand, they agreed.[57]

But plans for another new stateside theme park didn't generate enough enthusiasm to obscure the tragedy that was unfolding at Euro Disney. In December, PS Audit, a French unit of the accounting firm of Price Waterhouse, announced that the situation had grown serious: "The group will need financial support to face its contractual obligations in the 1994 accounting year." If a restructuring agreement between bank creditors and the Walt Disney Company was not made soon, "the group will have cash problems and will not be able to continue its activities." In other words, the Euro Disney Resort would be forced to shut down. "Euro Disney will require significant funding throughout 1994," a company spokesman observed. Without it, he added, the park "would face liquidity problems, but we will not start speculating on what the options are."[58]

In the Walt Disney Company's annual report issued late in 1993, Eisner finally expressed dismay at Euro Disney's struggles: he called the venture "our first real financial disappointment" and gave it a grade of "D"—as in "dreadful."[59] He also confirmed rumors of a poor outlook, admitting on December 31,

140

1993, that the Euro Disney Resort might have to close. Shortly thereafter, stock prices in Paris tumbled more than 6 percent to 30.9 francs ($5.23). One trader remarked, "I suppose it's more of a negotiating tactic than anything else. The stock is very sensitive to news."[60] But others saw it as more than a bluff. "Disney can't be seen by its stockholders to pump money into a bottomless pit," noted analyst Nigel Reed.[61] Eisner insisted that he meant business. In an interview with the French news magazine *Le Point*, he argued, "If an airplane engine lets you down during a flight, what are the options? Everything is possible today, including closure."[62]

AN UNHAPPY NEW YEAR

Disney officials cited a variety of external factors that had interfered with the new resort's success: a tough European recession, currency changes, high interest rates, and bad publicity, among others.[63] Debra Gawron, a Euro Disney spokesperson, noted that the poor financial climate had hit businesses across the country: "The economic downturn," she observed, ". . . really hit France this summer."[64] But Eisner was quick to point out that despite such problems, people throughout Europe had voted with their feet and come to the Euro Disney Resort in droves. "Attendance at the park is not a failure," he observed, "far from it, including in the low season."[65] More than eighteen million people had visited the park since its grand opening. Attendance and hotel bookings were better than the previous year's. And the 1992 animated film *Aladdin* had broken box office records for Disney films in France; it went on to become the number-one movie in Europe.[66] All that was needed for the new Magic Kingdom to flourish, reasoned Euro Disney executives, was some debt relief and a large infusion of cash.

Failing this, anything was possible. Eisner affirmed that the Walt Disney Company wanted to maintain a strong presence in France. But it could not rescue Euro Disney alone, without putting

141

itself into what he called "a financial black hole for a decade."[67] If push came to shove, he admitted, it would be better to surrender the battle in order to win the war. The Euro Disney Resort would not be permitted to bring the Walt Disney Company to its knees:

> We are currently at the heart of discussions with the banks, and it is difficult to predict how they will end up. . . . We have always said we would support Euro Disney up to March 31 [1994]. If an equitable accord is found by then between Walt Disney and all the banks and investors, Euro Disney will continue. That would be a happy ending in the Disney tradition. But if not, then there will be a more difficult ending.[68]

The "more difficult ending" Eisner was hinting at involved declaring bankruptcy. If the sixty lending institutions could not be persuaded to share the costs of restructuring, the Walt Disney Company was prepared to wash its hands of the failed venture and bid adieu to the Euro Disney Resort. Disney executives had already purged the project from their books the year before by taking a $350 million write-off. An additional $160 million loss—the amount it had paid for its 49 percent stake—would be painful, but not lethal.[69]

Such a scenario looked grim for all parties—especially the banks, who would be left holding the bag on a $4 billion investment. They would be the ones saddled with the job of running the park and hotel complex. But without the Disney name or characters to pull in crowds, their chances of making a go of it would be dodgy. Closing the park and selling off its assets would also present challenges, given that there was no market for giant, second-hand teacups or faux châteaux in Europe. Faced with this horrible vision of things to come, the bank syndicate, led by France's BNP and Banque Indosuez, commissioned a study to get a true picture of Euro Disney's finances. They wanted to determine if Euro Disney executives were overstating the resort's peril in an effort to scare the banks and squeeze more money from them.[70]

The lending consortium retained the accounting firm of KPMG Peat Marwick to look into the Euro Disney Resort and evaluate its prospects. Disney president Frank Wells promised full cooperation with the auditors. He insisted that Disney's own accountants from Price Waterhouse shadow their every move as they combed through Euro Disney's books. His concern was well-founded. The future of the Euro Disney Resort would depend on how sheaves of figures were interpreted. One miscalculation or false assumption could adversely affect the nature and scope of a refinancing agreement.[71] But Wells also knew that the KPMG team was looking for more than financial figures: they were searching for evidence that the Walt Disney Company was, in effect, calling the shots at Euro Disney. If proof could be found that the parent company was actually Euro Disney's operator, French bankruptcy law would prohibit Eisner's U.S.-based company from simply walking away from the complex—and its debts—in the case of financial failure.[72]

Most analysts recognized that while bankruptcy was an undeniable possibility, too many parties had a vested interest in keeping the Euro Disney Resort alive. For the Walt Disney Company, described by one reporter as "the most image-conscious of firms," public failure would add insult to injury on a grand scale. It would also lead to litigation and lock Disney out of the theme-park market in Europe indefinitely. For the French government, closing the park would mean losing some forty thousand jobs that had been created directly or indirectly by the Euro Disney Resort. And the banks, which sought to recoup their investment, certainly didn't want to end up with the park's assets or be stuck running the place. In other words, very little arm twisting would be required to convince all parties that they would be best served by saving the troubled Magic Kingdom.

This didn't mean that agreeing upon a financial restructuring package would be easy, however. Each side expected the

143

other to make greater concessions. Disney executives wanted the banks to convert some debt to equity and cut interest on remaining loans to lighten the park's $290 million in annual debt service. The banks wanted the Walt Disney Company to inject new capital, take part in a new rights issue, and cut the fees it was supposed to be paid out of Euro Disney's revenues and profits. Each side also wanted the other to purchase some of Euro Disney's assets, particularly its hotels.[73]

But the Walt Disney Company and the banking syndicate were not the only two parties involved. On January 31, an association representing some investors (holding 4 billion francs worth of Euro Disney convertible bonds) demanded representation at the negotiations. If excluded, they warned, legal action would result. Their primary concern was that the new restructuring package would place an unfair burden on bondholders—and they had reason to suspect that something of this nature might happen. After all, the prospectus that had lured them to invest in Euro Disney in 1991 featured the same profit projections that had been used in its initial share offer two years earlier—despite changes in the project's cost structure and the European economy. In addition, the prospectus had suggested that their funds would be put toward Phase II of the Euro Disney development, the Disney-MGM Studios Europe, which had since been tabled.[74]

On February 2, 1994, Euro Disney reported a loss of 553 million francs ($95 million) in the quarter ending in December—a figure 30 percent bigger than the previous year's. Least happy to get this bulletin were Euro Disney's bankers, who met for several hours that day to discuss the findings of KPMG Peat Marwick. The accountants had been unable to turn up any hard evidence that the Walt Disney Company was, in fact, pulling the strings at Euro Disney. But they confirmed suspicions that the ailing resort would need some combination of cash and debt relief totaling around 12 billion francs (nearly $2.5 billion) to survive. The bankers recognized that short-term survival was no guarantee of long-term profits. Yet they forged ahead and discussed a Disney proposal to restructure half of the $3.5 billion in debt and split the loss evenly between the banks and the Walt Disney Company.[75]

On March 14, 1994, exactly two weeks before the Walt Disney Company was to cut its financing of the Euro Disney Resort, an agreement to restructure its crippling debt and infuse it with capital was reached. The Euro Disney rescue plan, as it was called at a meeting of four hundred stockholders that day, was a complex arrangement. Under the plan, the Walt Disney Company would invest some $750 million in the struggling complex: $508 million would be plowed into new shares in a $1.1 billion rights issue and $240 million would be used to purchase certain park assets in a sale-leaseback arrangement favorable to Euro Disney.[76] The Walt Disney Company would also suspend for five years the collection of royalties and management fees. In return, the creditor banks would put up $500 million to buy shares in the new offering, forgive eighteen months of interest on Euro Disney's debt, and defer principal payments on it for three years. The restructuring, subject to approval from all sixty-three of the park's creditors, would cut the venture's debt burden nearly in half, to 10 billion francs ($1.73 billion) and allow Euro Disney to show a profit in the fiscal year ending September 1995.[77]

According to company officials, the Euro Disney rescue plan was to take effect "as soon as possible." But until it was ratified and implemented, the Walt Disney Company and lender banks agreed to tide Euro Disney over with enough cash to keep the park and hotel complex running without a reduction in services. An analyst from Salomon Brothers noted that the agreement had required all parties involved to make compromises. "Both sides—the French banks and Walt Disney—clearly capitulated," he observed. "Should the plan be approved, Walt Disney will clearly be more entwined in the performance of the Paris theme park."[78] In other words, the Walt Disney Company's increased stake in the venture would make it less likely to use bankruptcy as a bargaining chip in the future. Its own investment in the Euro Disney Resort would simply be too great to walk away from.

A NEW CAMPAIGN

Nearly one month before the refinancing package was assembled, Euro Disney executives made an important marketing decision. Ogilvy and Mather, the firm that had handled the massive account since the grand opening, would be kept on as the company's lead ad agency. But the choice had not been automatic. Gripped by the need to reinvigorate their promotional efforts for a spring relaunch, Euro Disney officials had invited a variety of top-notch firms, including D'Arcy Masius Benton and Bowles, DDB Needham, Euro RSCG, and TBWA de Plas to pitch ideas. They were looking for a fresh marketing offensive that would turn consumer attention away from balance sheets and back to Euro Disney attractions. After three months in review, the incumbent team won. Ogilvy and Mather, noted one Euro Disney executive, "has always done great creative work for Euro Disney."[79]

But until its selection as the resort's official advertising agency in February 1994, Ogilvy and Mather's role in the marketing effort had been limited to implementing campaigns created by Euro Disney's in-house creative department. One agency executive expressed dismay at this approach. "It's typical of Disney," he noted. "They give you an order and leave you in the dark. Then, if you win the budget, they call you in to tell you what their internal [ad] team has decided to let you do. An agency can't work like that. They must decide to do it themselves or trust the expert."[80] Euro Disney executives, however, dared to offer another alternative: an unusual staffing arrangement that would combine the talents of in-house and external planners. Under this scheme, Euro Disney people would go to Ogilvy and Mather to be part of a team of twenty creative and ten account staffers working on Euro Disney promotions. One insider explained the move. "We're building a creative team by shifting our people to work at Ogilvy," she noted. "The [Ogilvy and Mather] Paris office will be running everything for Europe and really taking charge."[81]

Its first assignment was to design a media campaign that was more suitable for a European setting. Frank Merkel, chairman of WOB Marketing, a business-to-business agency in Viernheim, Germany, felt that poor advertising—TV, print, and radio—had been behind the park's many struggles. "The entire marketing strategy of Euro Disney was to blame for the fiasco," he noted. First of all, Euro Disney had insulted Europeans with its imagery of American-style bigness. Overhead shots of the park and panoramic scenes of thousand-room hotels had emphasized the huge size of the development, making it seem overwhelming. Close-ups of Sleeping Beauty's château illuminated by sparkling lights and pixie dust, an image dear to most Americans since the early days of the *Disneyland* TV program, were seen as glitzy and materialistic in Europe. In the words of one Paris-based agency executive, "That ruined the magic." Dennis Speigel, president of Consultants International Theme Park Services, Cincinnati, concurred. Such ads, he noted, encouraged the French to see Euro Disney as "American imperialism—plastics at its worst."[82]

In the spring of 1993, Euro Disney broke with such ads and reinvented its approach by creating more descriptive work. "They got back on track," admitted Speigel. "But they could still do better."[83] Euro Disney planners at Ogilvy and Mather agreed. They went to work on creating an improved campaign that would target Disney-friendly territory and emphasize all the wonderful things the park had to offer. To reach the broadest audience, they adopted a dual marketing strategy. TV commercials directed toward children would feature popular Disney characters, and a series of print ads for adults would stress new attractions, special events, and package deals.[84]

Aladdin, star of the number-one film in Europe (it raked in $100 million in ticket sales in little over a month) stood at the center of the new TV and print ad campaign. A television spot featured him caught up in a world of excitement and endless celebration at the Magic Kingdom. Print ads, run in popular

147

magazines, built on the theme. In one, he was shown swooping down on his flying carpet to shake the hand of a little girl and invite her on a "magic vacation" to the Euro Disney Resort, "the kingdom where all dreams come true." The Aladdin ads also promoted a specially priced family vacation package: two days, one night, and one breakfast at a Euro Disney hotel for $95 per adult—and no charge for children. "We are positioning Euro Disney as the number one European destination of short duration, one to three days," commented one spokesman. "One of the primary messages is, after all, that Euro Disney is affordable to everyone."[85]

But that hadn't always been so. At one point, it was actually cheaper for British tourists to cross the Atlantic and visit Mickey Mouse in his natural habitat than go to France, where the pound was greatly devalued.[86] Alan Randall, head of sales and marketing at Thorpe Park, the United Kingdom's first theme park, pointed out that Euro Disney was expensive even when the economy was in full swing. A busload of twenty-five adults and twenty-five children, he observed, would pay $450 at Thorpe Park; the same group would pay some $1,500 at Euro Disney.[87] Planners knew that reversing the public perception of unaffordability was crucial if the Euro Disney Resort was ever to climb out of the red. They also knew that Euro Disney had to be marketed as much more than another park to escape price comparisons with less elaborate ventures. The Aladdin campaign helped to achieve both of these goals by enticing children with images of familiar characters from the big screen and offering parents special deals on family vacations.

THE LOSSES CONTINUE

In April 1994, as efforts got under way to supercharge Euro Disney's recovery with a brand-new ad campaign, tragic news hit: Frank Wells, president and chief operating officer of the Walt

Disney Company, had been killed in a helicopter accident during an Easter ski vacation in Nevada. Eisner was devastated. Not only did the news come as a personal shock, it also presented a serious business problem. The two had formed a strong team, with Eisner serving as "front man" and Wells taking a more low-profile role. Together, they had brought Disney's revenues from $1.5 billion to $8.5 billion and pushed up its stock value by 1,500 percent in a single decade.[88] Without his partner with him at the helm, Eisner feared, the entertainment empire they had built brick by brick might crumble. "Of all the people at the company to lose . . . ," he lamented.[89]

The situation in France was not much better. April 12, 1994, Euro Disney's second anniversary, lurked just around the corner, and its losses continued to mount. The nearly twenty million visitors to the park were below expectations—as were levels of guest spending and hotel occupancy. High operating costs continued to gouge at the resort's finances: its future as a magnet for regional development was on the line. "Euro Disney," proclaimed one reporter, "is going broke."[90] The news spread across Europe. In Spain, one newspaper ran a comic that showed Mickey Mouse panhandling near the Eiffel Tower. A British journal featured a cartoon with Mickey, Donald, Goofy, and Euro Disney's board of directors poised to fling themselves off an upper ledge of Sleeping Beauty's castle. A Swiss satire portrayed Euro Disney in the year 2001 as a camp for homeless people. And in France, a taxi driver noted that the resort had become Disney's "Berezina," the icy Russian river where Napolean lost ten thousand men in his retreat from Moscow.[91]

As before, many were pleased by Euro Disney's continuing struggles and argued that its planners could take full credit for their own undoing. "Disney came in here like conquerors, knowing everything . . . wanting advice from no one," commented Michel Colombe, mayor of Bailly-Romainvilliers. "They had a product they thought was perfect that they wanted to transpose in Europe. They didn't know how to adapt."[92] Others agreed, 149 claiming that the blind arrogance of Disney executives had led them to make two foolish assumptions: (1) Disney always triumphs, and (2) economies don't slow down.[93] Company executives defended their actions by arguing that critics had failed to appreciate the complexity of setting up an enterprise of Euro Disney's magnitude. "The amazing thing to me is the assumption we could do this without making mistakes," noted Steve Burke. "When you have a job that big . . . you become very focused, you rely on what you've done before . . . and simply don't have time to stand back. I don't think the initial team was arrogant so much as driven."[94]

Eisner agreed, noting that it was easy to latch onto errors that had been made in the past—without noticing the ones that had been strategically avoided. "Maybe I am just stubbornly optimistic or arrogantly insensitive on the creative side," he asserted, "but I think the park is the most fantastic product ever done by the company. A hundred years from now people will wonder how did this ever get built."[95] Bob Minick, president of J. R. Minick, a Dallas-based consultancy to theme parks, shared his assessment: "I visited [the park] and was very impressed."[96] Even Dominique Maquenhen, owner of the village cafe in nearby Bailly-Romainvilliers, expressed support for the Euro Disney Resort. "France has a big baby in its arms that weighs 20 billion francs," he remarked. "It's a beautiful baby. You can't go backward now."[97]

Eisner had no intention of doing so. In fact, he was already looking toward the future. Faced with a weak economy, declining profit growth, a string of box-office flops, and theme-park woes in Europe and the United States, he decided that the Walt Disney Company was in need of a tune-up. "We were reinventing ourselves before Frank's death," he admitted, "but this tragedy has forced us to speed up the process. I think you have to reinvent yourself every seven years or so, as businesses mature and situations change." At the forefront of Eisner's plan was international expansion. Foreign markets, he argued, represented the highest potential for growth—despite signs to the contrary at Euro Disney. "During the first ten years of this job," he noted, "we focused predominately on growing the domestic businesses. Now we have to start over again in places like China and India and develop new products for these markets."[98]

The Walt Disney Company's three divisions—theme parks, filmed entertainment, and consumer products—would be part of this new corporate thrust. Already, Disney had sixteen offices worldwide, serving forty-five countries. Its theme parks attracted people from all corners of the globe. Its animated films had been dubbed in twenty-five languages. And its TV programs had inspired the creation of some thirty-five *Disney Clubs*, broadcast internationally. But it was Disney's Consumer Products division (which oversees licensing, retailing, publishing, and records) that showed the greatest promise. In 1993, its operating income rose a full 26 percent to $356 million, thanks in no small part to the worldwide success of the Disney Stores. Most surprisingly of all, the Disney Store on the Champs-Élysées in Paris (open since fall 1993) was moving more merchandise than any of its 267 counterparts around the world.[99] Barton Boyd, president of Disney Consumer Products, noted that there were plans to open at least seventy new outlets each year. In 1994, one hundred new Disney Stores would open, he remarked, in England, France, Spain, Germany, Singapore, Hong Kong, Japan, Canada, and the United States.[100]

But the seemingly undefeatable Disney Stores would not be alone in seeking out new markets. Television, films, and even theme parks would continue to expand overseas too. Judson Green, president of Walt Disney Attractions, revealed that plans for yet another Magic Kingdom were already under way, perhaps somewhere in the Pacific Rim. However, he conceded, "the politics and economics have to be right before we make a major move."[101] Eisner noted the importance of looking forward in the midst of "the Euro Disney crisis" and admitted concern that his executives might become too cautious:

151

> There's not a meeting goes by that somebody doesn't say, "Ah, Euro Disney, Euro Disney. Can we afford to do this?" Okay, I've heard it. I can say we've learned. But I really do feel—about business and about life—that everybody has to make mistakes. And everybody should be encouraged to feel that if they make mistakes, it's okay. I have never wavered from the belief that I'm glad we did Euro Disney and that it is a monument to the creativity of our company. But there is also a reality of life known as economics, which always comes into the equation no matter how many pyramids you want to climb.[102]

Euro Disney, he reasoned, should serve as a lesson that Disney executives could learn from, not fear. For this reason, Eisner made it his mission to encourage executives to dream, to plan, to continue taking creative risks. Disney's America, the historical park near Manassas, Virginia, was but one of many bold projects on the docket that would help to restore Disney's image, he believed. A new animal park for Florida was also in the works, as was a new cruise ship business.[103]

Even with a slate of new projects, it was beginning to seem unlikely that the Walt Disney Company would achieve the 20 percent annual earnings growth that executives had set as their goal.[104] One former insider commented that sustaining such gains inevitably became more and more difficult. "They always need to top themselves," he noted. "It's like 'We're a shark. If we're not moving forward, we're dead.'"[105] Operating profits at Disney's U.S. parks were down 3 percent (to $152.3 million) in the first three months of 1994—due mainly to weak economies and a damaging earthquake in California. And the Euro Disney Resort was not helping matters. Attendance had dropped 10 percent in its second year, to 9.5 million, and executives expected no significant revenue growth until 1996. The Euro Disney rescue plan, it seemed, would need more time to save the day.[106]

ENTER THE PRINCE

On June 1, 1994, Euro Disney executives made an important announcement: a Saudi Arabian prince had decided to buy into the planned rights offering and invest up to half a billion dollars in the struggling theme park.[107] Described by one reporter as "a true grandson of the old desert pirate who created Saudi Arabia for power and profit," thirty-seven-year-old Prince Al-Waleed Bin Talal Bin Abdulaziz Al Saud had already made his mark as a shrewd businessman. In 1988, he bailed out the United Saudi Commercial Bank and named himself chairman. In the midst of the Persian Gulf War in 1991, he shocked Wall Street by pouring $590 million into Citicorp. Though its stock was at a low and some industry insiders predicted failure, the decision proved wise: his 10 percent interest doubled in value after only fifteen months—and quadrupled in value after three years.[108] Prince Al-Waleed, as he liked to be called, was following in his famous grandfather's footsteps.

Although the Euro Disney agreement was only a broad framework with lots of details to be worked out before the June 8 shareholder meeting, negotiators had set some parameters during months of top-secret proceedings. The Walt Disney Company would buy 49 percent of new shares issued in Euro Disney's $1.1 billion rights offering. The remaining 51 percent would be offered to existing stockholders at below-market rates (10 francs, or $1.76 per share, as compared with Euro Disney's then-current market price of $5.33) so that they might maintain their ownership proportions. Any unpurchased shares would be picked up by Euro Disney's lending banks and sold to Prince Al-Waleed, who would be permitted to buy up to $334 million—or 24.5 percent of the total (no more than half of the Walt Disney Company's stake). If existing shareholders bought a large portion of the new equity, the Walt Disney Company would sell the prince up to 13 percent of the total from its own shares, reducing its stake in the Euro Disney Resort to 36 percent.[109]

In the end, Prince Al-Waleed would own between 13 and   153

24.5 percent of the French venture, depending on demand for the rights offering. He would also provide Euro Disney with a three-year commitment of up to $100 million to finance the construction of a second convention center. The development promised to breathe new life into the Euro Disney Resort. After all, demand for convention space at Euro Disney had always been strong—even in the winter months. A second center would help to fill up hotels, especially on weekdays, with an expanding clientele: businesses. It also promised to move the entire operation to firmer financial ground, so that executives might revive the Disney-MGM Studios Europe, shelved since June 1992.[110] Euro Disney spokesman Jacques-Henri Eyraud expressed great enthusiasm for the new convention center. "We have always looked at small developments," he said, even those beyond the master plan.[111]

Analysts observed that the deal was a good one for the Walt Disney Company, even if it meant losing some ownership interest in the park. "They own so much already," said Jeff Logsdon, a managing director of Seidler Companies, "this is not a significant change." (The Walt Disney Company raked in some $8.5 billion in earnings from its assorted industries during the 1993 fiscal year.)[112] The high-profile deal also provided a swell of good publicity for the Euro Disney Resort—and the Disney name as a whole—in Europe. As noted by analyst Nigel Reed, it was "a positive sign that someone has confidence in the park."[113] Even creditors felt a sense of relief. "It's got to be seen positively," said one. "I am sure there is clearly a long-term commitment." Another Euro Disney banker agreed: "It makes us a lot more comfortable about the rights issue."[114]

But not everyone was convinced that Prince Al-Waleed's investment was a smart move. One Los Angeles attorney knowledgeable about the deal was puzzled. Arguing that Euro Disney's struggles were the result of poor attendance and spending levels—and not poor financial structuring—he exclaimed, "I'm surprised *anyone* would invest."[115] Most analysts, however, felt that the rescue package would put Euro Disney on solid financial footing for at least two years, which might help it to turn a profit by 1995 or 1996—when interest payments and license fees were scheduled to kick in again.[116] Jessica Reif at Oppenheimer and Company complimented Prince Al-Waleed's sharp business acumen: "It's a very intelligent investment. He's buying at the bottom."[117] Even the prince himself couldn't resist making a statement: "I don't give quotes. But you want one, here's one: 'Four years ago people were saying the investment in Citicorp did not look good. It was fantastic. Disney will be the same.'"[118]

As the Euro Disney rescue plan was closing, Eisner got a taste of his new partner's business style. He faxed a letter to Prince Al-Waleed, suggesting that they meet face-to-face. But his efforts were ultimately unsuccessful. According to aides of the prince, Eisner's Jewish faith presented problems in getting a quick visa to Saudi Arabia. And one remarked, "Al-Waleed didn't feel he had to hop when Eisner said hop."[119]

Any disappointment that Eisner may have felt from this snub, however, evaporated on July 29, 1994. His friend, former U.S. president George Bush, had talked François Mitterand into joining him for dinner that evening at L'Auberge de Cendrillon, near Le Château de la Belle au Bois Dormant. It was Mitterand's first visit to Euro Disneyland—after more than two years of vigorous refusal. When they emerged from the restaurant after their meal, Bush took notice of the press—and his pal's stony expression. Bush nudged him and said: "Smile. Come on, François, smile!" The next day, photos of the two men cheerfully waving from France's Magic Kingdom were front-page news. Eisner later reflected on the importance of this testimonial. "In a country in which the president helps to set the cultural agenda," he noted, "this image served as a powerful symbolic endorsement for the park."[120]

THE QUESTION OF SUCCESSION

One month after the Euro Disney rescue plan was approved, which effectively reduced the Walt Disney Company's stake in

155

the beleaguered theme park from 49 percent to 39 percent, tragedy struck again. This time it was Eisner. Suffering from clogged coronary arteries, he had to cut short a trip to Idaho to undergo emergency quadruple bypass surgery.[121] The fifty-two-year-old executive was a classic type A: overworked and under tremendous pressure. But his condition was more than a personal trauma: it was a corporate trauma as well. Frank Wells, president and chief operating officer of the Walt Disney Company, had not been replaced following his untimely death in April, just three and a half months before. If Eisner were to die or become incapacitated, with no heir apparent, there would be bedlam. The state of the entire Disney enterprise was hanging in the balance.

The severity of the situation did not escape Eisner. Moments before surgery, he did something unusual. "I made a list of candidates to replace me," he admitted, "and gave it to [my wife] Jane."[122] The secret list was never needed: his operation was successful. Two days later, Eisner was receiving guests and business calls at Cedars-Sinai Medical Center in Los Angeles, promising them all that he would be back on the job in as little as three or four weeks. But Roy Disney Jr. knew he wouldn't be able to wait that long. "I think we will see Michael back on the studio lot sooner than anyone realizes," he commented.[123]

Roy Disney's hunch proved to be right. Eisner was eager to settle the issue of succession once and for all. The obvious choice for the position of president, many thought, was Jeffrey Katzenberg, head of Disney's filmed entertainment division. Under his leadership, Disney had skyrocketed from last to first place among Hollywood studios. The movie powerhouse he built had also infused Disney's theme park and consumer products divisions with new energy (and revenues) by supplying a steady stream of ideas for new attractions and products.[124] Katzenberg had made it clear that he wanted the job. In fact, some said, he considered it his due. "Jeffrey wanted the recognition and the position within the company that he felt he had earned," commented one insider.[125]

But Eisner had decided against merely replacing Wells, his closest aide and chief strategist, with another person. After talking with a number of executives, both in and outside Hollywood, he realized that such an arrangement could never work. His friend Frank, he said, had left a void that was "impossible to fill."[126]

> I knew deep down that wasn't the way to go. I would have loved to have the company continue with Frank and do all these things we'd planned, but if Frank's not here any-more. . . . It's like some people, when they get divorced, they always seem to marry another woman who is exactly like the first wife. And it never works. I decided this was a new decade, and we had to do something different.[127]

Eisner's disinterest in stuffing another executive into the office once occupied by Wells, however, was coupled with serious doubts that Jeffrey Katzenberg was the right man for the job. For nineteen years, he had mentored Katzenberg, first at Paramount and then at Disney.[128] Eisner knew, perhaps better than anyone, the strengths and weaknesses of his young protégé. In the end, he decided that it would not be a good match. "I did not feel that [Katzenberg] should be president—for a lot of very logical reasons and also for some intuitional reasons," he later commented. "It was a hard decision, and I didn't make it in one day, and I didn't make it lying in the hospital. . . . I believe we had enough information over and over again that he should not have the job."[129]

On August 31, 1994, the Walt Disney Company announced the departure of Jeffrey Katzenberg. Stories differ as to which executive terminated the relationship. Even Eisner's account—"Jeffrey wanted a job I was not prepared to give him. So he left the company"—is mysteriously vague.[130] In any event, the move meant that the strong partnership between Eisner, Wells, and Katzenberg, which had rejuvenated the Walt Disney Company in the 1980s, had finally dissolved.[131] Eisner, the only remaining

157

Disney executive, still recovering from a serious operation, would have to go it alone for a while—or so it seemed. He quickly installed Joe Roth, who had been hired away from 20th Century Fox in 1992, as head of the Disney Studios and put Roy Disney Jr. in charge of the animated film division.[132]

Katzenberg, however, wasn't the only one to leave the Disney fold in August: Michael Montgomery, Euro Disney's chief financial officer, had announced his resignation just two weeks before. The park in France was still struggling. Matters became even worse with the release of an August 26 report from Paribas Capital Markets, which claimed that Euro Disney shares were worth only 1.6 francs ($.30)—and not 10 francs ($1.88), the price paid by investors in the new rights issue in June. The market reacted swiftly to the news. In only three days, share prices plummeted 27 percent to a record low of 7.55 francs ($1.40) on the Paris Bourse. Philippe Bourguignon asked stock market authorities to investigate irregularities in the share price and repeated expectations that the resort would be profitable by 1996. An article in *The Economist* painted a more dreary picture. "Investors in Euro Disney," it read, "might as well have climbed aboard Indiana Jones and the Temple of Peril. Jitters about the theme park's profitability are giving them a ride every bit as stomach-churning as Euro Disney's famous roller-coaster."[133]

A NEW NAME FOR A NEW DAY

In September 1994, Euro Disney executives announced that the name of their growing enterprise would be changed to Disneyland Paris. The decision came after months of internal discussion. "As Americans, we had believed that the word 'Euro' in front of Disney was glamorous and exciting," Eisner later explained. "For Europeans, it turned out to be a term that they associated with business, currency, and commerce. Renaming the park 'Disneyland Paris' was a way of identifying it not just with Walt's original creation but with one of the most romantic and exciting cities

158

in the world."[134] Renaming the park was also a way of giving Europe's Magic Kingdom a new lease on life. "Euro Disney" had become an unfortunate moniker after years of negative business news and controversy. It needed to be shed. The new name would be slowly incorporated into company logos and ads by reducing the size of the word "Euro," enlarging "Disneyland," and adding "Paris." But the legal name of the company operating the park would remain Euro Disney.[135]

The name change dovetailed with a new emphasis on marketing the theme park more aggressively to audiences outside of Europe. In the past, noted Jean-Marc Murro, sales manager for Disneyland Paris, promotional efforts had focused first on France, second on Europe, and lastly on other parts of the world. But no more. "[W]e have to make an effort to concentrate on all outside points," Murro observed. He added, "We have to do something [in the United States] to change perceptions."[136] In America, critics saw the Euro Disney venture as something similar to Coke's 1985 decision to change its formula: a major misstep by a master marketer.[137] One way in which Murro sought to reverse such perceptions was to invite three hundred American travel agents to visit the financially revitalized resort in November. If they could see for themselves the quality of Europe's Disney park against the magnificent backdrop of Paris, he reasoned, they might be more apt to sell clients on the idea of going there instead of to Disneyland or Walt Disney World. "We have to get a message out that we are OK."[138]

Murro also took special pains to reposition Disneyland Paris within the realm of leisure possibilities in Europe. Instead of continuing to market it as an all-out vacation destination like its world-famous counterpart in Orlando, he renewed the campaign to attract greater numbers of short-term visits. "Of course, visitors won't spend five days here," he commented, "but this could be the [place for the] first or the last night. Disneyland Paris is close to the Paris airports. We have buses to the airports. . . . We need to focus on this as a base to begin or end a trip."[139] As Disneyland

Paris continued to build toward its dream of a second theme park and added more attractions each year, the length of hotel stays would undoubtedly increase. One day, executives hoped, the resort might even approach the 94 percent occupancy rate of Walt Disney World hotels.[140] Until that time, it was best to think smaller and keep drawing new people in—so that they would want to return again and again as the park grew bigger and better.

Planners also promoted Disneyland Paris as the ideal site to stage meetings and events. But instead of merely publicizing the Hotel New York's Coliseum Convention Center, they made efforts to showcase other parts of the property as well. Festival Disney was touted as an exciting spot for lunches and themed parties. Buffalo Bill's Wild West Show was hyped as an unforgettable dinner experience that could accommodate groups as large as one thousand. And sections of the theme park itself—or even the whole thing—were made available to groups wishing to rent them before or after normal operating hours. The convention sales staff, in association with Tourisme 77, a local tourist board, was also equipped to arrange a variety of special events off-site. Cocktails at the Paris Opera, wine tasting at the Musée du Vin, medieval banquets at the thirteenth-century Caveaux St. Esprit in Provins, and "Dinner with Victor Hugo and Louis XIV" in the Grevin wax museum were just a sampling of the many packages available.[141] Disneyland Paris was aggressively positioned as a place where dreams could come true.

On November 3, 1994, a 21,000-square-foot annex was added to the Coliseum Convention Center. Housed in an all-weather tent, it was intended to help meet the demand for more meeting space until the more elaborate $100 million facility financed by Prince Al-Waleed could be built. The temporary annex increased the capacity of the existing convention center by nearly 65 percent. It also called attention to the success of Disneyland Paris's meetings operation, which had surpassed everyone's wildest expectations.[142]

But there were still a few dark clouds lingering over France's Magic Kingdom. One week earlier, it had announced a

$353 million loss in fiscal 1993. Although this figure compared favorably with the $1 billion loss of the previous year, theme park attendance had dropped another 10.2 percent, bringing the total number of visitors down to 8.8 million.[143] But executives were confident that the financial situation would stabilize. Prince Al-Waleed had just completed his purchase of 74.6 million shares of Euro Disney SCA in October, they reasoned, and the results would soon be felt.[144]

Michael Eisner hoped that such optimism was on target. The past two years, he reflected, had been filled with tragedy and turmoil. They had tested his very being. "You have an economic cloud in Europe," he noted, "and then the president of the company dies, then you have a kind of Shakespearean revolution going on inside the company, and then, on top of all that, you have a health problem . . . and God was playing his hand too, with fires and earthquakes in Southern California . . . then the tourist murders in Florida."[145] In addition, Eisner's plans to build Disney's America, a historical theme park near Manassas, Virginia, had crumbled before his very eyes. Opponents rallying against what one called "the raping and pillaging of America's history for a glorified hamburger stand" stirred up so much controversy that he suffered flashbacks to the early protests that afflicted Euro Disney.[146] The opponents' depth of feeling, one reporter observed, was almost French.[147] On September 28, 1994, Eisner officially abandoned plans to build the theme park on the three-thousand-acre Virginia site.[148]

It had been a rough period, through and through. "A lot of things were stacking up," Eisner recalled. "It tested whether or not we were a company that could deal in failure as well as success. It tested our management. It tested our board. It tested our major shareholders. And of course, it tested me."[149] The "Euro Disney crisis," as one writer had termed it early on, stood at the center of these difficulties. As the first Disney project in nearly a decade not to be received with universal acclaim, it broke the spell of invincibility that had fallen over Eisner and his golden team. As the first Disney theme park not to recover from an initial period of adjustment, it prompted executives to rethink their short- and long-term development strategies. As the first Disney venture that needed to be rescued from financial ruin, it demonstrated that fairy-tale endings weren't always engineered as easily as one might expect. Living happily ever after simply couldn't be guaranteed, not even in Europe's own Magic Kingdom.

But the experience of staring deeply into the eyes of doom had proven valuable, in its own way. By challenging Disney and Euro Disney executives to find solutions to unanticipated problems, it forced them to take creative risks and stretch the limits of their imaginations. It also demanded that they fine-tune their strategic planning skills before pushing further into the international marketplace. "Plussing" the property with new attractions had required them to think about how they might create a Disney park with a flavor all its own. Revamping shops and eateries with new merchandise and menu selections had compelled them to look more closely at the tastes of European audiences. Implementing fresh marketing initiatives had made them more sensitive to the subtleties of promotion and seasonal pricing. And negotiating a financial restructuring package with a consortium of banks, lawyers, accountants, shareholders, and a Saudi Arabian prince had taught them how to drive a hard bargain. As Euro Disney president Philippe Bourguignon had noted during the start-up process, "the test of whether our management works is not the park's initial difficulties. The test is how quickly we react to resolve them."[150] Disney and Euro Disney executives alike had reacted swiftly to this trial by fire, which called upon all of their resources and creative insights. It forced them to toughen up, reinvent the Disney entertainment formula for a new continent and a new century, and earn their success—instead of merely waiting for it to embrace them.

5 It's a Small World, Inc.

On July 25, 1995, some three years after its grand opening, Disneyland Paris surprised Europe by reporting its first quarterly profit: $35.3 million. The impact of the financial rescue package was beginning to be felt. Waves of tourists had started to swell, too, leading officials to predict a 14 percent increase in ticket sales for the fiscal year ending September 30. But these estimates proved to be conservative. When results for fiscal 1995 were released on November 15, Disney executives must have been beaming: theme park attendance had jumped a full 21 percent (from 8.8 million to 10.7 million) over the previous year, and hotel occupancy had climbed from 60 to 68.5 percent. Best of all, Disneyland Paris finished the year with a net profit of $22.8 million after debt payments.[1] The figure stood in stark contrast to the $366 million loss posted only one year before. Steve Burke, who had been promoted to president and chief operating officer of Disneyland Paris in February, commented on the sudden upswing. "Our goal was to break even in 1996," he noted. "This comes a year ahead of schedule, which for us is very good. We're now confident we can build on this new base."[2]

Europe's Magic Kingdom was in the black for the first time in its tumultuous history. Critics who had been circling overhead like buzzards, hungrily waiting for their forecasts to come true, grew alarmed. If this trend continued, they would suffer the public embarrassment of being proven wrong. Worse yet, they would have to confront their greatest fear: that France—and all of Europe—had fallen under the evil spell of an American mouse. The very idea that the beleaguered Disney enterprise might pull through after marching to the brink of failure was incomprehensible to such cynics. Even more offensive was the idea that the park might wind up being a real moneymaker for its parent corporation in the United States.

The dramatic turnaround performance of Disneyland Paris in the wake of financial restructuring merits close attention. Not only did it put a struggling resort on the path to profitability, it also set the stage for a transformation of entertainment landscapes across Europe. Both preexisting and new leisure parks would feel the impact of this latest Disney success story—creatively, operationally, and financially. And that impact cannot rightfully be reduced to the projection of American ideology onto continental soil. Disney art, after all, is not simply the product of a single national experience. As the Walt Disney Company plunges headlong into the multimedia landscapes of the twenty-first century, it stands poised to discover exactly how universal its creations are—as well as how far it might take the conviction that "It's a Small World."

CLIMB EVERY MOUNTAIN

When the results of fiscal 1995 were announced, Disneyland Paris executives were ecstatic—and undoubtedly more than a little relieved. They credited the financial rescue package with easing the high debt burden. They pointed to new marketing campaigns and tight cost controls, which had helped to push theme-park revenues up by 8.7 percent to $500 million and hotel revenues up to $360 million.[3] Company officials also identified one other reason for the dramatic upward surge in 1995: Space Mountain, the newest and most celebrated attraction at Disneyland Paris.

The decision to build the new ride, however, was not unquestioned. Imagineers had left vacant a spot at the center of

Discoveryland so that one day the popular stateside attraction could be installed to serve as the area's main visual magnet and "people-pump." Thinning crowds and worsening financial conditions, however, made it ever more difficult to justify the expense. Even Disneyland Paris executives who believed that it might help to increase ticket sales resisted plans to move forward with the colossal project. They simply couldn't afford to plow as much as $100 million into something that wasn't guaranteed to pay off. In the end, the Imagineers convinced them that the new attraction would create a second wave of interest in—and add force to the unique identity of—Europe's Disney park. "Discovery Mountain," as they planned to call it, was to be much more than a hand-me-down Space Mountain from other Disney parks. It would be an all-new attraction: something bigger and better than previous models that would strengthen the overarching motif of Discoveryland.[4]

The new name, however, failed to generate excitement in Europe. Philippe Bourguignon expressed concern that it sounded too much like a museum exhibit. Many of the park's customers (and cast members) were also reluctant to embrace the name. Despite repeated assurances that the ride would be "much more technical and much more fun than the Space Mountains in our other theme parks," they feared that Discovery Mountain would be something less than its legendary predecessors if its differences were substantial enough to warrant a name change.[5] After much discussion, Michael Eisner authorized the official renaming of Discovery Mountain. Henceforth, he decreed, it would be Space Mountain. The signs and electrified marquee reading "Discovery Mountain," which had already been installed, were quickly replaced. But the more understated "DM" monograms etched into the space vehicles and handrails were permitted to remain—as the symbol of a future that had been swept into the past.

The story, as related by Imagineer Tim Delaney, is ironic: it shows how perceptions can shape reality. Even more important, it attests to the great cultural currency of the Space Mountain—

and the Disney—name in Europe. Doubters, convinced that the original thrill ride could not be improved upon, were in for a big surprise. The new Space Mountain would share with its predecessors the basic premise of an indoor roller-coaster ride in the dark, but it also set out to accomplish something unique: the seamless marriage of architecture and ride technology with storytelling. Jules Verne's 1865 tale, *De la Terre à la Lune (From the Earth to the Moon)*, provided the thematic inspiration and guided Imagineers as they fleshed out ideas for how the adventure would be designed and experienced, both conceptually and physically.[6]

To blast guests into the story, Disney Imagineers created the first-ever inclined-ride catapult launch system. Located on the outside of the mountain, it would rocket passengers up a thirty-two-degree slope to the summit in 1.8 seconds before hurling them inside for a "fictional" journey through outer space. An on-board sound system, equipped with six speakers for each person, was also added to enhance visual effects with carefully synchronized music and sounds. But the most shocking feature of all in the new Space Mountain was a stretch of track with three inversion loops to spin passengers upside down in the darkness, dramatizing the climax of the Jules Verne tale with a touch of terror. Because of the ride's special intensity, Imagineers added one final feature: "la voie stellaire," an observation walkway that tunnels through the inside of the mountain at ground level so that interested onlookers could get a sense of the ride before deciding whether or not to venture inside.[7]

The Space Mountain created for Disneyland Paris was an all-new attraction, through and through. Its external appearance, electrified by gleaming shapes, colors, and Victorian styling, was equaled only by the adventure within. By blending drama, special effects, and carefully controlled motion through spaces charged with narrative meaning, the Imagineers succeeded in creating one of the premier thrill rides anywhere. Moreover, they succeeded in reinterpreting a famous Disney attraction for a new

166

park—and a new multinational audience. Its debut on June 1, 1995, more than three years after the park's grand opening, was celebrated with a musical appearance by Elton John that attracted other stars, including Yves Mourousi, Alain Madelin, Claudia Schiffer, and David Copperfield. At last, many concluded, Disneyland Paris was complete.[8] But of course, no Disney theme park is ever complete. In the words of a professor visiting from Sweden, the mountain created at the center of Discoveryland represented anything but a final chapter. "Space Mountain," he predicted, "will be the beginning of this park."[9]

THEME PARKS, THEME PARKS, EVERYWHERE

Disneyland Paris, similarly, has come to represent the beginning of the theme-park market in Europe. As early as the 1980s, when agreements with the French government were still being hammered out, companies across the Continent were scrambling to beat Disney to the punch. A March 1987 article in the *Economist* reported that the soon-to-be-built Euro Disney development would face competition from as many as sixteen other continental theme parks, built or planned.[10] The list included such long-standing favorites as Denmark's Tivoli Gardens and Legoland, Madurodam in Holland, and England's Alton Towers. And new proposals were coming in from both sides of the Atlantic: Marine World hoped to locate in France; Busch Gardens and Magic Mountain wanted to build in Spain; Wonderworld and Battersea Park were planning to open in Great Britain; Warner Brothers Movie World aimed to set up shop in Germany; and Universal Studios was shopping for sites in Paris and London. The goal for most was to be in operation by 1992, when the Summer Olympic Games in Barcelona (expected to draw an additional million tourists to the Continent) got under way.[11]

But this list was just the start. Less than six months after the *Economist* report, the total number of proposals for France alone had jumped to twenty-five. Theme parks seemed to be sprouting

167

up everywhere. Mirapolis, a $70 million park based on French and European folk tales, opened in May 1987 outside Paris. Big Band Schtroumpf, a $120 million park based on the Belgian Smurf cartoon characters, was built near Metz by a unit of French steelmaker Sacilor. Parc Astérix, a $200 million, 20-acre park designed around a popular French comic-book character, threw open its gates some twenty miles from the Disney site in the spring of 1989. And France Miniature, a $14.2 million, 9-acre diorama of France, opened in 1991 in Élancourt, west of Paris.[12] All of these ventures were tiny compared to the $4.4 billion, 4,800-acre Disney development—and none of them expected more than two to three million visitors per year. But their collective presence on the European landscape did not go unnoticed. "There's not enough room for all these parks," cried Pierre Mouchel, an officer at Banque Paribas, which owns 5 percent of Big Band Schtroumpf. "It's obvious we won't be able to build all the projects planned."[13]

The impending spread of theme parks across the European countryside was so alarming, in fact, that some communities, most notably in Great Britain, erected barriers to further construction. But industry experts were confident that European demand for the new pleasure gardens would grow. After all, they reasoned, there were some 2,000 successful theme parks operating throughout the United States. France alone would have to build another 383 parks to match this level in its own population.[14] Steve Burke agreed that the market was far from saturated. "The European theme park business is in the early parts of its growth cycle," he noted, "whereas in the U.S., it's very developed."[15] Burke went on to predict that the number of European theme park visitors would increase dramatically, from 45 million per year before Disney's arrival to 60 million per year (which was still only one-fourth the number of annual theme park visitors in the United States).[16]

Competition was of little real concern. In its many years of designing and operating theme parks, the Walt Disney Company had learned not to fear other entertainment ventures. Even parasitic operations located nearby, they had learned, ultimately helped to increase the flow of tourist traffic chez Mickey. "Let them promote the heck out of their Florida tour," Michael Eisner had remarked about the 1990 opening of a new Universal Studios theme park. "It'll only get more people to Florida, and they'll end up spending all of their time with us."[17] The theme-park pie in Europe, Disney executives firmly believed, was big enough to be sliced into many pieces. As long as the Walt Disney Company was able to offer unique entertainment at good value, they assured one another, it would be able to claim—and hold onto—the lion's share of the business.

Other theme park operators in Europe, who sought success on a smaller scale than the gargantuan Disney project, agreed that there was space for a multitude of different leisure experiences. Olivier de Bosrédon, director of Parc Astérix, admitted in a *Grand Public* magazine interview that this would not be the case if the tourist base was limited to a single national audience. After all, he argued, few French families could afford—or would agree—to spend hundreds of francs to visit both parks each year. But Disney was an international name. While the Magic Kingdom would certainly "steal" some of Astérix's French visitors, de Bosrédon reasoned, the runoff traffic from Disney's flood of foreign tourists promised to more than make up for this deficit.[18]

"REALIZING" THE FAKE

As the Euro Disney Resort helped to open France to a new multinational tourist trade, it also prompted changes in other area theme parks. Parc Astérix, France Miniature, and the rest could not simply rely on playing to French national identity. If they were to survive in the ever-changing market of European leisure entertainment, they would have to sell their version of French history to foreign tourists as well.[19] That meant putting up signs (and distributing guidebooks) printed in more than one language, offering a wide variety of souvenirs and menu selections,

169

and featuring attractions that would appeal to a broad cross-section of Europeans. It also meant promoting their ventures aggressively. Parc Astérix, which had enlisted the help of Economics Research Associates (a California-based group) to test the market waters in the 1980s, led the way by linking up with five other European parks. The network they created enabled them to coordinate marketing efforts, attract corporate sponsors, and increase revenue by reaching out to visitors from other countries.[20]

The design of the new parks in France was also influenced by American—namely Disney—models. At Parc Astérix, for instance, the guest entrance opens onto an avenue filled with shops that funnels visitors into the park, much like Main Street, U.S.A. But "Le Monde Antique," as this Roman-style commercial avenue is called, differs from the Disney version by adding twists and turns. While this layout denies visual access into the park, the mustachioed figure of Astérix perched atop a tall stone peak at the hub draws guests inward, much like the looming form of Sleeping Beauty's castle.[21] Other Disney-style attractions fill the park. The canal boat tours through Le Village d'Astérix recall the charm of bobbing past tiny hamlets in Storybook Land. La Rue de Paris, an attraction that traces French history in street tableaux from the Middle Ages to the nineteenth century, is France's answer to Main Street, U.S.A. And the spinning cauldron ride is little more than a disguised version of the Mad Hatter's teacups.

France Miniature, inspired by Holland's Madurodam (an imaginary Dutch village brought to life in tiny form), also takes cues from Disney theme parks. But instead of giving form to fictional places from the world of fairy-tale films, like Storybook Land, France Miniature takes a more literal approach. The hexagon-shaped park replicates the contours of the French countryside and features some 170 painstakingly crafted models of actual monuments, châteaux, factories, and entire villages, all cast at one-thirtieth actual size.[22] Tiny TGV trains and motorways crisscross a landscape dominated by the Eiffel Tower and more than thirty thousand bonsai trees. "Just like Hannibal," the park's brochure exclaims, "you cross the Alps and Mont Blanc is before you. Look! All of France is at your feet." Planners even included a small nuclear power station, a packaging plant, and an Esso refinery to demonstrate that this park was no Fantasyland.[23]

Both Parc Astérix and France Miniature were planned to package France for the tourist by scaling it down to its essential icons. But they were also created with the aim of educating children. Thiérry Coltier, one of the founders of France Miniature, noted that the pedagogical mission of his park set it apart from the competition. "The place is supposed to fall half-way between an open-air museum and an amusement park," he commented. "It should be fun, but also educative. It's really the only thing of its kind in France—we don't compete in the same category as Euro Disney and we're doing something quite distinct."[24] Nicolas Pérrard, marketing director of Parc Astérix, argued that his park also had a higher purpose. It had welcomed some two hundred thousand schoolchildren in 1994, he noted, to make learning French history fun. "Disney is based on fantasies, we are based on realities," Pérrard commented. "They are not based on a national culture, but on fairy tales."[25]

Pérrard's claim, which suggests how European theme parks defined themselves against the Disney model, is curious. If anthropomorphised buildings, flume rides down the River Styx, and animated figures of Victor Hugo and Toulouse-Lautrec—not to mention the cartoon likenesses of Astérix and his crew, wandering through the park—constitute historical "reality," what might be said to remain in the domain of artifice? More importantly, what have theme parks to do with authenticity at all? As architectural historian Joseph Rykwert has pointed out, "the ones which show a past or a remote place may, to some extent, pretend to [authenticity]." But that is all. "[I]nauthenticity, the creation of the quite unreal place," he argues, "is what a theme park is for."[26] The Parc Astérix mechanical facade that celebrates the storming of the Bastille in the French Revolution is fake. The Roman City, with its statuary and suspended gardens, is fake. The swordfights between characters suited in armor are also fake. The dioramas at France Miniature are fake, too—just like those at Euro Disney.

But in these worlds of absolute artifice there is a strange sense of legitimacy. "The authenticity" of such places, theorist Umberto Eco has observed, "is not historical, but visual. Everything looks real, and therefore it is real; in any case the fact that it seems real is real, and the thing is real even if, like Alice in Wonderland, it never existed."[27] Some counterfeit representations featured—and celebrated—at theme parks are copies of a familiar original. Others fit Plato's conception of the simulacrum: they are exact copies for which an original never existed.[28] Nonetheless, such representations are real in their own right and frequently, as cultural historian Miles Orvell has suggested, "more interesting than the real thing."[29] Despite claims of heightened authenticity at Parc Astérix and France Miniature, both ventures share with the Disney model to which they so violently struggle to react the desire to appear "real."

The line between reality and artifice becomes hopelessly blurred at Britain's Alton Towers. Built around a stately home owned by the Talbot family from 1412 to 1924, the park is a complex blend of history and fantasy. Guests visiting Alton Towers come into contact with what was once the largest family dwelling in all of Europe. But they experience it in a context that is far removed from the original. No longer the Staffordshire seat of the earls of Shrewsbury, nor even the small funfair into which it later evolved, the property has become a full-fledged theme park in the style of Disneyland. Rides, restaurants, shops, and shows compete for the attention of paying guests. Henry Hound, a dog character taken from the Talbot coat of arms and adopted as the company mascot in 1980, patrols the park, greets children, and poses for photos. One Disney executive visiting Alton Towers observed that its owner, John Broome, had started out with a distinct advantage over the Euro Disney complex being developed in France: Broome's central castle, he pointed out, was already built.[30]

Writer Joel Achenbach points to such places as examples of what he calls "creeping surrealism": the condition in which reality is slowly—and deceptively—replaced by artifice. "Lies have been raised to an art form," he notes, "information manipulated so delicately, so craftily, with such unparalleled virtuosity, that you can no longer tell the genuine from the fake, the virtuous from the profane. The technology of falsehood has far outraced the progress of our judgment." As a result, he argues, human agency is mercilessly restricted:

> People are confused. Alienated from nature, liberated from such primordial responsibilities as the growing of food, the making of clothes, the construction of shelter, people in the late 20th Century have entered a revolutionary phase in which they passively accept a cartoon version of reality that is projected upon them by an overwhelming assortment of unreliable, distortive and sometimes diabolical media. It's crazy as hell out there. There has arisen from this mess a strange sort of comfort with artifice and falsehood.[31]

Achenbach's suggestion that the fake appears more real each day cannot be questioned. New technologies make this possible. But his argument that people "passively accept" falsehood as truth is problematic. Given the huge success of Alton Towers in England (it is the single biggest tour-bus destination in Great Britain and the fourth most-visited theme park in Western Europe, drawing some three million visitors annually) and the flood of other fantasy theme parks opening up on both sides of the English Channel, it would seem more likely that people actively seek out artifice as a form of diversion and entertainment.[32]

The unqualified success of Denmark's Legoland since its opening in 1968 lends credibility to this conclusion. Filled with miniaturized landmarks from around the world—all built out of Lego bricks—the park is a collection of copies. Visitors can stroll through plastic safari landscapes complete with giraffes and

173

zebras, experience the majesty of Copenhagen's Amalienborg Palace, and discover the charms of the American West in a frontier town known playfully as "Legoredo." The purpose of these toy dioramas is not to deceive, but rather, to amaze guests with displays of meticulous accuracy. The fact that they are built entirely out of prefabricated rectangular bricks adds to the sense of wonder and curiosity about how long it might have taken to make them. The entertainment value of such imitation landmarks (and landscapes!) derives from the very fact that they are false—and that they are able to approximate reality, down to the tiniest details.

Few visitors walk away from Legoland believing that original monuments from around the world have been transplanted in Denmark. But the permeability of national borders—not to mention those separating reality and artifice—does become delightfully complex. The forty-six-foot-high version of Mount Rushmore, set into the side of a stony cliff and crafted entirely out of Legos, offers a unique case in point. As noted by cultural geographer John Dorst, "the Legoland Rushmore is an artificial monumental miniature of a gigantic enlargement that transforms a monumental natural landscape into a national monument."[33] But the Lego version is not simply a Danish copy of an American artifact. The original portrait busts in South Dakota were, in fact, carved out of the rock by the Danish-American sculptor Gutzon Borglum.[34] Dorst argues that it is becoming more and more difficult to determine who is importing and who is exporting in the world of postindustrial capitalism:

> The theme park as an industry and as a cultural institution, goes farther than perhaps any other contemporary phenomenon to call into question the old ways of thinking about how national cultures influence one another. As an industry, theme parks are thoroughly transnational in terms of ownership, design, production, operation, and clientele. More profoundly, as a mechanism of cultural production, theme

parks absorb all cultural distinctions by transforming them into images, each of which takes its place, like the individual brick in a Lego construction, as a unit in a commodity system of consumable similarities and differences.[35]

The blonde, blue-eyed Danes who wear feathered headdresses at "Legoredo"—much like the European cast members of Disneyland Paris who don cowboy hats and greet guests with a heavily accented "Howdy"—demonstrate Dorst's point that "the circularity of tourist appropriation is infinite." As other theme parks follow Disney's lead and set up shop in Europe and around the world, their transnational dimensions will undoubtedly continue to emphasize, with increasing strength, that the world we live in is shrinking.

FOLLOWING THE MOUSE

Disney's arrival in Europe is a defining moment in the theme park industry. Just as the 1955 opening of California's Disneyland marks a watershed in the development of American theme parks, 1992 signals the dawn of a new age for European leisure parks. "Disney's entry gave a further push to the [theme park] industry," noted one entertainment executive. "It drew visitors' attention, and obviously it put newer meaning as far as quality and expectations." More than this, it taught Europeans what a theme park was—as well as how one should be designed, marketed, and operated. When Parc Astérix opened in 1989, many of the people who ran it were recruits from the hotel and department store industries. Marketing director Nicolas Pérrard admitted that most "had little concept of what a theme park really was." But they learned quickly. By watching the Euro Disney operation take shape in France, executives transformed Parc Astérix from a confused jumble of attractions into a more coherent entertainment experience. "Thanks to Disney," Pérrard commented, "our people know what the product is."[36]

175

The Walt Disney Company also served as a catalyst for American businesses wishing to install theme parks in the seemingly rich European market. Port Aventura, a $400 million park financed by the Anheuser-Busch Companies and British entertainment group Tussauds (the wax museum people and the theme park division of Pearson P.L.C.), opened on May 1, 1995. Its location in Salou, along the Spanish Costa Dorada south of Barcelona, is significant: Disney officials had rejected the Catalonian site ten years earlier in favor of the Marne-la-Vallée region in France. Anheuser-Busch executives following in their wake snatched up 228 acres of the property shortly thereafter. The park they created features attractions that evoke far-off places, such as Polynesia and the American West, as well as a selection of thrill rides, like the Dragon Kahn roller-coaster, described by one guest as "sheer terror." Port Aventura planners learned from Disney's mistakes, too. John Collins, the park's director, cited Euro Disney's struggles as one reason Anheuser-Busch and Tussauds decided to wait before proceeding with hotel development. "[W]e have thoughts of developing a resort community, golf course—things like that," he noted. "But that's a long way down the road."[37]

Other American businesses also followed Mickey Mouse to Europe with hopes of claiming a share of the newly fertilized theme park market. Cultural critic Michael Medved felt that such a plan was inherently misguided. The Euro Disney Resort, he argued in February 1994, stood as a lesson to all the world that American commercialism would not be accepted in Europe's leisure landscapes. "Not that they'll learn," he seethed. "The same week that brought the first rumors of a Euro Disney shutdown also brought news that Warner Brothers was buying out Bavaria Studios' loss-making Bottrop-Kirchelen film theme park, situated in the Ruhr Valley."[38]

Warner Brothers Movie World, as the new $212 million park is called, opened in late spring 1996.[39] A full 40 percent larger than its counterpart on Australia's Gold Coast, the one-hundred-acre park features a selection of attractions, ranging from a Looney Tunes Village and a *Police Academy* stunt show to a roller-coaster ride inspired by the film *Lethal Weapon*. "We've taken [the] basic design, have watched closely what works and what doesn't and have expanded that concept," noted Joe Meck, general manager of the project (whose father was manager of Disneyland in the 1950s and 1960s). But Movie World executives also took cues from Euro Disney: they decided to close the park in the winter (thereby limiting its annual season to seven months) and directed early marketing campaigns at Germany and Holland. "While we would like to see families visiting from all over Europe," noted project planner Michael Reinert, "we have made sure of survival by meeting German demand." Executives also invested heavily in German travel and tour markets, which support some six thousand bus companies. "Bus packages," commented Meck, "are very popular in Europe and they will be a big part of our business."[40]

Universal Studios originally forecast a 1994 grand opening in Europe for its newest Hollywood studio tour. Executives were eager to crack open a new market. Even more important, they wanted to beat the Walt Disney Company (which had unveiled its studio theme park in Florida one year ahead of Universal's) at its own game by opening its gates a full two years before the widely publicized 1996 debut of the Disney-MGM Studios Europe.[41] "We're going to kick Disney's butt all over Europe," declared Jay S. Stein, head of MCA's recreational group, in March 1990.[42] The theme park they planned, much like its predecessors in California and Florida, was to be less concerned with creating and sustaining illusions than with shattering them. Attractions featuring popular Universal characters, such as E.T., Frankenstein, Phantom of the Opera, and a thirty-foot King Kong, would take guests behind the scenes to demonstrate how movie magic was created.[43] But as of early 1999, Universal Studios Europe has yet to open.

Indeed, the theme park market was becoming more and more global. But Americans were not the only ones looking to in-

177

stall leisure developments outside their national borders. Europeans also wanted a piece of the action. They followed Mickey's lead and began devising plans to enter the much more crowded U.S. market. Many new theme parks have been proposed. The Tussauds Group (which holds a 40 percent stake in Port Aventura and runs two other parks in Britain) announced its plans for a high-tech indoor entertainment complex on Forty-second Street in New York City. Lego World, the theme park division of Denmark's Lego Toy Company, is moving forward with two new theme park developments: one in Carlsbad, California (a one-hour drive from Disneyland), the other near Windsor, England.[44] And Warner Brothers has announced plans to open another Movie World theme park outside of London in 1999.[45]

BROADCASTING NATIONAL IDENTITY

The plethora of Hollywood studio theme parks planned for Europe, however, represents much more than an attempt to draw vacationing tourists. Executives at the Walt Disney Company, Warner Brothers, and Universal Studios imagine them as part of a long-term strategy to build movie-making empires across the Atlantic. For this reason, they included in their site plans big sound stages that would be used to shoot films and television shows. By setting up shop in Europe and taking on European partners, studio executives believe, they might sidestep Common Market rules and quotas regulating the amount of programming from outside regions, namely the United States. The new state-of-the-art facilities promise to safeguard—and even increase—the distribution of their respective products, while expanding the participation of European talent in a rapidly globalizing entertainment industry.

France has been most suspicious of American media. Its response to the introduction of the VCR, notes writer John Huey, illustrates the degree to which cultural protectionism has asserted itself. The government originally slapped a 33 percent tax on both foreign-made VCRs and pre-recorded tapes to curb spending on such imports. It also withheld the release of films on videocassette for a period of one year (instead of the six months customary elsewhere), which effectively killed the video business. Government officials further required that the pay-TV channel Canal Plus show 50 percent French programs. Under that rule, some estimate, the network would have had to air some 200 French films annually—an impossibility, given that France produces only 130 films each year.[46] "France's preferred weapon against the cultural invaders of Paramount, CNN, and MTV," noted one writer, "is quotas. Anything non-European must be strictly rationed. The majority of what appears on TV and radio must be European—preferably French."[47]

France also took steps to persuade other countries of the European Economic Community to adopt its protectionist philosophy. The fact that American films had moved from a one-third box-office share at the end of the 1960s to one-half ten years later was scary enough to preservationists. But American films have since come to dominate the market in Europe, claiming between 80 and 90 percent of the receipts. In 1991, the ten highest-earning films in France were all American.[48] The wild success of Disney's *Lion King* (1994), heralded by one *Paris Match* reporter as "the commercial event of 1994," did little to assuage fears that Hollywood was colonizing Europe.[49] In January 1995, François Mitterand implored the European Parliament in Strasbourg, France, not to allow American films, fast food, blue jeans, and slang to wash away that which made Europe unique. "Europe must be more than economic balance sheets and tons of freight," he proclaimed. "I would say, but I don't want to exaggerate, that it needs a soul. . . . Europeans must love Europe."[50]

Mitterand's impassioned words were a call for joint action. And, because France held the rotating presidency of the European Union for the first half of 1995, entitling it to set the agenda for all fifteen member states, the issue of cultural protectionism was kept alive. The revision of a 1989 European Union directive known as

179

Television Without Frontiers (which required member states to "reserve for European works . . . a majority proportion of their transmission time") topped France's list. If restrictions on imports of non-European (meaning American) films, television shows, and music were not tightened, officials argued, the long-term consequences would be devastating. The excitement over interactive TV, video-on-demand, and music delivered over the Internet, not to mention the wave of studio theme parks soon to be installed on European soil, only strengthened their resolve. If they failed to take a stand, many believed, it would soon be too late.[51]

But others felt that it already was too late for the types of measures France had in mind. Cultural quotas and regulations were at best a shaky solution. And "Fortress Europe," as Steven Ross, chairman of Time Warner, has called it, promised to be no more effective than the Maginot Line, France's last greatest attempt to wall itself off from invaders.[52] Unless French leaders wished to see history repeat itself, cultural critic John Andrews argued, with new technologies once again rendering such barriers obsolete, they would have to devise a new strategy for cultural protection and preservation.[53] Others, including Mark Hunter, author of a book on French minister of culture Jack Lang, agreed. "France," he declared, "has yet to learn that you do not legislate taste by decree."[54]

That efforts to promote the national film industry by quadrupling its subsidies in the 1980s had failed to keep attendance at French movies from shrinking was proof that cultural nationalism could not be purchased—especially if the quality wasn't there. "You have to ask if the kind of cinema they're promoting has any relation to what the public wants to see," Hunter commented. "What nobody wants to say is that American movies are doing so well in France because some of them are pretty good, and some of the auteur cinema is second rate."[55] Keiji Matsushima, director of account services at Japan's Dentsu, the world's largest ad agency, agreed. "American movies are the only ones that are really international," he asserted. "Americans know how to entertain people. The French, the British, and the Japanese filmmakers are too intoxicated with themselves. They don't give a damn about audiences; they want their names in history books."[56]

Even Jeanne Moreau, François Truffaut's star and collaborator, shared this view. In a *Newsweek* article, she complained that the new generation of French directors was more interested in bureaucratic maneuvering for subsidies than in appealing to popular taste. As a result, France's ability to draw audiences and compete in the marketplace had slipped dramatically. More disturbing still, the strict programming quotas set by governmental officials were forcing French producers to churn out cookie-cutter copies of what some considered to be "American banalities." Time and cost constraints, critic John Andrews noted, prevented them from straying from familiar formulas:

> French TV is full of soaps that make *Dynasty* look like Shakespeare. It boasts a French music channel called MCM (which is a rather good copy of MTV), and it broadcasts a subsidized news channel called EuroNews—a vain attempt to compete with CNN. In his determination to block Europe's gates to any audiovisual or cultural *cheval de Troie,* [French Minister of Culture] Toubon doesn't seem to have asked himself which is the more powerful force of cultural infiltration: an original American program, or a Frenchified copy of similar ideas and characters. According to the law, what makes a film or program French, or European, is simply where the film is shot—not where the ideas come from. And Toubon and his allies are determined to keep the European cameras rolling by keeping the products of American ones out.[57]

But as popular culture scholar Todd Gitlin has pointed out, the task of assigning nationality to a film—or an entire film operation—has become increasingly complex in recent years. "*Terminator 2,*" he observed, "with its Austrian-born star, its French

181

co-financing, and its Spanish-language gags, might as well come from the moon or the Cayman Islands" as the United States.[58] An American film studio in Europe (or a collection of them) supported by European investment and operated with the help of European talent would prove to be equally difficult to classify in the rapidly changing media landcapes of the twenty-first century.

For Europeans intent on defending continental values in the face of changing technology, the move toward Marshall McLuhan's vision of a global village promises to be problematic.[59] Not only will it require monitoring and censorship on the grandest of scales, it might even mean risking the very culture they seek to preserve in the first place. The words of cultural critic Andrews are worth quoting in full:

> A nation's soul cannot be manufactured by regulatory fiat. And a nation's culture, the expression of its soul, cannot be preserved in a regulatory museum; it must evolve. There will always be subsidies for the arts—from state support for opera in Britain to tax incentives for film production in Ireland. But to set quotas is to stifle the conversations and the evolution that keeps culture alive. French TV soaps with their guaranteed market share are no better than the American ones, while the good French pop groups, like Les Négresses Vertes, don't need any state-guaranteed FM air time.[60]

Andrews concluded:

> What is at risk in the arguments over culture is France's—and Europe's—stake in the future. Any culture or nation that does not come to grips with the technologies changing our lives is, quite literally, living in the past. . . . If Europe falls even further behind on [the information superhighway] it will no longer have to worry about its cultures, for it will have effectively put them all in a museum.[61]

The irony is painful. But it promises to grow even more so, such champions of globalization have argued, if protectionists effectively sacrifice what they are trying to guard simply because they refuse to believe that cultures can peacefully coexist. "[T]he word Americanisation," says Professor Rob Kroes of the University of Amsterdam, "is unduly alarmist. It reduces the complex processes of cultural influence, of borrowing, imitation and reception, to the stark binary form of a zero-sum game. In a field of two opposite alternatives, of a Europeanism as opposed to Americanism, any degree of Americanisation implies an equal degree of de-Europeanization."[62] Others have agreed with the ridiculousness of such a model. "The French language will no more weaken just because it incorporates 'le weekend' than English has been weakened by using words like sang-froid," noted one, "nor will French cuisine disappear because there is a McDonald's in every town."[63] Daniel Toscan du Plantier, president of the French film promoter UNIFRANCE, concurred: "One can like hamburgers and still want to keep cassoulet."[64] British columnist Peregrine Worsthorne went further, claiming that Americana has become so prevalent in Europe that many have come to view it as modern, global culture as opposed to a transatlantic import. "I'm not sure McDonald's and Coca-Cola are even associated any longer with America," she noted. "They've been here for so long now."[65]

As the Norwegian media researcher Helge Ronning has suggested, it is possible that American popular culture is becoming everyone's second culture.[66] Writer John Huey has characterized it as the driving force behind the "global pop culture Zeitgeist."[67] And Gitlin has argued that it is "the closest approximation there is today to a global lingua franca, drawing urban classes in most nations into a federated culture zone."[68] As people from Australia to Zimbabwe switch from the local news to the American Oscar ceremonies and back again, he asserts, they acquire a certain fluency in both their own cultures and the developing global semiculture. The "bilingualism" that is activated

183

by this constant movement between two worlds repositions them as citizens of a transnational system.[69]

THE ABCs OF VERTICAL INTEGRATION

On July 31, 1995, the Walt Disney Company announced that it had made a deal to purchase Capital Cities/ABC for $19 billion in cash and stock. Described by reporters as "a miracle" and "the most significant attempt yet to dominate the converging fields of entertainment, information and multimedia," it united one of the premier movie studios with the top-rated television network.[70] More than this, it neatly closed a forty-year circle in the life of the two media giants.[71] ABC had agreed to invest in Walt Disney's first theme park during the 1950s in exchange for a weekly *Disneyland* television show, and the deal had proven to be smart for both companies. Disney CEO Michael Eisner and Capital Cities chairman Thomas Murphy hoped that a new alliance would bring them continued success as they marched into the multimedia landscapes of the twenty-first century.[72]

For both, the union seemed like a marriage made in heaven. The Walt Disney Company brought to the table many assets, including a cast of characters that played well around the world, a powerful television and movie studio, a collection of popular theme parks, some four hundred retail stores, a record and book arm, the Disney Channel pay-TV service, and a professional hockey team. Capital Cities/ABC (created in a March 1985 merger) also had much to offer. Not only did it own the most profitable network (with 225 affiliate broadcasters) and eight of the best-managed television stations in the country, it boasted the nation's largest radio network (21 stations), seven newspapers (including the *Kansas City Star* and the *Ft. Worth Star-Telegram*), an 80 percent stake in the ESPN sports cable channel, interests in other cable networks such as Lifetime and A & E, and a list of trade magazines. Capital Cities/ABC also had a depth of management talent that could help to fill the gaps left by recent departures at the Walt Disney Company.[73] Reporter Dan Reed summed up the strengths of the new partnership: "You're talking about being able to put the best content producer in the entertainment industry together with the best delivery system available. This deal has 'synergies' written all over it."[74]

But the Disney deal was different from other media mergers. Unlike the 1990 buyout of Warner Brothers by Time Incorporated and Viacom's 1994 acquisition of Paramount and Blockbuster Entertainment, both of which had faced severe difficulties trying to reorganize, there was little overlap between the Eisner and Murphy conglomerates. As one observer noted, "Disney produces entertainment. Capital Cities/ABC exhibits it."[75] Each business complemented the other—and they promised to fit together, like two halves of an amulet. "Imagine promoting a Disney sports movie like 'Mighty Ducks' on ESPN, or [ABC's] 'Grace Under Fire' at Disneyland," said Paul Marsh of Natwest Securities Corporation. "Imagine creating the world's largest media company, with $4 billion in cash flow. That's what we're looking at."[76] Eisner agreed: "[T]he synergies go on and on."[77]

Capital Cities/ABC would be a fully owned subsidiary of the Walt Disney Company: it would remain headquartered in New York and ABC president Robert Iger (who signed a five-year contract with Eisner) would continue to direct its strategic operations. "Mike told me, and I trust him," Iger said, "that this will be my entity to run."[78] The independence of production and distribution units promised to make the new corporation less prone to the internal power struggles that had gripped other mergers. It also greatly reduced the likelihood of layoffs, such as those that followed the mergers of brokerage firms and banks in recent years. If anything, some analysts predicted, the combined total of some ninety thousand employees would increase as the enhanced Walt Disney Company expanded into new frontiers of communication and entertainment.[79]

The international market stood out as the most immediate prospect. In fact, the opportunity to expand overseas, both Eisner

185

and Murphy stated, was the key to the merger. For more than half a century, the Walt Disney Company had maintained a global presence, circulating its films, comics, and consumer products to the far reaches of the world. Disney theme parks and Disney Stores had, more recently, contributed to this effort. But Eisner knew that more could be done. The first year that Hollywood took in more revenue from overseas theaters than domestic movie houses was 1994. "I could see how I could protect [Disney] for five or six more years being alone," Eisner said. "But I didn't know how I could protect it for another 20 years without some partner to compete in Europe, to get into India and China, to keep access for our children's programs."[80]

The Disney–Capital Cities/ABC merger provided the solution. In the words of analyst Lloyd Rixe, "Disney . . . is now in a position to become a dominant player, maybe even the dominant player, in the world of entertainment. And not just in the United States, but globally."[81] Christopher Dixon, an analyst at Paine Webber, concurred. "This creates a company with global reach that can meet the ongoing demand for American entertainment in the multichannel environment around the world," he noted. "It gives them two very strong brand names and the scale to go up against Viacom, Time Warner and News Corp."[82] But more than this, the merger created the world's largest entertainment company, a one-of-a-kind global powerhouse with combined sales of $20.7 billion; it pushed the leading media conglomerate, Time Warner (with its $16 billion in revenues), back to a distant second place.[83]

Disney's market share in television alone promised to increase greatly. Before the merger, its stakes in foreign TV stations were limited to Britain's GMTV and Germany's Super RTL. ABC, on the other hand, had entered into coproduction deals with local TV programmers from Brussels to Beijing. And ESPN International Networks were hooked up to seventy million homes in 130 countries. The thought of beaming ESPN and the Disney Channel (which already had fourteen million subscribers in America) around the world was enough to make most Disney executives lick their lips. And the opportunities for cross-promotion—selling related merchandise, films, and even theme-park vacations—were almost too many to comprehend.[84] "The professionals immediately understood the synergy of the deal," noted Mario Gabelli, a money manager with a large stock interest in both companies. "This is about globalism. Advertisers like Procter & Gamble and Coca-Cola are going around the world and want the frequency and reach broadcasters provide."[85]

In short, the Walt Disney Company did not simply go out and buy a network. Eisner dismissed the idea as "70s thinking." What was needed to survive—and profit from—changes in the rapidly advancing world of digital and global entertainment, he argued, was "new century thinking." In other words, both producers and consumers of media would have to update their understanding of mass communication to include new technologies, new distribution capabilities, new affiliations, and new audiences. "Exportation of U.S. intellectual product has been going on forever," Eisner commented, "but now it can be more organized. This is the real beginning of U.S. companies being global."[86] Alan Schwartz, managing director at Bear Stearns and Company, who represented Disney on the ABC transaction, affirmed that the merger could be seen both as a business opportunity and as a long-term survival strategy: "As the global markets develop, the ability to leverage across product lines is becoming more and more important."[87]

A MICKEY MOUSE MONOPOLY?

Naturally, the Disney–Capital Cities/ABC merger caused some concern—especially in media circles. Would network programming be affected by Disney entertainment standards? Would smaller rivals be squashed? Would Ted Koppel be issued a pair of mouse ears (as one editorial cartoon suggested) to be worn while delivering the news on *Nightline*? ABC anchors and reporters,

187

worried about protecting their journalistic integrity, were wary of how the deal might unfold. During an interview with Michael Eisner and Thomas Murphy on *Good Morning America*, the normally pleasant Charlie Gibson remarked, "I never thought I'd work for a guy named Mickey." Eisner ribbed him: "So you don't like the deal, do you, Charlie?" But Gibson stonewalled. He turned to the camera instead and asked, "Don't you think this would be a good time for a commercial, everybody?"[88]

Gibson was not alone in his displeasure. Paul Fussell, professor of English at the University of Pennsylvania, could barely contain his revulsion at the thought of Mickey Mouse heading up America's top-rated network. "The taste of the Disney products," he snorted, "has always seemed to me gravely sub-adult."[89] Harold Bloom, professor of humanities at Yale University and author of *The Western Canon,* shared the academic disdain for all things Disney. "It's a disaster," he said of the Disney-ABC deal. "At the end of this road lies cultural homogenization of the most ghastly kind."[90] Antitrust experts and economists worried that skeptics in the right wing of the intellectual community might be correct: the possibility that ABC would revamp its programming in the coming years to include nothing but sweet-as-sugar Disney shows was only too easy to imagine.

But these were fears, not facts. Harvard economist Bruce Scott argued that the Walt Disney Company and other media conglomerates were less interested in squeezing consumers or competitors in the United States than in acquiring the financial strength to prosper on a global basis.[91] It was in Disney's own best interest, after all, to continue offering programs that people—and advertisers—wanted. If this meant buying television shows from rival production companies, even DreamWorks SKG (the studio created by ex–Disney executive Jeffrey Katzenberg, Steven Spielberg, and David Geffen) they would do it. "[W]e're not looking to dominate or even be the majority player [in supplying shows to ABC]," Eisner commented. "We want ABC to pick the best shows and the best people that will get the biggest audiences."[92] Such a strategy would be the key to retaining its number-one position in America—and in a global marketplace of more than five billion people.

Many industry insiders believed Eisner's claim that he would not put the "sin" back in synergy and drive the little guys out of business. Garth Ancier, programming chief at the Warner Brothers television network and former president of Disney's TV division, commented that "no network can survive supplying itself."[93] Tom Werner, of Carsey-Werner (which produced *Roseanne* and *Grace Under Fire*) agreed. "[G]ood programming," he asserted, "is the fuel for the whole network."[94] And Rod Perth, president of programming at the USA Network, also failed to see any cause for alarm. "Disney will run ABC like they do [Los Angeles independent station] KCAL-TV," he remarked. "They'll buy the programs that work for them, from anywhere."[95]

The Disney–Capital Cities/ABC deal did, however, accelerate consolidation in the entertainment industry by triggering a frenzy of matchups and alliances. Companies like Turner Broadcasting Systems, the Sony Corporation, and the Seagram Company (MCA's new owner) began nosing around, looking for partners that would give them leverage to compete with the Walt Disney Company and ABC in the international marketplace. But Westinghouse was the first to close a deal. On August 1, 1995 (one day after the Disney buyout was made public), it unveiled a much-expected $5.4 billion takeover of CBS. Shortly thereafter, MCI announced its plan to invest $2 billion in Rupert Murdoch's News Corporation in exchange for a 10 percent stake. Bill Gates's Microsoft announced its intention to team up with NBC (which was owned by General Electric). And on March 19, 1996, Michael Jackson and Prince Al-Waleed Bin Talal Bin Abdulaziz Al Saud (whose investment had helped to save Disneyland Paris) announced the formation of a new international media company dedicated to the promotion of family values. "Kingdom Entertainment represents a long-awaited dream come true," Jackson

189

said at the Paris press conference, adding that during his concert tours, he "began to appreciate that global family entertainment could bring peace to the world."[96]

For many, the tide of mergers was frightening: it suggested an Orwellian future dominated by a handful of giants. But industry experts argued that there would be little possibility of huge corporations monopolizing the media—and the minds—of millions. Five-hundred-station cable companies, video-on-demand satellite broadcasts, direct-to-video movies, computer games, and on-line services stood as compelling proof, they reasoned, that no one company, no matter how large, could dominate the multimedia landscape.[97] "Sony, General Motors and other large companies are not the market powers they once were," said David Resler, chief economist at Nomura Securities, a Japanese-owned brokerage firm. "One of the lessons of history is, one thing we should not worry about is size."[98] John Malone, CEO of Tele-Communications Incorporated, agreed, pointing to Rupert Murdoch—who owns a movie studio, the Fox TV network, a satellite TV delivery system in Europe and Asia, and interests in long-distance company MCI—as an example of what vertically integrated companies of the future might look like. "Their existence," he observed, "does not require them to wipe out everybody else. You'll still have a lot of independent players at various levels. You'll still have a lot of diversity in terms of voice."[99]

But some weren't so sure. Bruce Erickson, professor of business and government at the University of Minnesota's Carlson School of Management, expressed reservation: "If you're a program producer with creative ideas, you may be forced to produce within four or five large conglomerates, rather than take a chance and do your own thing outside the bureaucracies."[100] Brad Grey, of Brillstein-Grey Entertainment, was also cautious about what the Disney–Capital Cities/ABC deal might mean: "The universe is shrinking. Independents will have fairly rough seas to navigate."[101]

190

EVERYTHING'S COMING UP DISNEY!

On February 8, 1995, the Federal Communications Commission gave final approval to the Disney–Capital Cities/ABC deal, creating the world's largest entertainment company. The only condition imposed was that the Walt Disney Company would have to sell either the radio stations or a newspaper in both the Fort Worth and Detroit markets.[102] Shortly thereafter, investor Warren Buffett, who controlled twenty million shares (or 13 percent) of Capital Cities/ABC stock, elected to take only shares of Walt Disney Company stock in exchange for his $2.5 billion stake in Capital Cities/ABC. The move was seen as a vote of confidence in the new Disney conglomerate, which had offered shareholders some latitude on how they would be paid. Had Buffett opted for cash instead, some felt that it would have signaled doubts about the prospects for success and continued growth. John Reidy, media analyst for Smith Barney, offered the most succinct interpretation: "It says he believes in this global diversified company."[103]

The future looked bright for the new Walt Disney Company. As noted by Martin Sosnoff, an investment manager at Atlanta Sosnoff Capital, "the fundamentals of the new Disney are all good. Video sales are great. Attendance at the theme parks is up. Euro Disney has been rationalized now. And Capital Cities/ABC is as good a broadcast operation as there is. The only question is one of its growth rate."[104] But there was no question in Eisner's mind. He had promised shareholders 20 percent annual growth beginning in 1997. "The Eisner legacy at Disney has been creating growth," observed Timothy Pettee, media analyst at Alliance Capital in Minneapolis. "Eisner said that five years ago nobody at Disney envisioned then what are now its great growth vehicles: the Disney Channel, its multimedia productions, some of its incremental hotel developmental work. Those are all now major components of Disney's growth rate."[105]

The trend, many believe, is sure to continue. The success of *Beauty and the Beast* at the Palace on Broadway, followed by the

191

much-celebrated *Lion King*, has launched the Walt Disney Company into the world of legitimate theater. The opening of Walt Disney Galleries in several Disney Stores has demonstrated that the market for animation cels and upscale character merchandise has yet to be fully tapped. The unveiling of a new Animal Kingdom in Florida (1998), two Disney cruise ships (1998), and TokyoSea (a second theme park for Japan, in 2000) are adding choices to an ever expanding landscape of Disney entertainment.[106] Disney's restoration of the New Amsterdam Theater on Forty-second Street at Times Square (not to mention its talks to buy Rockefeller Center, where the NBC Studios are located) promises to give Mickey Mouse a powerful and lasting presence in the Big Apple. Disney's hiring by the Royal Canadian Mounted Police to oversee the licensing and marketing of its image suggests that Disney executives have just begun to crack open the international market. And plans for continuing expansion outside of Disneyland Paris— which have, so far, included a new convention center, a Planet Hollywood restaurant, an eight-screen Gaumont theater, and a $980 million new town (complete with a 150-store shopping mall and 1,500 family homes)—would seem to suggest that all thoughts of failure in France have been abandoned.[107]

Perhaps most ambitious of all are the Walt Disney Company's plans to make its founder's dream of a residential community blossom. Celebration, a $2.5 billion city of twenty thousand located just ten minutes away from the Magic Kingdom in Florida, differs from what Walt originally envisioned EPCOT to be in the mid-1960s. But it still seeks to offer citizens "a life they can't find anywhere else in the world."[108] According to Eisner, Celebration is intended to be "a community of tomorrow with the values of yesteryear."[109] Small-town architecture of the 1940s has revived the front porch, the backyard garages and alleys, the picket fences, the sidewalks, and the curbside rows of tall trees in an effort to capture (or invent) the sense of community that was lost in the rush to suburbia that began after World War II.[110] The Disney Institute, designed to offer "discovery vacations" with week-long courses in everything from animation to rock-climbing, complements Celebration's unique mission by helping to create what project director Doug McGuire calls "a small college-town feel."[111] Whether or not the Mayberry-style community will provide a remedy for the social ills gripping American society remains to be seen. But Vincent Scully, Sterling Professor Emeritus of Art History at Yale, has pointed to Celebration as "the most important thing happening in architecture."[112]

Celebration is not the only place where people might live the Disney experience, however. "These days," observed reporter Mitchell Landsburg, "it seems we're all living in Disney's America. With its purchase of ABC . . . the company founded by Walter Elias Disney in 1923 deepened its claim on the American psyche, from Main St. to Tomorrowland." In his title, Landsburg diagnosed the situation as "Disney Overload":

> It would be hard to name another company that has ever exercised such influence on American culture. It would be hard to find another company so widely admired—even loved—by Americans. As a nation, we flock to Disney films, and then replay them—over and over and over—on Disney videotapes. We read Disney books to our Disney-pajama-clad children. We watch Disney shows on Disney TV. We make pilgrimages to Disneyland and Disney World, where we stay in Disney hotels and eat Disney food. We buy Disney products at Disney stores, and listen to Disney records of Disney songs. By next year, we will be able to send our children to a Disney school (near Orlando, Fla.) and educate ourselves at the Disney Institute, an adult-education resort in Florida where, the *Wall Street Journal* observed, "Goofy can get in touch with his inner self." The world of Disney is becoming anything but a small, small world.[113]

Landsburg is right. It is hard to imagine a single area of modern life left untouched by the Walt Disney Company. It is even more difficult to imagine a world without the ubiquitous Mouse. As Disney executives bring their growing enterprise into the next century, the question remains: How much is too much? Anthony Fonzo, a forty-two-year-old army systems analyst, admitted his fondness for Disney art. "I think of entertainment that's been with me my entire life," he said. When asked if Disney's presence had grown too overpowering, Fonzo responded with a statement that would have made Mickey smile: "I don't think so."[114]

But others beg to differ. British critic Stephen Bayley predicts that Eisner's goal of 20 percent annual growth will be impossible to meet—especially in Europe. The Walt Disney Company will soon run up against a brick wall, he argues, when the public tires of being force-fed Disney ideology—and when technology renders the traditional theme park formula obsolete.

> Maybe the synthetic and saccharine easy-listening experience will soon acquire a period charm. Euro Disney has plans through to 2017, but I wonder if new technology will make it redundant before then. You don't have to be a happy-clappy Silicon Valley hippie to see that computer-driven virtual reality is set to upstage Euro Disney before the millennium. The first stage of the separation of tourism from travel may have been to jet in jumbos of credulous, uninquisitive proles to look at synthetic tableaux, board them for the night and jet them back again, but the crucial second stage will be to make them stay at home strapping on virtual-reality body stockings and having a Davy Crockett experience, complete with wood fires, mosquitoes and chipmunk droppings . . . in the easeful, unthemed comfort of home. All thanks to high definition television and some fiendishly powerful chips.[115]

"I like to think that by the turn of the century Euro Disney will have become a deserted city," he added, "similar to Angkor Wat or Arc-et-Senans: a haunting reminder of a knowing, but innocent, past age. Those hungry for the tourist experience or avid for entertainment will let the fingers of their virtual-reality gloves do the walking."[116]

Bayley's vision is not grounded in wishful thinking alone. Japan's Sega Enterprises is developing technology that promises to reinvent the traditional amusement park.[117] Building on the success of its game systems (which are in millions of homes worldwide), Sega executives have assembled an experienced team of some 850 specialists to bring interactive entertainment to the next level. Hisashi Suzuki, director of research and development, has proudly observed that "no other company in high-technology amusement has this many people."[118] And Hayao Nakayama, president of Sega Enterprises, has made no bones about his primary goal. "Our target," he admitted, "is Disney."[119]

A new ride called Scramble Training offers a peek into the future of virtual reality entertainment. Unlike Disney's Star Tours attraction, for instance, which takes passengers on a simulated space ride straight out of *Star Wars* (a movie screen at the head of the cabin serves as the "windshield"), Scramble Training functions as part film and part communal video game: the passengers are the ones who steer and shoot. They control the adventure—and the scores they earn offer an incentive to try again and again. The advantage of such rides, aside from their increased interactivity, is that operators need only insert a new software package to experience an entirely different adventure. Sega executives view the technology as a major breakthrough that will enable them to thrill audiences without having to painstakingly "imagineer" entire landscapes in three dimensions. One observer described the new computerized rides as "Disneyland in a box."[120]

If all goes according to plan, Sega will build a series of small (one- to five-acre) theme parks (costing between $10 million and $50 million each) filled with such rides in the not-too-distant future. Fifty are slated for Japan and another fifty for the United States.[121] Sega even has plans to tap into the European market by opening an indoor amusement center, modeled after its Yokohama Joypolis park, in London.[122] Other companies are developing high-tech theme parks too. Namco, a leading Japanese arcade game maker, which scored big with a Tokyo facility called the Wonder Egg, has made plans to expand in Japan and the United States. Paramount is working on a virtual reality "Star Trek" attraction (based on the "holadeck" installed on the ships of the Star Fleet). Sony is said to be developing an ambitious high-tech theme park operation. And Edison Brothers Stores of St. Louis have already opened three "Exhilarama" virtual reality amusement centers in the United States.[123]

"Theme parks," notes multimedia artist Brian Eno, "are a relatively new cultural form that is going to become more and more a place for artists to look."[124] On-line theme parks known as MUDs, which enable people to experience the digital thrills of high-tech simulation on a computer screen, without virtual-reality goggles and gloves, hold enormous potential for in-home entertainment. Writer Kevin Kelly has stated that the impact of MUDs will be revolutionary: "They will have all the richness and emotional power and generational identity that music gave us. A vast visual MUD—where you can explore a world that you can also partly make, if you care to—will become the center for a new youth culture."[125] But it is doubtful that MUDs will ever replace the Disney theme parks in America, Japan, or Europe. As noted by media scholar Marshall McLuhan, people desire—and need—more than just visual stimulation. "The visual is the only sense that produces the attitude of noninvolvement," he observed. "Where stress on visual qualities merely leaves us looking on as spectators, sound and smell and touch and movement are profoundly involving.[126]

Walt Disney's instinctive grasp of this point lives on as a powerful legacy. His animated and live-action films have entertained millions. His television programs have brought stories to life in homes across the globe. And his theme parks have offered conceptual and physical passage to worlds of fantasy once confined to the screen. By bringing cinematic adventure to life in three-dimensional form, these imaginative settings have surprised, amused, and touched audiences around the world. Most importantly of all, they have engaged enthusiasts and critics alike in an ongoing discussion of American culture. Disneyland Paris, the most ambitious and controversial Disney project to date, has furthered this process by prompting new dialogue about America's role in the international system. Its continuing evolution promises to cast light on new questions of representation, appropriation, and globalization. As the Walt Disney Company plunges into new frontiers of multimedia communication and entertainment, it remains to be seen what twists will be encountered in the road ahead. Echoing over these crossings are the words of Walt Disney, as he escorted Billy Graham through his flagship park in California more than thirty years ago: "This is the real world here. The fantasy world is outside."[127]

Notes

INTRODUCTION

1. "Euro Disney Grand Opening," CBS (11 April 1992).

2. John Huey, "Eisner Explains Everything," *Fortune* 131 (17 April 1995), p. 58.

3. Ibid., pp. 59–60.

4. John Hench (Imagineer), interview by author, 22 June 1995.

5. Liane Bonin, "Tragic Kingdom," *Detour Magazine* (April 1998), p. 69.

6. Martha Sawyer Allen, "The Mouse Trap," *Minneapolis Star Tribune* (10 January 1997), sec. B, pp. 5, 8; Don L. Boroughs, "Mickey Mouse Walks Away from a Fight," *U.S. News and World Report* 117 (10 October 1994), p. 103; "Eisner: Disney Pushing to Become 'Aggressive' 'Contender' on Internet," *Minneapolis Star Tribune* (30 April 1998), sec. D, p. 5.

7. Viewed at http://web.mit.edu/disney.html on 1 April 1998.

8. "Eisner: $565 Million in Stock Options," *Los Angeles Times* (4 December 1997), sec. A, pp. 1, 36.

9. Greg Burkman, "The Man Behind the Magic," *Seattle Times* (11 January 1998), sec. M, p. 2.

10. "Cheers and Jeers," *TV Guide* (9–15 May 1998), p. 13.

11. Ibid.

12. Bonin, p. 70.

13. Faith Popcorn, *Clicking: 17 Trends That Drive Your Business—and Your Life* (New York: HarperCollins, 1997), pp. 298–299.

14. Mark Dolliver, "Clinging to a Belief That What's Big Must Be Bad," *Adweek* (19 January 1998), p. 16.

15. Rob Kroes et al., eds., "Introduction," in *Cultural Transmissions and Receptions: American Mass Culture in Europe* (Amsterdam: VU University Press, 1993), p. vii.

16. John Dorst, "Miniaturising Monumentality: Theme Park Images of the American West and Confusions of Cultural Influence," in Kroes, p. 263.

17. Pope is cited in Thomas J. Schlereth, *Artifacts and the Material Past* (Nashville: American Association for State and Local History, 1980), p. 3.

18. Woodyard is cited in Barry James, "Not Without Qualms, France Cedes Space to Disney's World," *International Herald-Tribune* (9 April 1992), sec. 1, p. 1.

19. Jennifer Allen, "Tragic Kingdom," *New Republic* (10 and 17 January 1994), p. 16.

20. Stephen Birmingham, "Once Upon a Time . . . There Lived the Greatest One-Man Show on Earth . . . in the Magic Land of Hollywood," *McCall's* (July 1964), p. 121; and Paul Jerome Croce, "A Clean and Separate Space: Walt Disney in Person and Production," *Journal of Popular Culture* 25 (Winter 1991), p. 94.

21. Robert de Roos, "The Magic Worlds of Walt Disney," *National Geographic Magazine* 124 (August 1963), p. 178.

1. A DISNEYLAND FOR EUROPE

1. On February 6, 1986, Walt Disney Productions would officially change its name to the Walt Disney Company.

2. Janet Castro, "Mickey Mouse Goes to Paris," *Time* 126 (30 December 1985), p. 62.

3. Alan Brown, "Tokyo: Mickey's First Trip Abroad," *Travel and Leisure* (22 August 1992), p. 110.

4. Charles Vial, "Les Comptes de Fées: Euro Disney Ouvre Ses Portes a Marne-la-Vallée," *Le Monde* (12–13 April 1992), p. 11.

5. Robert Treichler, "Mickey Mouse Goes Continental," *World Press Review* 38 (July 1991), p. 41.

6. Ray Bradbury, "L'Homme Qui a Changé Notre Histoire," in Gilles Anquetil, et al., "Invasion Culturelle Américaine: Cette Souris, Est-Elle Dangereuse?" *Le Nouvel Observateur* (3 January 1986), p. 25.

7. On August 13, 1983, only four months after opening to the public, Tokyo Disneyland broke Disneyland's attendance record for a single day with a total of 94,378 guests. And after its first year, Tokyo Disneyland's annual attendance rate nearly surpassed that of Disney's flagship park in California (which, after twenty-eight years, was drawing some 9.9 million visitors per year). See Ron Grover, *The Disney Touch: How a Daring Management Team Revived an Entertainment Empire* (Homewood, Ill.: Business One Irwin, 1991), p. 186; and Treichler, p. 41.

8. "European Preferences," *New York Times* (2 April 1984), p. 16. See also Steven Bergsman, "In France, Little Flipping Over Euro Disneyland," *Barron's* (14 October 1991), p. 50.

9. Stewart Toy, "An American in Paris," *Business Week* (12 March 1990), pp. 60–61, 64. See also George Sivell, "Autumn Target Set for $1

Billion Euro Disneyland Flotation," *Times* (London) (26 May 1989), p. 27A; and Steven Greenhouse, "Playing Disney in the Parisian Fields," *New York Times* (17 February 1991), sec. 3, p. 1.

10. Allan K. Sloan, "Europe Is Ripe for Theme Parks," *Los Angeles Times* (22 August 1990), sec. D, p. 3. See also Grover, pp. 185–187.

11. Vial, p. 11.

12. Sloan, sec. D, p. 3; Grover, pp. 185–187.

13. Woodyard and Wells are quoted in Barry James, "Not Without Qualms, France Cedes Space to Disney's World," *International Herald-Tribune* (9 April 1992), sec. 1, pp. 1, 3.

14. Vial, p. 1.

15. Michael Eisner, *Work in Progress* (New York: Random House, 1998), p. 264.

16. Grover, pp. 186–187.

17. Martin Waller, "Men of Vision Seek £580 Million in the Mud of Euro Disneyland," *Times* (London) (14 September 1989), p. 29A.

18. "Mouse Trapped in France," *New Statesman and Society* 6 (20 August 1993), p. 6.

19. Grover, pp. 187–188.

20. Vial, p. 11.

21. "Euro Disneyland Off to Not-So-Fun Start," *Chicago Tribune* (25 September 1988), sec. 7, p. 12F.

22. "Spain Tries to Prove It's a Mickey Mouse Place," *Times* (London) (29 May 1985), p. 8C.

23. "Hi-Ho! Hi-Ho! Culture High and Low," *Harper's Bazaar* 275 (September 1987), p. 210. See also Toy, pp. 60–61, 64; Greenhouse, p. 1; and Grover, p. 188.

24. Eisner, pp. 264–265; Grover, p. 188. For discussion of Arthur D. Little's methodology, see Robert Anthony, "Euro Disney: The First 100 Days," Harvard Business School Case Study #9-693-013, 4 June 1993, p. 9.

25. Fitzpatrick is cited in Greenhouse, p. 6.

26. Castro, p. 62.

27. Barbara Rudolph, "Monsieur Mickey," *Time* 137 (25 March 1991), pp. 48–49. See also David Lawday, "Where All the Dwarfs Are Grumpy," *U.S. News and World Report* (28 May 1990), pp. 50–51; and Vial, p. 11.

28. P. J. O'Rourke, "Inside EPCOT Center," *Harper's* 267 (August 1983), p. 43.

29. Lawday, pp. 50–51.

30. MCA president Sidney J. Sheinberg was the first to describe Mickey Mouse as the "Ravenous Rat" and made no secret of his plans to pit Universal Studios against Disney theme parks in the United States and Europe. See Kevin Kelly and Linda Bernier, "It's King Kong vs. the 'Ravenous Rat,'" *Business Week*, no. 3019 (5 October 1987), p. 54.

31. Peter Mikelbank, "Slipping Paris a Mickey," *Washington Post* (31 March 1991), sec. F, p. 1.

32. Mikelbank, sec. F, p. 1.

33. Lawday, pp. 50–51.

34. Martha Zuber, "Mickey-sur-Marne: Une Culture Conquérante?" *French Politics and Society* 10 (Summer 1992), p. 70.

35. Ibid., p. 66.

36. Julian Nundy, "Disneyland Would Like to Set Trap for Mickey and Company," *Chicago Tribune* (19 January 1987), sec. 1, p. 12. See also Rudolph, pp. 48–49.

37. Ibid.

38. The economies of the five neighboring villages were expected to undergo a dramatic change. According to the *Quotidien du Maire*, a weekly published by the Tesson publishing group, each one would collect about 83 million francs (or $16.5 million) on a developed property tax in the first five years. The SAN would collect some 170 million francs (about $34 million) annually from the "taxe professionnelle," or business tax. But these projections were based on the assumption that 11 million people would visit the park its first year. If attendance fell short of this mark and Euro Disney failed to generate enough tax revenues, only the Seine-et-Marne region would be compensated in full. The villages had no such guarantee. For discussion, see Zuber, pp. 70–71.

39. Ibid., p. 67. See also "Mickey Hops the Pond," *The Economist* (28 March 1987), p. 75.

40. "Disney Park Plans Criticized," *Atlanta Constitution* (20 December 1985), sec. A, p. 19.

41. Paul Lewis, "A French Disneyland Near Paris Is Approved," *New York Times* (22 March 1987), sec. I, p. 6. See also Grover, p. 189.

42. Unemployment in France had become a hot political issue. Many political leaders who might have preferred to oppose the Euro Disney project knew that it would provide thousands of sorely needed jobs, both on- and off-site. It also promised to attract many other investors to the depressed outskirts of Paris. For discussion, see Richard Turner and Peter Gumbel, "Major Attraction: As Euro Disney Braces for Its Grand Opening, the French Go Goofy," *Wall Street Journal* (10 April 1992), sec. A, p. 1; and Zuber, p. 67.

43. Alan Tillier, "Disney Is Not Funny in France," *Times* (London) (16 March 1986), p. 56G.

44. Grover, p. 190.

45. Nundy, p. 12.

46. "Disney in Europe," *New York Times* (13 March 1987), sec. 4, p. 4.

47. Gerard Petitjean, "La Stratégie de la Souris," *Le Nouvel Observateur*, no. 1430 (2–8 April 1992), p. 40.

48. "What Other Newspapers Are Saying," *Chicago Tribune* (4 April

1987), sec. 1, p. 11; "Mickey Hops the Pond," p. 75 . See also "Disney in France," *New York Times* (25 March 1987), sec. 4, p. 3; "French Bonanza for Monsieur Mickey Mouse," *Times* (London) (23 March 1987), p. 6D; and Mikelbank, p. 1.

49. Toy, pp. 60–61, 64.

50. For discussion of the Disney-MGM Studios, see Michael Kiernan, "The Tight-Budget, No-Hassle Way to See Disney World," *U.S. News and World Report* 106 (5 June 1989), p. 62; and Matthew Cooper, et al., "Empire of the Sun," *U.S. News and World Report* 108 (28 May 1990), p. 48.

51. "£800 Million for Disney Project in France," *Times* (London) (28 April 1989), p. 28A. For an explanation of how the Disney Company set up the Euro Disney project as a French version of a limited partnership, see Grover, pp. 190–191.

52. Shawn Tully, "The Real Estate Coup at Euro Disneyland," *Fortune* 113 (28 April 1986), p. 172. See also George Sivell, "Mickey Mouse Weaves a Magic Deal," *Times* (London) (29 May 1989), p. 23B.

53. Terry Ilott and Michael Williams, "MCA Plays Catch-Up in Global Parks," *Variety* 342 (18 March 1991), pp. 1, 110. See also Rudolph, pp. 48–49; and Greenhouse, p. 1.

54. According to a report in the *Wall Street Journal,* the French government paid farmers four francs (80 cents) per square meter of land and then resold it to the Walt Disney Company at twelve francs ($2.40) per square meter—still a bargain price. But in an interview in the French journal *Projet,* Fitzpatrick noted that Disney paid some 530 francs ($106) per square meter for the land after it was "viabilisé," or equipped with electricity, water, and sewage disposal. See Alexandra Tuttle, "The French Dance to Disney's Looney Tunes," *Wall Street Journal* (13 April 1992), sec. A, p. 16; Toy, pp. 60–61, 64; Grover, p. 192; and Zuber, p. 72.

55. Tully, p. 172.

56. Ibid.

57. In a radio interview, Fitzpatrick asserted that the TGV station was not a gift from the French government: the Euro Disney Resort would pay for it. See Frank J. Prial, "Dreyfuss, a Driver and Disneyland-by-the-Marne," *New York Times* (13 August 1985), sec. I, p. 2; Sivell, "Mickey Mouse Weaves Magic Deal," p. 23B; and Zuber, p. 72.

58. Ilott and Williams, "MCA Plays Catch-Up," pp. 1, 110. See also Tully, p. 172; and Lewis, p. 6.

59. "Disney Looks to Be the Clear Winner in Magic Kingdom," *Times* (London) (9 October 1989), p. 30A.

60. Toy, p. 60.

61. Bernard Poupard, "Marne en Disney: Les Enjeux de Développement de Marne-la-Vallée et de l'Euro Disneyland," *Études* 371 (December 1989), pp. 625–638.

62. Jacques Neher, "Disney Park Gets European Accent," *Chicago Tribune* (3 April 1989), sec. 4, p. 1. See also Greenhouse, p. 1.

63. The Euro Disney Resort was expected to create four "exterior" jobs for every one at the theme park and hotel complex. For discussion, see "Euro Disneyland Financing Gains," *New York Times* (8 July 1988), sec. 4, p. 12; Grover, p. 192; Lewis, p. 6; Castro, p. 62; and Vial, p. 11.

64. Greenhouse, p. 6.

65. "Disney Park Plans Criticized," p. 19. See also Richard Kuisel, *Seducing the French: The Dilemma of Americanization* (Berkeley: University of California Press, 1993), p. 227.

66. Anquetil, p. 26; Jim Henderson, "Euro Disney: Oui or Non?" *Travel and Leisure* 22 (August 1992), p. 83.

67. Alan Riding, "Only the French Elite Scorn Mickey's Debut," *New York Times* (13 April 1992), sec. A, p. 1.

68. Ibid. See also Kuisel, p. 228.

69. Riding, sec. A, p. 13.

70. Toy, p. 60; Dave Kehr, "It's Not All Ooh-La-La Over French Disney Park," *Chicago Tribune* (8 June 1991), sec. 1, p. 1.

71. Kuisel, p. 229.

72. The term "Coca-Colonization" is borrowed from Frederic Ferney, "L'Amér Look des Anti-Américains," *Le Nouvel Observateur* (3–9 January 1986), p. 26.

73. Richard Corliss, "Voila! Disney Invades Europe. Will the French Resist?" *Time* 139 (20 April 1992), p. 82.

74. André Glucksmann, "American Magic, in an Homage to Its Roots," *International Herald-Tribune* (9 April 1992), sec. 1, p. 3.

75. Todd Gitlin, "World Leaders: Mickey, et al.," *New York Times* (3 May 1992), sec. 2, p. 1.

76. Riding, sec. A, p. 13.

77. Stephen Bayley, "In This Sterile Diorama, Life Is But a Theme," *International Herald-Tribune* (9 April 1992), sec. 1, p. 1.

78. Ibid., p. 3.

79. Corliss, p. 82.

80. Anquetil, p. 22.

81. Denis Lacorne, "Disneyland et Euro Disneyland," *Esprit* (June 1986), pp. 105–113; Jacques Juillard, "Invasion Culturelle Américaine: Cette Souris, Est-Elle Dangereuse?" *Le Nouvel Observateur* (3–9 January 1986), p. 21.

82. Anquetil, p. 27.

83. Gitlin, p. 30.

84. Riding, sec. A, p. 1.

85. Kuisel, p. 229.

86. Rudolph, p. 49.

87. Gitlin, p. 1.

88. James Lileks, "The French Turn Up Their Noses at Disney? Well, Excusez Mouse!" *Minneapolis Star Tribune* (26 April 1992), sec. F, p. 8.

89. Zuber, p. 68.

90. Kuisel, p. 229.

91. Petitjean, p. 41.

92. Turner and Gumbel, sec. A, p. 1.

93. Zuber, p. 64. See also *Facts on File* (New York: Facts on File, 27 March 1987), p. 205; and "Mickey Hops the Pond," p. 75.

94. Mikelbank, p. 1.

95. Anquetil, pp. 22.

96. Mikelbank, p. 1.

97. Anquetil, p. 21.

98. Kehr, p. 1.

99. Kuisel, pp. 228–229. See also Gitlin, p. 1.

100. "Jack Lang: Fasciné par Orlando," *Le Monde* (12–13 April 1992), p. 9.

101. Corliss, p. 82.

102. Riding, sec. A, p. 13; and Kuisel, p. 229.

103. Riding, sec. A, p. 13; and Kuisel, p. 229.

104. Janice Randall, "In Paris Today, à la Mode Means à l'Américaine," *France Today* (Autumn 1986), pp. 36–39; "Les Français Aiment Les États-Unis," *Le Figaro* (4 November 1988); and Kuisel, p. 229.

105. Glucksmann, sec. 1, p. 3.

106. Ibid.

107. Jean Cau is cited in "Intellectuals Attack Euro Disney," *Wall Street Journal* (7 April 1992), sec. A, p. 10.

108. Glucksmann, sec. 1, p. 3.

109. "Intellectuals Attack Euro Disney," sec. A, p. 10.

110. Mikelbank, p. 1.

111. Adam Gopnik, "Basic Instinct: Why Are the French Importing Sex?" *New Yorker* 71 (4 December 1995), p. 98.

112. Lileks, sec. F, p. 8.

113. Kuisel, pp. 229–230.

114. Turner and Gumbel, sec. A, p. 1.

115. Mitchell Martin, "Mob Pelts Disney Chiefs," *Washington Post* (6 October 1989), sec. D, p. 2. See also George Sivell, "Disneyland Postpones £1 Billion Flotation," *Times* (London) (25 April 1989), p. 25B.

116. Martin, p. 2; Sivell, "Disneyland Postpones £1 Billion Flotation," p. 25B.

117. Joann S. Lublin, "Will Sneezy Be Making Cold Calls to Sell European Disneyland?" *Wall Street Journal* (13 September 1989), sec. C, p. 1. See also Martin Waller, "Mickey Mouse Stakes for Sale," *Times* (London) (13 September 1989), p. 25H.

118. "Europe to Aid Disney Park," *New York Times* (5 October 1989), sec. 4, p. 19. See also Grover, p. 195.

119. Grover, p. 195.

120. Zuber, p. 69.

121. Martin, p. 2.

122. Marc Fumaroli, "Le Défi Américain," *Le Nouvel Observateur*, no. 1430 (2–8 April 1992), p. 42.

123. Stephen Leather, "European Sell-Out for Disney," *Times* (London) (12 October 1989), p. 25B. See also "Disney Premium of 172P," *Times* (London) (7 November 1989), p. 25B.

124. "A Disneyland for Hungary?" *New York Times* (8 August 1988), sec. 4, p. 2.

125. Kehr, p. 1.

126. Eisner, p. 269.

127. "Euro Disneyland Revises Plans," *Wall Street Journal* (26 October 1990), sec. A, p. 12. See also "Euro Disneyland Spending is Raised," *New York Times* (4 May 1990), sec. 4, p. 5; and Rudolph, pp. 48–49.

128. Kehr, p. 1.

129. Greenhouse, p. 1.

130. Ibid.

2. DESIGNING THE EURO DISNEY RESORT

1. Ron Grover, *The Disney Touch: How a Daring Management Team Revived an Entertainment Empire* (Homewood, Ill.: Business One Irwin, 1991), p. 196. See also Michael Eisner, *Work in Progress* (New York: Random House, 1998), p. 277.

2. Eisner is quoted in Grace Wagner, "It's a Small World After All," *Lodging Hospitality* 48 (April 1992), p. 26.

3. Peter Mikelbank, "Slipping Paris a Mickey," *Washington Post* (31 March 1991), sec. F, p. 1.

4. Paul Lewis, "A French Disneyland Near Paris Is Approved," *New York Times* (22 March 1987), sec. I, p. 6.

5. Eisner, p. 270.

6. For discussion of Levitt's N.I.H. Syndrome, see David Ogilvy, *Ogilvy on Advertising* (New York: Vintage Books, 1985), p. 178.

7. "The American Dream and the Great Escape," *Economist* 298 (11 January 1986), p. 85.

8. Edward Sotto III (Imagineer), interview by author, 28 June 1995.

9. Ibid. See also Richard Turner and Peter Gumbel, "Major Attraction: As Euro Disney Braces for Its Grand Opening, the French Go Goofy," *Wall Street Journal* (10 April 1992), sec. A, p. 14.

10. Richard V. Francaviglia, "Main Street, U.S.A.: A Compari-

son/Contrast of Streetscapes in Disneyland and Walt Disney World," *Journal of Popular Culture* 15 (Spring 1981), pp. 141–156. See also by the same author, "Main Street, U.S.A.: The Creation of a Popular Image," *Landscape, A Magazine of Human Geography* 21 (Spring–Summer 1977), pp. 18–22.

11. The power lines were ultimately ruled out as an impediment to the parades, which feature towering floats. Sotto interview.

12. Turner and Gumbel, p. 14.

13. John O'Toole, *The Trouble with Advertising: A View from the Inside* (New York: Times Books, 1985), p. 73.

14. Sotto interview.

15. Ibid., and Marvin Davis (retired Imagineer), interview by author, 26 July 1995.

16. Much of Euro Disneyland was designed to be weatherproof. The moving sidewalks from the 12,000-space parking lot are protected by a colorful circuslike canopy; the ticket booths at the Main Gate entrance are sheltered by the Hotel Disneyland; and the waiting areas for many of the attractions—and even some rides, themselves—are covered to protect guests from the sloppy weather conditions of northern France. Eisner personally ordered the installation of thirty-five fireplaces throughout the Euro Disney Resort, most of which ended up in the Hotel District. Turner and Gumbel, pp. 1, 14.

17. Jacques Neher, "Disney Park Gets European Accent," *Chicago Tribune* (3 April 1989), sec. 4, p. 1; and Stewart Toy, "An American in Paris," *Business Week*, no. 3149 (12 March 1990), pp. 60–61, 64.

18. Dated renderings of Frontierland attractions for the Euro Disney Resort indicate that Imagineers dropped the name "Westernland" in the early months of 1989. A panoramic image of the area by Frank Armitage, completed on April 1, 1989, is the first to be filed under the "Frontierland" designator. Walt Disney Imagineering, Information Research Center, Glendale.

19. For further discussion of the decision to enhance American themes at the Euro Disney Resort, see Dave Kehr, "It's Not All Ooh-La-La Over French Disney Park," *Chicago Tribune* (8 June 1991), sec. 1, p. 1; and Catherine Watson, "Bonjour Pardner: Continent Will Get Goofy (and Mickey and Donald) with Euro Disney Opening," *Minneapolis Star Tribune* (29 March 1992), sec. G, pp. 1–2.

20. Janice Randall, "In Paris Today, à la Mode Means à l'Américaine," *France Today* (Autumn 1986), p. 38.

21. Robert Athearn, *The Mythic West in 20th Century America* (Lawrence: University Press of Kansas, 1986), p. 259. See also Richard Kuisel, "Vive l'Amérique" in Seducing the French: The Dilemma of Americanization (Berkeley: University of California Press, 1993), pp. 212–230.

22. Disney Imagineers were well aware of the controversy generated by language issues in France. To mollify such concerns, Disney Imagineers used English signage and narrations only in sections of the park that were to be seen as distinctly American—and even then, they made special efforts to select Latin-based names that multinational audiences would be able to understand. Jean-Marie Gerbeaux, Euro Disney's French spokesman, reassured would-be guests that the new Disney theme park would not be a strictly "American" venture: "We are a French company in France and the official language of Euro Disneyland is French. But English will be on the same level." See Kehr, sec. 1, p. 1.

23. Michael Steiner, "Walt Disney, the Mythic Frontier, and the Architecture of Reassurance" (paper delivered at the annual meeting of American Studies Association, Pittsburgh, 10 November 1995), p. 3. See also Neher, sec. 4, p. 1.

24. Tony Baxter Interview, *Euro Disney* (Paris: Connaissance des Arts, 1992), pp. 64–66.

25. Marjorie Robins, "Mickey Goes to France: Awfully American for Grown-Ups," *Los Angeles Times* (3 May 1992), sec. L, p. 1.

26. For discussion of the historical meaning and significance of American Indians in Europe, see Robert E. Bieder, "Marketing the American Indian in Europe: Context, Commodification and Reception" in Rob Kroes, et al., eds., *Cultural Transmissions and Receptions: American Mass Culture in Europe* (Amsterdam: VU University Press, 1993), pp. 15–23; and C. F. Feest, ed., *Indians and Europe: An Interdisciplinary Collection of Essays* (Aachen: Rader Verlag, 1987).

27. "Worlds of Wonder," *Newsweek,* special issue (Fall–Winter 1991), p. 15.

28. Tom Morris (imagineer and creative director of Euro Disneyland), interview by author, 27 July 1995.

29. For discussion of Disneyland's Haunted Mansion, which was filled with "light" instead of "fright," see Randy Bright, *Disneyland: Inside Story* (New York: Harry N. Abrams, 1987), pp. 204–208.

30. While the iconography of *Psycho* (1960) served as a source of inspiration for Phantom Manor, it was not the only one. An early Disneyland concept sketch by Harper Goff (1951) predated the famous horror film by nearly a decade. It features a haunted house with gabled roofs perched high atop a hill at the end of Main Street. Its look—complete with crooked fences, gnarled trees, and broken shutters—would all be reproduced at Phantom Manor in France. Bruce Gordon and David Mumford, *Disneyland: The Nickel Tour* (Santa Clarita, Calif.: Camphor Tree Publishers, 1995), p. 260.

31. Disney Imagineers increased the level of fright—and gore—in this attraction for European audiences, whom they thought would

demand scariness in a haunted house. Writer David Lawday, who spent his childhood in London, agrees that continental audiences are more accustomed to dark tales than Americans: "Europe's youth are raised more on dark deceit than on Disney-grade fun. The aptly named world of the German brothers Grimm remains standard fare." But Disney Imagineers had no intention of creating an atmosphere of pure terror and toned down several scenes that provoked complaints from parents. For discussion, see David Lawday, "Dateline: 'Ow-Dee' to Frerè Mickey," *U.S. News and World Report* 112 (13 April 1992), p. 18.

32. For discussion of how Disney rides function as movie cameras, see Christopher Finch, *The Art of Walt Disney: From Mickey Mouse to the Magic Kingdoms* (New York: Harry N. Abrams, 1973), p. 392; Stephen M. Fjellman, *Vinyl Leaves: Walt Disney World and America* (Boulder, Colo.: Westview Press, 1992), p. 258; Margaret J. King, "Disneyland and Walt Disney World: Traditional Values in Futuristic Form," *Journal of Popular Culture* 15 (Spring 1981), p. 120; and Karal Ann Marling, "Disneyland, 1955: Just Take the Santa Ana Freeway to the American Dream," *American Art* 5, nos. 1–2 (Winter–Spring 1991), p. 197.

33. Kehr, sec. 1, p. 1.

34. Steiner, p. 3.

35. Baxter interview, *Euro Disney,* pp. 79–80.

36. Edward W. Said, "Orientalism: The Cultural Consequences of the French Preoccupation with Egypt" in Robert Tignor, ed., *Egypt: Al-Jabarti's Chronicle of the French Occupation, 1798* (New York: Markus Wiener Publishing, 1993), pp. 169–180.

37. Edward W. Said, *Orientalism* (New York: Vintage Books, 1979), pp. 1–2.

38. Said defines "Orientalism" as "a way of coming to terms with the Orient that is based on the Orient's special place in European Western experience." Ibid., p. 1. For discussion of how French North Africa inspired the visual memory of Delacroix, see Timothy Wilson-Smith, *Delacroix: A Life* (London: Constable, 1992), pp. 93–110.

39. This description is taken from a scrolled word portrait at the introduction to the film *Algiers* (1938).

40. Anthropologist Stephen Fjellman, who describes Adventureland at Walt Disney World as "the cartoon history of colonialism and empire," suggests that the new North African theme of Europe's Adventureland was inspired by the exoticism of France's former territories. For discussion, see Fjellman, p. 225; and Eric Smoodin, ed., *Disney Discourse: Producing the Magic Kingdom* (New York: Routledge, 1994), pp. 15–16.

41. Baxter interview, *Euro Disney,* pp. 79–80.

42. The desert theme of Adventureland corresponded nicely with the release of *Aladdin* (which premiered in the United States on Novem-

ber 25, 1992, and on November 24, 1993, in France). "Disney à la Mode de Chez Nous," *En Coulisse,* no. 3 (September 1993), p. 4.

43. Baxter interview, *Euro Disney,* pp. 83–84.

44. Fjellman, p. 225.

45. Baxter interview, *Euro Disney,* p. 80.

46. *The HarperCollins Guide to Euro Disneyland 1992* (London: HarperCollins Publishers, 1992), p. 41.

47. Steven Greenhouse, "Playing Disney in the Parisian Fields," *New York Times* (17 February 1991), sec. 3, p. 1.

48. Watson, sec. G, p. 1.

49. Turner and Gumbel, p. 14.

50. The futuristic castle idea was captured on paper by Imagineer Tim Delaney. Walt Disney Imagineering, Information Research Center, Glendale.

51. Isabelle Leouffre, "Welcome to France, Mickey," *Paris Match,* no. 2238 (16 April 1992), p. 97. See also Gerard Petitjean, La Stratégie de la Souris," *Le Nouvel Observateur,* no. 1430 (2–8 April 1992), p. 43; and "Introduction," *Euro Disney,* p. 13.

52. Morris interview. See Richard Reeves, "Parlez-Vous Disney: Mickey Mouse Is Learning French," *Travel and Leisure* (February 1991), p. 42. See also Lewis, sec. I, p. 6; Mikelbank, sec. F, p. 1; and Neher, sec. 4, p. 1.

53. Morris interview.

54. Baxter interview, *Euro Disney,* p. 79.

55. David R. Smith, ed., *Walt Disney: Famous Quotes* (Lake Buena Vista, Fla.: Walt Disney Company, 1994), p. 62.

56. Tim Delaney (Imagineer), interview by author, 6 July 1995.

57. The term "concreteland," a disparaging sobriquet for Tomorrowland, is borrowed from Fjellman, p. 354.

58. Delaney interview.

59. *HarperCollins Guide,* p. 49.

60. In all, Michael Eisner ordered $8–10 million in "extras" for Le Visionarium. Turner and Gumbel, p. 14.

61. "Euro Disneyland Guest Guide" theme park brochure, p. 17.

62. Walt Disney Imagineering, Information Research Center, Glendale.

63. So successful would Discoveryland be in tapping into people's desires to relive yesteryear from a new angle that Imagineers would use it as a model for the revamping of Tomorrowland at Walt Disney World in Florida (completed in February 1995). For discussion of nostalgia for the future, see Fjellman, pp. 354–355. For discussion of the transformation of Tomorrowland in Florida, see Kevin Rafferty, et al., "It's a Great Big Beautiful Tomorrow(land) . . . ," *Disney Magazine* 30 (Winter 1994), pp. 20–23.

64. O'Toole, p. 134.

65. The Euro Disney golf course was designed by architect Ronald Fream. "Golf Euro Disney," *En Coulisse* 3 (15–30 October 1992), p. 8.

66. Eisner, p. 276.

67. Cathleen McGuigan, "Après Mickey, Le Deluge," *Newsweek* 119 (13 April 1992), p. 64.

68. According to Wing Chao, senior vice president of the Walt Disney Design and Development Company, insiders referred to these high-profile architects as the "Gang of Five." Wing Chao, interview by author, 7 July 1995. See also Wing Chao interview, *Euro Disney,* pp. 42–43.

69. Robert A. M. Stern interview, "Hotel Cheyenne," *Euro Disney,* p. 46.

70. Coccoli is cited in Wagner, p. 27.

71. Suzanne Stephens, "Manifest Disney," *Architectural Record* 180 (June 1992), p. 54.

72. Chao interview, *Euro Disney,* pp. 43, 46.

73. *Euro Disney,* pp. 10, 46–47.

74. McGuigan, p. 65.

75. Stern interview, *Euro Disney,* p. 46.

76. *Euro Disney,* p. 10.

77. McGuigan, p. 65.

78. Suzanne Stephens, "That's Entertainment," *Architectural Record* 178 (August 1990), p. 75.

79. Stephens, "Manifest Disney," p. 55.

80. Dana Aiken interview, "Disneyland Hotel," *Euro Disney,* pp. 23–24.

81. Originally, the Hotel Disneyland was designed to be six stories tall, but it was scaled down to four stories when Imagineers realized the overpowering effect it would have upon an already reduced-scale Main Street, U.S.A., inside the park. Sotto interview.

82. "Festival Disney," *Euro Disney,* p. 61.

83. For discussion of Buffalo Bill's Wild West Show at the Euro Disney Resort, see John F. Sears, "Bierstadt, Buffalo Bill, and the Wild West in Europe," in Rob Kroes, et al., eds., *Cultural Transmissions and Receptions: American Mass Culture in Europe* (Amsterdam: VU University Press, 1993), pp. 3–14; Richard Slotkin, "Buffalo Bill's 'Wild West' and the Mythologization of the American Empire," in Amy Kaplan and Donald E. Pease, eds., *Cultures of U.S. Imperialism* (Durham: Duke University Press, 1993), pp. 164–181; Shanna Smith, "Where the Buffalo Roam," *Disney Magazine* 30 (Fall 1995), pp. 26–28; Kenneth Whyte, "The Carsen Show," *Saturday Night* 108 (February 1993), pp. 48–52, 62–69; and Watson, sec. G, p. 2.

84. Stephens, "Manifest Disney," p. 56.

85. Michael Graves Interview, "Hotel New York," *Euro Disney,* p. 30.

211

86. Eisner, p. 278.

87. Antoine Grumbach Interview, "Sequoia Lodge," *Euro Disney,* pp. 37, 39.

88. McGuigan, p. 66. See also Richard Corliss, "Voilà! Disney Invades Europe. Will the French Resist?" *Time* 139 (20 April 1992), p. 84.

89. For discussion of *Paris, Texas,* see Peter Beicken and Robert Phillip Kolker, *The Films of Wim Wenders: Cinema as Vision and Desire* (Cambridge: Cambridge University Press, 1993), pp. 114–137.

90. McGuigan, p. 66; Corliss, p. 84.

91. Stephens, "Manifest Disney," p. 57.

92. Stephens, "That's Entertainment," p. 121.

93. McGuigan, p. 65.

94. Stephens, "That's Entertainment," p. 72.

95. Baxter Interview, *Euro Disney,* p. 84.

3. MARKETING A NEW MAGIC KINGDOM IN EUROPE

1. "Euro Disney Grand Opening," CBS (11 April 1992).

2. Kathleen O'Steen, "Grand Opening of Euro Disney," *Variety* 347 (20 April 1992), p. 30.

3. Walt Disney is cited in "The Euro Disney Look" guidebook, the Euro Disney Resort (1992), p. 12.

4. Alan Riding, "Only the French Elite Scorn Mickey's Debut," *New York Times* (13 April 1992), sec. A, p. 13.

5. Terry Ilott and Michael Williams, "Disney Puttin' on the Blitz: Euro Theme Park Partners Find Themselves Picking Up the Tab," *Variety* 346 (2 March 1992), p. 80.

6. Steven Greenhouse, "Playing Disney in the Parisian Fields," *New York Times* (17 February 1991), sec. 3, p. 1.

7. Nicole Swengly, "Of Mice and Marketing Men," *Times* (London) (24 October 1990), p. 183.

8. Robert Treichler, "Mickey Mouse Goes Continental," *World Press Review* 38 (July 1991), p. 41.

9. "French Given a Preview of Disney Park," *Atlanta Constitution* (6 December 1990), sec. F, p. 7; Barbara Rudolph, "Monsieur Mickey," *Time* 137 (25 March 1991), p. 49.

10. E. S. Browning, "Disney Gets Many Helping Hands to Sell the New Euro Disneyland," *Wall Street Journal* (1 April 1992), sec. B, p. 4; Howard Rudnitsky, "Creativity with Discipline," *Forbes* 143 (6 March 1989), pp. 41–42; and Ilott and Williams, p. 80.

11. Ilott and Williams, p. 80.

12. Ibid. See also Stewart Toy, "An American in Paris," *Business Week,* no. 3149 (12 March 1990), p. 61; Rudnitsky, pp. 41–42; Browning, sec. B, p. 4.

13. Browning, sec. B, p. 4.

14. Ibid.

15. "Euro Disney Resort Quiz," *En Coulisse* 2 (15–31 March 1992), p. 3; Rudnitsky, pp. 41–42.

16. "Nestle: La Collection Magique," *En Coulisse* 3 (1–15 June 1993), p. 5.

17. Browning, sec. B, p. 4.

18. The joint marketing effort between Euro Disney and P & O was expected to give a major boost to passenger numbers on ferries between England and France, especially on the key Dover-Calais route. But it was also expected to help save the ferry business as a whole. The long-awaited Eurotunnel, scheduled to open in June 1993, posed a major threat to surface travel across the English Channel. For more discussion, see two articles by Janet Porter: "P & O European Ferries Signs Marketing Pact with Disney," *Journal of Commerce* 338 (5 June 1991), sec. B, p. 3; and "Mickey Mouse May Rescue Ferry Firms," *Journal of Commerce* 338 (26 June 1991), sec. A, p. 6.

19. Ilott and Williams, p. 1.

20. Greenhouse, p. 1.

21. Ilott and Williams, p. 80.

22. Ibid. See also Jacques Neher, "Disney Park Gets European Accent," *Chicago Tribune* (3 April 1989), sec. 4, p. 1.

23. Nicholas Powell, "Costume Requirements at Euro Disneyland Called a Mickey Mouse Idea," *Minneapolis Star Tribune* (10 March 1991), sec. G, p. 5.

24. Judson Gooding, "Of Mice and Men," *Across the Board* 29 (March 1992), p. 40. See also Diane Summers, "Disney's Cast of Thousands," *London Financial Times* (18 February 1991), p. 10.

25. Catherine Watson, "Bonjour Pardner: Continent Will Get Goofy (and Mickey and Donald) with Euro Disney Opening," *Minneapolis Star Tribune* (29 March 1992), sec. G, p. 2.

26. The competition for positions at Euro Disney was so fierce that some French nationals actually found it easier to secure positions in the "France" pavilion at Epcot Center in Florida. Gooding, pp. 42–43. French cast member, interview by author, Walt Disney World, 14 September 1992.

27. Chris Tighe, "Queuing for Flawed Fantasy," *London Financial Times* (13–14 June 1992), p. 5. See also Rone Tempest and Joel Havemann, "Euro Disney Proves It Is 'A Small World After All,'" *Sunday Punch* (Ikeja, Nigeria) (20 September 1992), unpaginated.

28. Gooding, pp. 42–43. Tempest and Havemann, unpaginated.

29. The Euro Disney workforce was as diverse as the park's visitors: 61 percent French; 9 percent British; 3 percent Dutch; 3 percent Irish; 2 percent German; 1 percent Danish; 1 percent Belgian; and 1 percent

Portugese. The remaining 19 percent of cast members came from other areas as near as Morocco and as far away as New Zealand. Summers, p. 10; Tempest and Havemann, unpaginated. On cast member housing, see Tighe, p. 5; and Grace Wagner, "It's A Small World After All," *Lodging Hospitality* 48 (April 1992), p. 31.

30. Sanjay Varma, executive vice president of resorts, is cited in "Interviews," *En Coulisse* 3 (1–15 November 1992), pp. 4–5.

31. Some 270 Euro Disney supervisors were brought to America to learn how the operation would run in Europe. Two hundred managers from Disney parks in California and Florida were brought to France to help them set up shop. Charlene Marmer Solomon, "How Does Disney Do It?" *Personnel Journal* 68 (December 1989), pp. 50–57. See also "Euro Disney Annual Report," 1990.

32. Toy, p. 61.

33. Euro Disney executives maintained that because appearance guidelines were made known before cast members signed their employment contracts, all new hires had voluntarily agreed to abide by those rules. One official noted that "[n]ot one of the 8,000 to whom we have offered jobs has declined because of the dress code. For that matter, every company in France has appearance standards, notably companies like Air France." See Gooding, pp. 43–44.

34. Powell, sec. G, p. 5; Riding, sec. A, p. 13.

35. The "Euro Disney Look" controversy came on the heels of another publicized conflict between Euro Disney and a group of French subcontractors employed by Gabo, which had recently declared bankruptcy. The subcontractors claimed that they were entitled to an extra 850 million francs ($157 million) over and above agreed-upon price estimates because Euro Disney execs had continually altered the projects they were working on. Fitzpatrick refused to pay. "There may have been an assumption that we were innocents abroad, that we were pushovers," he noted. "But we are very tough businessmen. We are not going to go over budget." This dispute, widely covered by the press, was one of the first incidents in which Euro Disney was portrayed as a giant Yank corporation beating up on local companies that were too small to defend themselves. In the end, Euro Disney agreed to pick up 60 percent of the debts owned by Gabo to the subcontractors, at a cost of about 17 million francs ($3 million)—a move that helped to defuse subcontractors' threats to cause problems at the grand opening. For a full discussion, see "Euro Disney Immune," *Variety* 346 (10 February 1992), p. 36; "Mickey Mouse to Le Rescue," *Variety* 346 (17 February 1992), p. 49; and Ilott and Williams, p. 80.

36. According to the text of "Euro Disney Look," women's fingernails are permitted to extend 7 mm beyond the fingertip. Lipstick "in the pinks, reds or natural colors" and eye makeup (in the form of mascara

and eyebrow pencil), far from being "banned," are actually encouraged in order "to complement [the cast member's] appearance." Women's heels are not to exceed 10 cm in height. And acceptable dress and skirt length "ranges from top of the knee to mid calf," not "8 cm above the knee—no more, no less," as Perrin-Boucher stated. See "The Euro Disney Look," pp. 1, 5, 7.

37. Ibid.

38. Powell, sec. G, p. 5.

39. Watson, sec. G, p. 2.

40. Wagner, p. 31.

41. Rudolph, pp. 48–49.

42. Michael Williams, "No Mickey Mouse Opening for Star-Studded EuroDisney Bow," *Variety* 347 (20 April 1992), p. 33. See also Michael Eisner, *Work in Progress* (New York: Random House, 1998), p. 282.

43. Ilott and Williams, p. 1.

44. For splashy treatment of the celebrities in attendance at the grand opening, see also "Mickey Soirée Privée," *Paris Match* 2239 (23 April 1992), pp. 66–71; and "La Parade des Stars," *Paris Match* 2239 (23 April 1992), pp. 72–75.

45. "Euro Disney Grand Opening," CBS (11 April 1992).

46. Ibid.

47. Ibid.

48. Williams, p. 33.

49. O'Steen, p. 30.

50. Williams, p. 33.

51. Ibid.

52. Ibid.

53. Paul Noglows, "Euro Disney Gives Stateside Stock Near-Term Muscle," *Variety* 347 (20 April 1992), p. 61.

54. "Euro Disney Resort Quiz," p. 3.

55. Robert Anthony, "Euro Disney: The First 100 Days" (Harvard Business School Case Study #9-693-013, 4 June 1993), p. 1; Riding, sec. A, p. 13.

56. Williams, p. 42. See also Eisner, p. 282.

57. Riding, sec. A, p. 13.

58. Eisner, p. 285.

59. Riding, sec. A, pp. 1, 13.

60. Jim Henderson, "Euro Disney: Oui or Non?" *Travel and Leisure* 22 (August 1992), p. 84.

61. Tighe, p. 5.

62. Anthony, p. 13.

63. Guest letter sent to the Euro Disney Resort, Entertainment Department.

64. Riding, sec. A, p. 1.

65. *HarperCollins Guide,* p. 12.

66. Eisner, p. 283.

67. "Euro Disney: The Not-So-Magic Kingdom," *The Economist* 324 (26 September 1992), pp. 87–88; and S. G. Warburg Securities, "Euro Disneyland: Offer for Sale" (5 October 1989), cited in Anthony, p. 9.

68. Anthony, p. 14.

69. Tighe, p. 5.

70. "Euro Disney Grand Opening," CBS (11 April 1992).

71. Michael Skapinker, "Mickey Mouse Outfit Suffers Culture Shock," *London Financial Times* (23 April 1992), p. 19.

72. Anthony, p. 14.

73. Skapinker, p. 19.

74. Anthony, p. 14.

75. Richard Turner, "Euro Disney's Fitzpatrick Denies Report That 3,000 Workers Quit Over Low Pay," *Wall Street Journal* (27 May 1992), sec. B, p. 10.

76. Turner, sec. B, p. 10; Anthony, p. 13.

77. Michael Williams, "Mart Trips Mousetrap as French Dis Disney," *Variety* 347 (1 June 1992), p. 89.

78. "Mickey Mouse Diplomacy," *Minneapolis Star Tribune* (18 June 1992), sec. D, p. 2; "Euro Disney Draws Over 1.5 Million in First Seven Weeks," *Wall Street Journal* (5 June 1992), sec. B, p. 5.

79. Michael Williams, "Euro Disney Stock Falls After Release of Figures," *Variety* 347 (8 June 1992), pp. 30, 34.

80. Ibid.

81. "Euro Disney's $2.3 Billion Expansion Delayed," *Engineering News Record* 228 (15 June 1992), p. 5.

82. Roger Cohen, "Euro Disney Sees Loss; Disney Profit Rises 33%," *New York Times* (24 July 1992), p. D3; Terry Ilott and Michael Williams, "Euro Disney Predicts Losses for First Year," *Variety* 348 (27 July 1992), p. 46; and "Euro Disney Draws Over 1.5 Million in First Seven Weeks."

83. Ilott and Williams, "Euro Disney Predicts Losses," p. 39.

84. Anthony, p. 2. See also Williams, "Euro Disney Stock Falls," p. 30.

85. Jennifer Allen, "Tragic Kingdom," *New Republic* (10 and 17 January 1994), p. 16; "French Farmers Blockade Euro Disneyland," *Investor's Business Daily* (29 June 1992), p. 25.

86. As Euro Disney executives were predicting a loss for its first fiscal year, the Walt Disney Company (which owned 49 percent of the Euro Disney Resort), announced that earnings for its fiscal third quarter ending June 30 had increased 33 percent. Such strong performance was the result of increased attendance at Disney's Stateside parks and huge sales of consumer goods. For a full discussion, see Cohen, p. D3; "Disney Reaps 33% Earnings Jump," *Variety* 348 (27 July 1992), p. 73.

87. Cohen, sec. D, p. 3.

88. Ibid.

89. Ilott and Williams, "Euro Disney Predicts Losses," p. 46.

90. Cohen, sec. D, p. 3.

91. Anthony, p. 15.

92. Alan Liddle, "Guests Walk a Not-So-Fine Line at Euro Disney's Attractions," *Nation's Restaurant News* 26 (23 November 1992), p. 54.

93. Walt Disney Company Quarterly Reports, cited in Anthony, p. 15.

94. "La 'Dream Team' en Tournée à Travers la France," *En Coulisse* 2 (15–30 September 1992), p. 8.

95. Stewart Toy, et al., "The Mouse Isn't Roaring," *Business Week* (24 August 1992), p. 38.

96. Gary Mead, et al., "A Question of the Mouse's Attraction," *London Financial Times* (13–14 June, 1992), p. 5.

97. Toy, et al., "Mouse Isn't Roaring," p. 38.

98. Euro Disney executives also announced plans to cut hotel prices in the off-season. The Hotel Santa Fe, for example, which had already reduced room rates by 36 percent to 550 francs (or $110), would slash them down to 450 francs ($90). Even the Hotel Disneyland, a five-star vacation residence, cut its nightly rates from $410 per night to $275 for the off-season. For discussion, see "Euro Disney Group Cuts Room Rates at Six Hotels," *Nation's Restaurant News* 26 (17 August 1992), p. 2; "Euro Disney Hotel Closes for Winter," *Los Angeles Times* (20 September 1992), sec. L, p. 4.

99. "Euro Disney: Un Nouveau Élan," *En Coulisse* 3 (15–30 October 1992), pp. 4–5.

100. Terry Ilott and Michael Williams, "Report Casts Pall as Theme Park Gets Gall," *Variety* 348 (7 September 1992), pp. 35, 69.

101. Ibid., p. 69.

102. "Fan Mail," *En Coulisse* 3 (1–15 October 1992), p. 5.

103. "5,000 Smiles," *En Coulisse* 3 (1–15 October 1992), p. 8; "Olé!" *En Coulisse* 2 (1–15 September 1992), p. 4; "The Cast Members' New Smile," *En Coulisse* 3 (15–30 October 1992), p. 2; "Passage du Flambeau," *En Coulisse* 3 (1–15 October 1992), p. 3; "Publicité: L'Émotion Retrouvée," *En Coulisse* 2 (15–30 September 1992), p. 8; "Deux Cow-Boys à Euro Disney," *En Coulisse* 3 (1–15 October 1992), p. 8.

104. "Euro Disney Communiqué Spécial" (12 October 1992).

105. Euro Disney Information Presse, "The Impact of Euro Disney on the Economy and Tourism After Six Months in Operation" (30 October 1992), pp. 1–3.

106. Jean-Philippe Geurand, "La Belle et La Bête," *Actuacine* 121 (October 1992), cover story, unpaginated; "Sortie Officielle," *En Coulisse* 3 (1–15 November 1992), p. 8.

107. "West Side Store," *En Coulisse* 2 (1–15 September 1992), p. 4; "What's News," *En Coulisse* 3 (15–31 December 1992), p. 5.

108. "Unconventional," *En Coulisse* 3 (1–15 November 1992), p. 3. See also Terry Ilott, "Disney Defers Payments to Help ED Stock Price," *Variety* 348 (19 October 1992), p. 54.

109. Comprehensive Euro Disney Media Plan, base plan (October 1992–September 1993).

110. Eisner, pp. 283–285.

111. Robert Fitzpatrick and Philippe Bourguignon revealed in the fiscal 1992 report that after 172 days of operation, Euro Disney's attendance had reached 6.8 million and hotel occupancy was averaging 74 percent. The theme park accounted for 2.6 billion francs (or 68 percent of the total), and the resort hotels accounted for 1.2 billion francs (or 32 percent of the total). "Overall," they noted, "our financial performance for the year was impacted by several factors. Revenues reflected lower levels of attendance, occupancy and per capita spending than expected, as well as generally weak economic conditions throughout Europe. Also, the initial level of operating costs, including staffing, was established based upon the anticipated attendance and occupancy. This factor, together with high start-up costs and other expenses, eroded operating margins for the period. Also, high French interest rates had a significant impact on the Group's financing costs. . . . We expect that the Group will sustain a loss during the first six months of fiscal 1993 due to the effect of the seasonal low period of attendance, but we anticipate significant improvement in the second half of the year. However, we do not anticipate that we will achieve profitability for the entire year. Overall, while our short-term outlook is cautious, the growing enthusiasm for the Euro Disney Resort concept in the European market gives us great confidence for the long-term success of this Company." Euro Disney Information Presse, "Euro Disney S.C.A. Announces Fiscal 1992 Results, Proposed Dividend and Deferral of Management Fee to the Walt Disney Company" (19 November 1992), pp. 1–3.

112. "How to Raise a Reindeer," *En Coulisse* 3 (1–15 December 1992), pp. 4–5.

113. "Christmas Season Press Event—November 20/22," *En Coulisse* 3 (15–30 November 1992), p. 4.

114. Ilott, "Disney Defers Payments," p. 54.

115. "What's News."

116. "Club Bénévole," *En Coulisse* 3 (15–30 November 1992), p. 5; "Club Bénévole," *En Coulisse* 3 (15–30 June 1993), p. 6.

117. "Euro Disneyland, Le Vent En Poupe," *En Coulisse* 3 (1–15 February 1993), p. 2.

118. "Euro Disney: Un Nouveau Élan."

119. "New Program: Show Time," *En Coulisse* 3 (1–15 December 1992), p. 3.

120. "Going to Bat for Quality," *En Coulisse* 3 (15–30 June 1993), p. 5.

121. "Lettre de Robert Fitzpatrick," Euro Disney Communiqué Special (15 January 1993).

122. "Fitzpatrick Out at Euro Disney," *Nation's Restaurant News* 27 (25 January 1993), p. 2.

123. "Décollage," *En Coulisse* 3 (1–15 February 1993), p. 1.

124. "Mickey's World Tour," *En Coulisse* 3 (1–15 February 1993), p. 2.

125. Euro Disney Media Plan, memo by Anne Marie Verdin and Nathalie Moride (January 1993).

126. Burke is quoted in Michael Williams, "Le Mouse Gets His First Candle," *Variety* 350 (12 April 1993), p. 47.

127. "Star Nights" targeted people ages 18–35 with ads featuring Zorro. Unlike other Euro Disney commercials, which showed the park through the eyes of children and animated film characters, the Zorro spots encouraged potential visitors to see the park through the eyes of the night. *Pariscope* devoted a full page to "Star Nights" (June 23–July 14) and promoted a contest offering two hundred free-entry passports to winners. The Virgin Megastore on the Champs-Élysées was decorated with the silhouette of Zorro and the colors of the "Star Nights" campaign. Ads were shown on giant stadium screens during Prince, Dépêche Mode, and Johnny Halliday concerts. Zorro masks and brochures were distributed all over Paris. For discussion, see "Sous le Signe de la Nuit," *En Coulisse* 3 (1–15 June 1993), pp. 1–2.

128. Williams, "Le Mouse Gets His First Candle," p. 1.

129. "Le Château en Gâteau: Good Enough to Eat!" *En Coulisse* 3 (15–30 April 1993), p. 2.

130. Williams, "Le Mouse Gets His First Candle," p. 1.

131. "Happy Birthday Euro Disney Resort," *En Coulisse* 3 (1–15 May 1993), pp. 6–7.

132. "Houba!" *En Coulisse* 3 (15–31 January 1993), p. 8; "Marsupilami's First Visit: Houba!" *En Coulisse* 3 (15–30 April 1993), p. 4.

133. "Fun Facts," *En Coulisse* 3 (1–15 May 1993), p. 8.

134. "Les Filleuls de Mickey: Un An Déjà," *En Coulisse* 3 (15–30 April 1993), p. 4.

135. "Rencontre Avec Roy Disney," *En Coulisse* 3 (15–30 April 1993), p. 2.

136. Stephen Grey, "It's Euro Birthday Party Time for Mickey," *Daily Express* (13 April 1993).

137. "Une Image en Pleine Mutation," *En Coulisse*, no. 1 (July 1993), p. 3.

138. Anthony, p. 16.

139. "Une Image en Pleine Mutation."

140. Williams, p. 47.

141. Tim O'Brien, "Year 1: Euro Disney Keeping Its Chin Up," *Amusement Business* 105 (12–18 April 1993), p. 18.

142. Williams, "Le Mouse Gets His First Candle," p. 1.

143. "Milestone Met!" *Op Sheet*, no. 17 (25 April–May 1 1993).

144. Peter Bart, "Enter the Euro Yank," *Variety* 347 (1 June 1992), p. 24.

4. RESCUING THE EURO DISNEY RESORT

1. "Euro Disney Continues Strategic Reexamination," *En Coulisse Communiqué* (8 July 1993), p. 1.

2. Michael Williams, "Euro Disney Awash in Red Ink," *Variety* 351 (19 July 1993), p. 38.

3. Michael Medved, "The Business," *Sight and Sound* 4 (February 1994), p. 4.

4. Jane Sasseen, "Disney's Bungle Book," *International Management* 48 (July–August 1993), pp. 26–27.

5. Elaine Ganley, "Euro Disney Learns to Say 'In the Red' in French: Vast Regional Development Plans on Hold," *Star-Ledger* (10 April 1994), p. 3.

6. Michael Meyer, "Of Mice and Men," *Newsweek* 124 (5 September 1994), p. 41.

7. John Huey, "Eisner Explains Everything," *Fortune* 131 (17 April 1995), pp. 59–60.

8. "Tourisme: Une Année Difficile," *En Coulisse*, no. 2 (August 1993), p. 4.

9. Robert Anthony, "Euro Disney: The First 100 Days" (Harvard Business School Case Study #9-693-013, 4 June 1993), p. 9; and Steven Greenhouse, "Playing Disney in the Parisian Fields," *New York Times* (17 February 1991), sec. 3, p. 1.

10. "Euro Disney Continues Strategic Reexamination," p. 1.

11. Williams, p. 38.

12. Anthony, pp. 10, 18.

13. Richard Martin, "Foodservice Pioneer Nunis Keeps the Dream Alive," *Nation's Restaurant News* 26 (23 November 1992), p. 58.

14. Tim O'Brien, "Euro Disney's New Attractions Aimed at Increasing Attendance," *Amusement Business* 105 (12–18 April 1993), p. 18; "Constructive Marvels," *En Coulisse* 3 (1–15 May 1993), p. 12.

15. Ibid. See also "Euro Disneyland," *Disney Magazine* 29 (Winter 1993), p. 58; and "A Living Legend," *En Coulisse* 3 (15–30 June 1993), pp. 1–2.

16. O'Brien, p. 18. See also "Et Si On Se Faisait Un Peu de Cinéma?" *En Coulisse* 3 (1–15 December 1992), pp. 1–3; and "The Old Mill Gets a Face-Lift," *En Coulisse* 3 (15–30 June 1993), p. 2.

17. "Le 29 Juin: Bienvenue Sur Endor!" *En Coulisse* 3 (15–30 June 1993), p. 2; and O'Brien, p. 18.

18. O'Brien, p. 30.

19. On August 14, 1993, just two weeks after its inauguration, Le Temple du Péril proved worthy of its name. Apparently, the ride's security system detected a problem and shut it down, bringing vehicles to an immediate halt. All eight passengers (from France, Germany, and the Netherlands) were brought to the hospital for examination of whiplash-related injuries, and three were released later that day. For discussion of the attraction, see ibid; and "Euro Disneyland," p. 58. For information on the accident, see Frederic Constans, "Huit Blessés Chez Indiana Jones," *Le Journal du Dimanche* (15 August 1993), p. 6; and "Info.," *En Coulisse Hebdo*, no. 2 (18–25 August 1993), p. 1.

20. Although the Storybook Land attraction was scheduled to open in 1993, a string of delays prevented it from premiering until May 1994. Bruce Crumley, "Ogilvy, Mickey and Pals to the Rescue," *Advertising Age* 65 (21 March 1994), p. 42.

21. The Walt Disney Company, which purchased the rights to L. Frank Baum's Oz stories in 1954, had never before featured an Oz-themed attraction at any of its parks. Anne K. Okey, "A New Storybook Land for Euro Disneyland," *Disney Magazine* 29 (Fall 1994), p. 31; and O'Brien, p. 30.

22. O'Brien, p. 18.

23. Stewart Toy, "Euro Disney's Prince Charming?" *Business Week* (13 June 1994), p. 42.

24. O'Brien, p. 18.

25. Andrew Phillips, "Where's the Magic?" *Maclean's* 106 (3 May 1993), p. 47.

26. "Evolution," *En Coulisse*, no. 3 (September 1993), p. 3.

27. The price of theme park tickets was reduced by more than 20 percent in the off-season (and lifted by 10 percent in the peak season). Nightly rates were also lowered by some 30 percent at all Euro Disney hotels in the low season (except the 575-room Hotel New York, which operated a successful convention center). For discussion, see Nadine Godwin, "Disneyland Paris is New Address in France for Mickey and Minnie," *Travel Weekly* 53 (24 October 1994), p. 36.

28. Euro Disney executives also went to great lengths to patch up relations with European tour operators. "We didn't realize the importance of catering to groups and tour operators initially," Burke noted. "They play a much larger role here than in the U.S. We now pay a lot more attention to them." Sasseen, p. 27.

29. "Interview: Changing of the Guard," *En Coulisse* 2 (15–30 September 1992), p. 5.

30. Rick Lyman, "Euro Disney Attendance Is Disappointingly Mickey Mouse," *Journal of Commerce* 397 (10 August 1993), sec. A, p. 9.   221

31. "Mouse Trapped in France," *New Statesman and Society* 6 (20 August 1993), p. 6.

32. Michael Eisner, *Work in Progress* (New York: Random House, 1998), p. 283.

33. Lyman, sec. A, p. 9.

34. Calvin Sims, "Makeover at Disney," *Minneapolis Star Tribune* (3 May 1994), sec. D, p. 8.

35. Michael Williams, "No Mickey Mouse Opening for Star-Studded Disney Bow," *Variety* 347 (20 April 1992), p. 42. See also Eisner, p. 283.

36. Sasseen, p. 26.

37. Chris Tighe, "Queuing for Flawed Fantasy," *London Financial Times* (13–14 June 1992), p. 5; and Lyman, sec. A, p. 9.

38. Ganley, p. 3.

39. "Mouse Trapped in France," p. 6.

40. "Communiqué: Communication Interne" (23 Jun 1993), p. 1.

41. Sasseen, p. 27.

42. "Evolution," p. 3.

43. Sasseen, pp. 26–27.

44. Ibid., p. 27.

45. "Tourisme: Une Année Difficile"; and "Euro Disney Continues Strategic Reexamination."

46. "Euro Dis Lowers Hotel Prices," *Variety* 352 (25 October 1993), p. 152.

47. "Of Mice, Men and Money," *Economist* 329 (13 November 1993), p. 79; and Stewart Toy, "Is Disney Headed for the Euro-Trash Heap?" *Business Week* (24 January 1994), p. 52.

48. Williams, "Euro Disney Awash in Red Ink," p. 38.

49. Sasseen, p. 27; and "Of Mice, Men and Money," p. 79.

50. "Euro Disney's Woes Continue," *Business Week* (1 November 1993), p. 58; and "Storm Clouds Over Disney Land," *Business Week* (1 November 1993), p. 43.

51. "Of Mice, Men and Money," p. 79.

52. "Euro Disney's Woes Continue," p. 58.

53. "Jiminy Cricket! Eisner Says Euro Disney May Close," *Minneapolis Star Tribune* (1 January 1994), sec. D, p. 4; Toy, "Is Disney Headed for Euro-Trash Heap?" p. 52; and "Of Mice, Men and Money," p. 79.

54. Charles Fleming, et al., "A Goofy Kind of Year," *Newsweek* 122 (18 October 1993), p. 57.

55. "France: Euro Disney," *Facts on File* 54 (19 May 1994), p. 367; "Dreams Can Come True," *Minneapolis Star Tribune* (16 November 1995), sec. A, p. 17.

56. Analyst Emanuel Gerard is cited in Fleming, p. 57. See also "Storm Clouds Over Disney Land," p. 43; Sims, sec. D, p. 1; and Toy, "Is Disney Headed for Euro-Trash Heap?" p. 52.

57. "Disney Plunges Ahead Despite Recent Losses," *Engineering News Record* 231 (22 November 1993), p. 14.

58. Lisa Gaines, "Lackluster Financial Results Could Force Euro Disney to Shut Down," *Travel Weekly* 52 (30 December 1993), p. 21.

59. Bruce Crumley and Christy Fisher, "Euro Disney Tries to End Evil Spell," *Advertising Age* 65 (7 February 1994), p. 39; "Meltdown at the Cultural Chernobyl," *Economist* 330 (5 February 1994), p. 65; Jolie Solomon, et al., "Mickey's Trip to Trouble," *Newsweek* 123 (14 February 1994), p. 39; Meyer, p. 45; and Eisner, p. 288.

60. "Jiminy Cricket!" sec. D, p. 1.

61. Toy, "Is Disney Headed for Euro-Trash Heap?" p. 52.

62. "Jiminy Cricket!" sec. D, p. 1.

63. "Meltdown at the Cultural Chernobyl," p. 66.

64. Lyman, sec. A, p. 9.

65. "Jiminy Cricket!" sec. D, p. 4.

66. Crumley and Fisher, p. 39.

67. Eisner, p. 288.

68. "Jiminy Cricket!" sec. D, pp. 1, 4.

69. "Meltdown at the Cultural Chernobyl," pp. 65–66.

70. Ibid. See also Toy, "Is Disney Headed for Euro-Trash Heap?" p. 52; and Crumley and Fisher, p. 39.

71. Toy, "Is Disney Headed for Euro-Trash Heap?" p. 52; and "Meltdown at the Cultural Chernobyl," p. 65.

72. "Meltdown at the Cultural Chernobyl," p. 65.

73. Ibid., pp. 65–66. See also Toy, "Is Disney Headed for Euro-Trash Heap?" p. 52.

74. "Meltdown at the Cultural Chernobyl," p. 66.

75. Ibid., p. 65; Solomon, p. 34.

76. Thomas G. Donlan, "An Empty Vision," *Barron's* 74 (1 August 1994), p. 51.

77. "Cash Infusion for Euro Disney," *Travel Weekly* 53 (21 March 1994), p. 8; Crumley, p. 42; "Euro Disney Rescue Plan Is Accepted by Bankers," *Minneapolis Star Tribune* (15 March 1994), sec. D, p. 3; "France: Euro Disney," p. 367; and Eisner, p. 291.

78. "Euro Disney Rescue Plan Is Accepted," p. 3D.

79. Crumley, p. 42. See also "Euro Disney Looks for New Agency Partner," *Adweek* 34 (29 November 1993), p. 14; and "Euro Disney Agency Decision Near?" *Advertising Age* 65 (14 March 1994), p. 41.

80. Crumley and Fisher, p. 39.

81. Crumley, p. 42.

82. Crumley and Fisher, p. 39.

83. Ibid. See also Sasseen, p. 27.

84. Crumley, p. 42. See also Toy, "Euro Disney's Prince Charming?" p. 42.

85. Crumley and Fisher, p. 39.

86. "Mouse Trapped in France," p. 6.

87. Crumley and Fisher, p. 39.

88. Sims, sec. D, p. 1.

89. Huey, p. 52. See also Anne K. Okey, "Frank G. Wells: In Celebration of an Extraordinary Life," *Disney Magazine* 29 (Summer 1994), p. 12.

90. Ganley, p. 3.

91. Solomon, p. 35. See also Martin Walker, "Disney's Saccharin Turns Sour," *World Press Review* 41 (March 1994), p. 36.

92. Ganley, p. 3.

93. Solomon, pp. 35–36.

94. Ganley, p. 3.

95. Sims, sec. D, p. 8.

96. Crumley and Fisher, p. 39.

97. Ganley, p. 3.

98. Sims, sec. D, p. 1.

99. Donlan, p. 51.

100. Sims, sec. D, pp. 1, 8.

101. Ibid., p. 8.

102. Huey, p. 60.

103. Ibid., pp. 63–64.

104. Donlan, p. 51.

105. Solomon, pp. 35–36. See also Sims, sec. D, p. 1.

106. Toy, "Euro Disney's Prince Charming?" p. 42; Sims, sec. D, p. 8.

107. Michael Meyer, "A Charming Prince to the Rescue?" *Newsweek* 123 (13 June 1994), p. 43.

108. Donlan, p. 51; Meyer, "Charming Prince" p. 43; John Rossant, et al., "How Disney Snared a Princely Sum," *Business Week* (20 June 1994), p. 61; and Toy, "Euro Disney's Prince Charming?" p. 42.

109. Toy, "Euro Disney's Prince Charming?" p. 42. See also "Prospectus: Euro Disney S.C.A." (17 June 1994), p. 1; "Prince Rescues Euro Disney," *Engineering News Record* 232 (13 June 1994), p. 16.

110. "Saudi Prince Buys Into Euro Disney," *Advertising Age* 65 (6 June 1994), pp. 49, 54; "Saudi Prince to Buy Shares in Euro Disney Offering," *Travel Weekly* 53 (13 June 1994), p. 55; and Toy, "Euro Disney's Prince Charming?" p. 42.

111. "Prince Rescues Euro Disney," p. 16.

112. "Saudi's Disney Investment May Ease a Few Minds," *Minneapolis Star Tribune* (3 June 1994), sec. D, p. 3.

113. Toy, "Euro Disney's Prince Charming?" p. 42.

114. "Saudi's Disney Investment," sec. D, p. 3.

115. Meyer, "Charming Prince" p. 43.

116. Toy, "Euro Disney's Prince Charming?" p. 42.

117. Meyer, "Charming Prince" p. 43.

118. Ibid.

119. Rossant, p. 62.

120. Eisner, p. 399.

121. Meyer, "Of Mice and Men," p. 42; Huey, p. 60.

122. Huey, p. 45.

123. "Succession Becomes Issue at Disney," *Minneapolis Star Tribune* (19 July 1994), sec. D, p. 3.

124. Before Katzenberg joined the Walt Disney Company, movies brought in only 1 percent of the company's operating income. Less than one decade later, they were generating 43 percent of the company's revenues. Katzenberg made other contributions as well. He spearheaded Disney's acquisition of Miramax, put together a partnership with Merchant-Ivory, made a games deal with Sega, and teamed up with three regional Bell companies to deliver video programming over phone lines. See ibid.; Huey, p. 46; and Meyer, "Of Mice and Men," pp. 43, 44, 46.

125. Meyer, "Of Mice and Men," p. 43.

126. Ibid., p. 44.

127. Huey, p. 56.

128. Meyer, "Of Mice and Men," p. 43.

129. Huey, p. 56.

130. Ibid.

131. Katzenberg would go on to found DreamWorks SKG, a new Hollywood studio with movie mogul Steven Spielberg and music heavyweight David Geffen. Less than one year later, he stated that all was well and that he was "going 150 miles an hour with the top down and no rear-view mirror." Huey, p. 59. See also Russ Britt, "Hollywood's Eyes Are on DreamWorks," *Minneapolis Star Tribune* (23 October 1995), sec. E, p. 4; Richard Corliss, "Hey, Let's Put on a Show!" *Time* 145 (27 March 1995), pp. 54–60; "Euro Disney's Roller-Coaster Ride," *Economist* 332 (3 September 1994), p. 66; and Andrew E. Serwer, "Analyzing the Dream," *Fortune* 131 (17 April 1995), p. 71.

132. Meyer, "Of Mice and Men," p. 44. See also Ken Auletta, "The Human Factor," *New Yorker* 70 (26 September 1994), pp. 54–56; and "Disney Waxes Roth," *New Yorker* 70 (5 September 1994), pp. 35–36.

133. By week's end, following a public relations campaign directed at journalists and analysts, Euro Disney stock had largely regained its value and closed at 9.45 francs ($1.68) per share. For discussion, see Bruce Crumley, "Euro Disney's Fragile Condition," *Advertising Age* 65 (5 September 1994), p. 38; and Peter C. Du Bois, "More Grumpy News for Euro Disney," *Barron's* 74 (5 September 1994), p. MW12; and "Euro Disney's Roller-Coaster Ride," p. 66.

134. Eisner, p. 292.

135. Godwin, p. 1. See also "Disney Renames French Theme Park," *Advertising Age* 65 (19 September 1994), p. 51.

136. Godwin, pp. 1, 36.

137. Solomon, p. 35.

138. Godwin, p. 36.

139. Ibid., p. 38.

140. Solomon, p. 37.

141. Nadine Godwin, "Park Stages Special Events for Meetings Delegates," *Travel Weekly* 53 (17 October 1994), p. 73.

142. Nadine Godwin, "Euro Disney Convention Center To Be Expanded," *Travel Weekly* 53 (17 October 1994), p. 73.

143. "Euro Disney Posts $353 M Loss," *Advertising Age* 65 (7 November 1994), p. 64.

144. Prince Al-Waleed and his United Saudi Commercial Bank purchased a full 24.6 percent share in the French theme park and hotel complex. He would trim back his holdings to 20 percent in February 1995 in compliance with a special condition imposed by the Walt Disney Company: that no shareholder could own more than half the equity of Euro Disney's American parent. For discussion, see "Prince Completes Disney Buy," *Travel Weekly* 53 (24 October 1994), p. 77; and "Saudi Prince May Reduce Park Stake," *New York Times* (3 February 1995), sec. D, p. 5.

145. Huey, pp. 46–47.

146. J. D. Podolsky and Jane Sims Podesta, "An Uncivil War," *People Weekly* (18 July 1994), p. 70.

147. Donlan, p. 51.

148. "Disney Won't Build Theme Park at Civil War Site," *Minneapolis Star Tribune* (29 September 1994), sec. A, p. 2. For discussion of Disney's America, see also Don L. Boroughs, "Mickey Mouse Walks Away from a Fight," *U.S. News and World Report* 117 (10 October 1994), p. 103; Kirstin Downey Grimsley, "Disney Packs Its Bags," *Washington Post* (3 October 1994), p. 1; Lisa Gubernick, "The Third Battle of Bull Run," *Forbes* 154, special issue (17 October 1994), pp. 67, 70, 72, 74; Cliff Hocker, "Forward Spin: If We Help Build It, People Will Come," *Black Enterprise* 25 (October 1994), p. 17; Richard Lingeman, "Disneyburg Address," *Nation* 259 (11 July 1994), p. 40; Russell Miller, "Past Imperfect," *New Republic* 211 (8 August 1994), pp. 12, 14, 16; "The New Civil War: Making a Stand," *Conde Nast Traveler* 29 (September 1994), pp. 146–151; Mary Beth Regan, et al., "Mickey Does Manassas," *Business Week* (29 November 1993), p. 46; Jolie Solomon, et al., "Disney: A Sudden Surrender in Virginia," *Newsweek* 124 (10 October 1994), p. 46; William Styron, "Slavery's Tragedy Would Be Cheapened by Disney's Theme Park," *Minneapolis Star Tribune* (7 August 1994), sec. A, p. 27; and Catherine Watson, "A Theme Park Built on Blood and Bones," *Minneapolis Star Tribune* (5 December 1993), sec. G, p. 1.

149. Huey, p. 48.

150. Sasseen, p. 27.

5. IT'S A SMALL WORLD, INC.

1. One article remarked on the posted profits of Disneyland Paris with skepticism, noting that "all but $400,000 came from Euro Disney buying back bonds that could have been converted into stock." But increasing numbers of visitors surely had something to do with the success of the resort too. "Dreams Can Come True," *Minneapolis Star Tribune* (16 November 1995), sec. A, p. 17. See also "Euro Disney Makes Money, Finally," *Orlando Sentinel* (16 November 1995), pp. C1, C5; and John Tagliabue, "Step Right Up, Monsieur! Growing Disneyfication of Europe's Theme Parks," *New York Times* (23 August 1995), sec. C, p. 19.

2. "Dreams Can Come True," sec. A, p. 17; "Euro Disney Taps Steve Burke to be Firm's President," *Wall Street Journal-Europe* (3 February 1995), p. 5.

3. Ibid. See also "Euro Disney Makes Money, Finally," sec. C, pp. 1, 5.

4. Tim Delaney (Imagineer), interview by author, 6 July 1995. See also Michael Eisner, *Work in Progress* (New York: Random House, 1998), p. 284.

5. Tim O'Brien, "Euro Disney's New Attractions Aimed at Increasing Attendance," *Amusement Business* 105 (12–18 April 1993), p. 18.

6. Patrick Alo, "From the Earth to the Moon and Back Again!" *Disney Magazine* 31 (Winter 1995), pp. 26–28.

7. Delaney interview; Alo, p. 28.

8. "Disneyland Paris: Pour Space Mountain, le Show-Biz Redevient Enfant," *Paris Match*, no. 2403 (15 June 1995), p. 39.

9. Delaney interview.

10. "Mickey Hops the Pond," *Economist* (28 March 1987), p. 75.

11. Di Carlo Rossanigo, "Topolino and Soci Sbarcano in Europa," *Fortune* (June 1991), p. 126; Stewart Toy, et al., "An American in Paris," *Business Week* (12 March 1990), p. 61; Kevin Kelly and Linda Bernier, "It's King Kong vs. the 'Ravenous Rat,'" *Business Week* (5 October 1987), p. 54.

12. Ibid. See also Roger Cohen, "The Glories of France in Miniature," *New York Times* (4 July 1993), sec. 5, p. 18; John Dorst, "Miniaturising Monumentality: Theme Park Images of the American West and Confusions of Cultural Influence," in Rob Kroes, et al., eds., *Cultural Transmissions and Receptions: American Mass Culture in Europe* (Amsterdam: VU University Press, 1993), p. 263; "Mickey Hops the Pond," p. 75; and Martha Zuber, "Mickey-sur-Marne: Une Culture Conquérante?" *French Politics and Society* 10 (Summer 1992), p. 77.

13. "Mickey Hops the Pond," p. 75; Kelly, p. 54.

14. Kelly, p. 54.

15. "Saudi Prince May Reduce Park Stake," *New York Times* (3 February 1995), p. D5.

16. Tagliabue, sec. C, p. 19.

17. Ronald Grover, "Theme Parks: This Slugfest Is No Fantasy," *Business Week* (23 March 1987), p. 38.

18. Zuber, p. 77.

19. Ibid.

20. Tagliabue, sec. C, p. 19.

21. *Bienvenue au Parc Astérix* (Paris: Les Éditions Albert Réné/ Goscinny-Uderzo, 1991).

22. An important prototype for France Miniature was Tobu World Square, a park near Nikko, Japan, which features 1/25th-scale models of 102 of the world's greatest landmark attractions. France Miniature, however, limited its scope to the landmarks of France. Eric Hubler, "The Many Worlds of Fun in Japan," *New York Times* (4 July 1993), sec. 5, p. 17.

23. Cohen, p. 12.

24. Ibid., p. 18.

25. John Tagliabue, "A Comic-Strip Gaul Battles Disney," *New York Times* (15 August 1995), p. 3.

26. Joseph Rykwert, "Is Euro Disney a Substitute for Paris?" *Times Literary Supplement*, no. 4668 (18 September 1992), p. 6.

27. Umberto Eco, *Faith in Fakes: Essays* (London: Secker and Warburg, 1986), p. 16. For discussion of how history has been modified and brought to life in the present, see David Lowenthal, *The Past Is a Foreign Country* (Cambridge: Cambridge University Press, 1985).

28. Frederic Jameson, "Postmodernism, or The Cultural Logic of Late Capitalism," *New Left Review* 146 (July–August 1984), p. 66.

29. Miles Orvell, "Understanding Disneyland: American Mass Culture and the European Gaze," in Kroes, et al., p. 247.

30. Rykwert, p. 6. See also "Nice Idea, Shame About the Weather," *Economist* 298 (11 January 1986), p. 86.

31. Joel Achenbach, "Reality to Be Cancelled?" *Miami Herald* (13 December 1987), p. 18.

32. In 1995, the most-visited theme parks in Western Europe were Euro Disneyland (8.8 million); England's Blackpool Pleasure Beach (7 million); Denmark's Tivoli Gardens (3.8 million); Italy's Gardaland (3 million); and Alton Towers (3 million). See "At Play in the Old World," *New York Times* (23 August 1995), sec. C, p. 19; and "Nice Idea" p. 86.

33. Dorst, p. 267.

34. Henry Wiencek, *The World of Lego Toys* (New York: Harry N. Abrams, 1987), p. 135.

35. Dorst, p. 267.

36. Tagliabue, "Step Right Up, Monsieur!" sec. C, p. 19.

37. Anheuser-Busch holds a 20 percent share of Port Aventura, which its Busch Entertainment group helped to design. But the park is also backed by Catalan savings bank La Caixa and Spanish electricity firm Fecsa. See "An Answer to Disney," *Minneapolis Star Tribune* (2 May 1995), p. 2D; and Tagliabue, "Step Right Up, Monsieur!" p. C19.

38. Michael Medved, "The Business," *Sight and Sound* 4 (February 1994), p. 4.

39. Tim O'Brien, "Germany's Warner Bros. Movie World on Schedule for Late Spring Debut," *Amusement Business* 108 (15–21 January 1996), pp. 17, 24. See also Peggy Salz-Trautman, "Can Bugs Top Mickey's Act?" *World Press Review* 41 (March 1994), p. 36.

40. O'Brien, "Germany's Warner Bros.," p. 17.

41. Grover, p. 38.

42. Toy, p. 61.

43. Kelly, p. 54. See also "The American Dream and the Great Escape," *Economist* 298 (11 January 1986), p. 86.

44. Tagliabue, "Step Right Up, Monsieur!" sec. C, pp. 1, 19. See also Dorst, p. 265.

45. "E! Entertainment Report," Amy Powell, KARE 11 News, Minneapolis (February 1996).

46. John Huey, "America's Hottest Export: Pop Culture," *Fortune* 122 (31 December 1990), p. 60.

47. John Andrews, "Culture Wars," *Wired* 3.05 (May 1995), p. 130.

48. In addition to the flood of Hollywood films in Europe was the powerful impact of MTV, watched by some 7.3 million Europeans every day. Between 1987 and 1994, its viewership in Europe increased by 6,100 percent. See Andrews, p. 132; Elizabeth Neuffer, "The World Looks Anew at America," *Boston Globe* (9 October 1994), p. 22.

49. Elisabeth Chavelet, "Hollywood, L'Envers du Succès," *Paris Match*, no. 2381 (12 January 1995), p. 87.

50. Andrews, p. 130.

51. Ibid., pp. 130, 132.

52. Huey, p. 58.

53. Andrews, p. 130.

54. Huey, p. 60.

55. Ibid.

56. Ibid., p. 51.

57. Andrews, p. 134.

58. Todd Gitlin, "World Leaders: Mickey, et al.," *New York Times* (3 May 1992), sec. 2, p. 30.

59. Marshall McLuhan and Bruce R. Powers, *The Global Village: Transformations in World Life and Media in the 21st Century* (New York: Oxford University Press, 1989).

60. Andrews, p. 138.

61. Ibid.

62. Rob Kroes, et al., eds., *Cultural Transmissions and Receptions: American Mass Culture in Europe* (Amsterdam: VU University Press, 1993), p. 303.

63. Andrews, p. 138.

64. Neuffer, p. 23.

65. Ibid., p. 22.

66. Gitlin, p. 1.

67. Huey, p. 51.

68. Gitlin, p. 1.

69. Ibid.

70. Maureen Dowd, "Good News, Mouseketeers: Disney's Taking Over the World," *Minneapolis Star Tribune* (8 August 1995), sec. A, p. 9; "That Mouse Will Really Roar Now," *Minneapolis Star Tribune* (1 August 1995), sec. D, p. 1.

71. The deal also represented a personal homecoming, of sorts, for Michael Eisner, who had launched his career as an ABC programming executive from 1966 to 1976. See Bill Carter, "Merger Has Makings of a TV Juggernaut," *Minneapolis Star Tribune* (1 August 1995), sec. A, p. 11; and David Lieberman, "Disney Intent on Big Role in World Market," *USA Today* (1 August 1995), sec. A, p. 2.

72. Nancy Gibbs, "Easy as ABC." *Time* 146 (14 August 1995), pp. 24–30.

73. Sallie Hofmeister and Jane Hall, "Disney to Buy Cap Cities/ABC for $19 Billion, Vault to No. 1," *Los Angeles Times* (1 August 1995), sec. A, pp. 15–16; David Lieberman, "Disney Buys ABC for $19B," *USA Today* (1 August 1995), sec. A, p. 1; and "A Mighty Bucks Merger," *Minneapolis Star Tribune* (1 August 1995), sec. A, p. 10.

74. Dan Reed, "Mouse Roars," *Minneapolis Star Tribune* (10 February 1996), sec. D, p. 1.

75. Mike Meyers, "Experts Ponder: Is This a Merger of Peril or Promise?" *Minneapolis Star Tribune* (1 August 1995), sec. A, p. 10.

76. "That Mouse Will Really Roar Now," sec. D, p. 1.

77. Carter, sec. A, p. 11.

78. To facilitate the merger, Capital Cities chairman Thomas Murphy, age 70, opted to retire from active management and accept a seat on the Disney board. "On a personal basis," he reflected, "this is the high point of my career: seeing these two companies agreeing to go forward together." See ibid.; James Kim, "A Career Capper for Cap Cities' CEO," *USA Today* (1 August 1995), sec. B, p. 3; and Reed, sec. D, p. 1.

79. Reed, sec. D, p. 1; Meyers, sec. A, p. 10; Hofmeister and Hall, sec. A, p. 15.

80. Lieberman, "Disney Intent on Big Role," sec. A, p. 2.

81. Reed, sec. D, p. 1.

82. Hofmeister and Hall, sec. A, p. 1.

83. Ibid.

84. "Prime-Time Passions," *Economist* 336 (5 August 1995), p. 55.

85. Hofmeister and Hall, sec. A, p. 15.

86. Lieberman, "Disney Buys ABC," sec. A, p. 1.

87. "Mighty Bucks Merger," sec. A, p. 10.

88. Dowd, p. 9A; Michael Hiltzik and Claudia Eller, "Chemistry Made Talks Quick, Quiet," *Los Angeles Times* (1 August 1995), sec. A, p. 14; and "Mouse That Roared," *USA Today* (1 August 1995), sec. A, p. 10.

89. Mitchell Landsburg, "Disney Overload," *Minneapolis Star Tribune* (7 August 1995), sec. D, p. 1.

90. Ibid.

91. Meyers, sec. A, p. 10.

92. Jefferson Graham, "Will DreamWorks' Deal with Network Dissolve?" *USA Today* (1 August 1995), sec. D, p. 1; Jefferson Graham, "Disney Says ABC Won't Be Its Puppet," *USA Today* (1 August 1995), sec. D, p. 1; Lieberman, "Disney Intent on Big Role," sec. A, p. 2; and Meyers, sec. A, p. 10.

93. Graham, "Disney Says ABC," sec. D, p. 1; and Dowd, sec. A, p. 9.

94. Ibid.

95. Ibid.

96. Hofmeister and Hall, sec. A, pp. 15–16; "Prime-Time Passions," p. 55; "Not Such a Small World," *USA Today* (1 August 1995), sec. B, p. 1; and "King of Pop, Saudi Prince Teaming Up in Business," *Minneapolis Star Tribune* (20 March 1996), sec. B, p. 5.

97. "Prime-Time Passions," p. 56.

98. Meyers, sec. A, p. 10.

99. Kevin Maney, "Merger Mania Spreads to Disney World," *USA Today* (1 August 1995), sec. B, p. 2.

100. Meyers, sec. A, p. 10.

101. Graham, "Disney Says ABC," sec. D, p. 1.

102. Time Warner ultimately took back the top slot when its proposed $7.5 billion buyout of the Turner Broadcasting Company was approved by federal antitrust regulators. Reed, sec. D, p. 1.

103. The standard selection of most Capital Cities/ABC investors was a share in Disney stock and $65 cash for each Capital Cities/ABC share. See "Buffett Gives Disney Vote of Confidence in Purchase," *Minneapolis Star Tribune* (8 March 1996), sec. D, p. 2.

104. Reed, sec. D, p. 3.

105. Ibid.

106. For discussion of Disney's involvement in theatrical projects, see "Disney Plans Next Musical: 'King David,'" *Minneapolis Star Tribune* 231

(24 December 1995), sec. F, p. 7; and Bruce Handy, "Endpaper: Disney Does Broadway," *New York Times Magazine* (9 October 1994), p. 88. For treatment of the Disney Galleries, Disney's Animal Kingdom, and the Disney Cruise Line, respectively, see E. Scott Reckard, "Disney Not Just for Kids," *Minneapolis Star Tribune* (30 November 1994), sec. D, pp. 1, 4; "Disney's Wild Animal Kingdom Guided by Prestigious Panel," *Walt Disney World Eyes and Ears* (13 July 1995), p. 2; Marci Schmitt Boettcher, "Mickey Goes Cruising," *Minneapolis Star Tribune* (28 April 1995), sec. D, p. 2; and Gene Sloan, "Mickey at Sea," *USA Today* (31 July 1998), sec. D, pp. 1–2.

107. For discussion of the Walt Disney Company's plans for New York City, see "Disney to Invest in Rockefeller," *Minneapolis Star Tribune* (17 August 1995), sec. D, p. 3; Handy, p. 88; Landsburg, sec. D, p. 4; and Reed, sec. D, p. 3. For more information on the Royal Canadian Mounted Police and Celebration, respectively, see "Mounties Hire Disney to Market Their Image," *Minneapolis Star Tribune* (29 June 1995), sec. D, p. 3; and "Euro Disney to Build New Town Near Paris-Based Theme Park," *Minneapolis Star Tribune* (13 March 1996), sec. D, p. 3.

108. Walt Disney is quoted in David R. Smith, ed., *Walt Disney: Famous Quotes* (Lake Buena Vista, Fla.: Walt Disney Company, 1994), p. 53.

109. "Celebrating Twenty Years of Magic," *Newsweek*, special issue (Fall/Winter 1991), pp. 8, 10.

110. Robert A. M. Stern is a principal designer of Celebration. But other big names in architecture were also retained to help plan the development, including Michael Graves, Philip Johnson, Cesar Pelli, Aldo Rossi, and Helmut Jahn. For discussion, see Steve Berg, "Mr. Disney's Neighborhood," *Minneapolis Star Tribune* (10 December 1995), sec. A, pp. 1, 16; and "Celebrating Twenty Years of Magic," pp. 8, 10.

111. The Disney Institute, with more than eighty programs in nine different tracks (culinary arts, design arts, entertainment arts, environment, lifestyles, performing arts, sports and fitness, story arts, and youth), opened on February 9, 1996. See "New Disney Institute Offers Unique Discovery Vacations," *New York Times* (30 April 1995), summer travel guide, p. 7. See also "Celebrating Twenty Years of Magic," pp. 8, 10; and "Disney Institute," *Walt Disney World Eyes and Ears* (13 July 1995), pp. 1, 4.

112. Interest in Celebration was so great that the Walt Disney Company was forced to hold a lottery for the chance to build one of its first 351 homes or rent one of its first 170 apartments. Some 4,500 people turned out for the lottery drawing. Berg, sec. A, p. 16.

113. Landsburg, sec. D, p. 1.

114. Ibid., sec. D, p. 4.

115. Stephen Bayley, "In This Sterile Diorama, Life Is but a Theme," *International Herald-Tribune* (9 April 1992), p. 3.

116. Ibid.

117. For discussion, see "Sega's American Roots," *New York Times* (4 July 1993), sec. 3, p. 6.

118. Andrew Pollack, "Sega Takes Aim at Disney's World," *New York Times* (4 July 1993), sec. 3, p. 1.

119. Ibid.

120. Ibid.

121. Some industry experts predict that Sega Enterprises, which sold its American arcade business in 1990, will never build so many parks and will proceed with caution in the changing media landscapes of the coming century. See "Big Plans for Theme Parks," *New York Times* (4 July 1993), sec. 3, p. 6.

122. Tagliabue, "Step Right Up, Monsieur!" sec. C, p. 1.

123. "Big Plans for Theme Parks," p. 6.

124. Kevin Kelly, "Eno: Gossip is Philosophy," *Wired* 3.05 (May 1995), p. 204.

125. Ibid.

126. Marshall McLuhan, "A Garland of Christmases Past and a Glimpse of Christmas Future," *McCall's* 95 (December 1967), p. 97.

127. "Celebrating Twenty Years of Magic," p. 10.

Bibliography

BOOKS

Adams, Judith A. *The American Amusement Park Industry: A History of Technology and Thrills.* Boston: Twayne Publishers, 1991.

Appelbaum, Stanley. *The Chicago World's Fair of 1893: A Photographic Record.* New York: Dover Publications, 1980.

Athearn, Robert. *The Mythic West in 20th Century America.* Lawrence: University Press of Kansas, 1986.

Banham, Reyner. *Los Angeles: The Architecture of Four Ecologies.* Harmondsworth: Penguin, 1971.

Barbera, Joe. *My Life in 'Toons: From Flatbush to Bedrock in Under a Century.* Atlanta: Turner Publishing, 1994.

Beard, Richard R. *Walt Disney's EPCOT Center: Creating the New World of Tomorrow.* New York: Harry N. Abrams, 1982.

Beicken, Peter, and Robert Phillip Kolker. *The Films of Wim Wenders: Cinema as Vision and Desire.* Cambridge: Cambridge University Press, 1993.

Bercovitch, Sacvan. *American Jeremiad.* Madison: University of Wisconsin Press, 1979.

Bienvenue au Parc Astérix. Paris: Les Éditions Albert Réné/Goscinny-Uderzo, 1991.

Bright, Randy. *Disneyland: Inside Story.* New York: Harry N. Abrams, 1987.

Bryman, Alan. *Disney and His Worlds.* London: Routledge, 1995.

Caeser, James W. *Reconstructing America: The Symbol of America in Modern Thought.* New Haven: Yale University Press, 1998.

Canemaker, John. *Winsor McCay: His Life and Art.* New York: Abbeville Press, 1987.

Cholodenko, Alan, ed. *The Illusion of Life: Essays on Animation.* Sydney: Power Publications, 1991.

Coleman, Barbara J. *Fitting Pretty: The Media Construction of Adolescent Girls in the 1950s.* Ph.D. dissertation, University of Minnesota, 1995.

Cronon, William. *Changes in the Land: Indians, Colonists and the Ecology of New England.* New York: Hill and Wang, 1983.

Culhane, John. *The American Circus: An Illustrated History.* New York: Henry Holt and Company, 1990.

Dorfman, Ariel, and Armand Mattelart. *How to Read Donald Duck: Imperialist Ideology in the Disney Comic.* New York: International General, 1971.

Driver, Tom F. *The Magic of Ritual: Our Need for Liberating Rites That Transform Our Lives and Our Communities.* San Francisco: HarperCollins, 1991.

Eaton, Faith. *The Miniature House.* New York: Harry N. Abrams, 1990.

Eco, Umberto. *Faith in Fakes: Essays.* London: Secker and Warburg, 1986.

Eisner, Michael. *Work in Progress.* New York: Random House, 1998.

Eliot, Marc. *Walt Disney: Hollywood's Dark Prince.* New York: Birch Lane Press, 1993.

Euro Disney. Paris: Connaissance des Arts, 1992.

Feest, C. F. *Indians and Europe: An Interdisciplinary Collection of Essays.* Aachen: Rader Verlag, 1987.

Finch, Christopher. *The Art of Walt Disney: From Mickey Mouse to the Magic Kingdoms.* New York: Harry N. Abrams, 1973.

Findlay, John M. *Magic Lands: Western Cityscapes and American Culture After 1940.* Berkeley: University of California Press, 1992.

Fjellman, Stephen M. *Vinyl Leaves: Walt Disney World and America.* Boulder: Westview Press, 1992.

Flower, Joe. *Prince of the Magic Kingdom: Michael Eisner and the Re-Making of Disney.* New York: John Wiley and Sons, 1991.

Gordon, Bruce, and David Mumford. *Disneyland: The Nickel Tour.* Santa Clarita, Calif.: Camphor Tree Publishers, 1995.

Grant, John. *Encyclopedia of Walt Disney's Animated Characters.* New York: Harper and Row, 1987.

Greene, Katherine, and Richard Greene. *The Man Behind the Magic: The Story of Walt Disney.* New York: Viking Press, 1991.

Griffin, Al. *Step Right Up Folks!* Chicago: Henry Regnery, 1974.

Grover, Ron. *The Disney Touch: How a Daring Management Team Revived an Entertainment Empire.* Homewood, Ill.: Business One Irwin, 1991.

The HarperCollins Guide to Euro Disneyland 1992. London: HarperCollins Publishers, 1992.

Henry Ford Museum and Greenfield Village: An Illustrated History. Santa Barbara: Albion Publishing Group, 1993.

Hine, Thomas. *Populuxe: The Look and Life of America in the '50s and '60s, From Tailfins and TV Dinners to Barbie Dolls and Fallout Shelters.* New York: Alfred A. Knopf, 1987.

Huizinga, Johann. *Homo Ludens: A Study of the Play-Element in Culture.* London: Routledge and Kegan Paul Limited, 1949.

Kasson, John F. *Amusing the Million: Coney Island at the Turn of the Century.* New York: Hill and Wang, 1978.

Klein, Norman M. *Seven Minutes: The Life and Death of the American Animated Cartoon.* London: Verso, 1993.

Koenig, David. *Mouse Tales: A Behind-the-Ears Look at Disneyland.* Irvine, Calif.: Bonaventure Press, 1994.

Kroes, Rob, et al., eds. *Cultural Transmissions and Receptions: American Mass Culture in Europe.* Amsterdam: VU University Press, 1993.

Kuisel, Richard. *Seducing the French: The Dilemma of Americanization.* Berkeley: University of California Press, 1993.

Leach, William. *Land of Desire: Merchants, Power, and the Rise of a New American Culture.* New York: Pantheon Books, 1993.

Lewis, R. W. B. *The American Adam: Innocence, Tragedy, and Tradition in the Nineteenth Century.* Chicago: University of Chicago Press, 1955.

Leyda, Jay, ed. *Eisenstein on Disney.* London: Methuen, 1988.

Lowenthal, David. *The Past Is a Foreign Country.* Cambridge: Cambridge University Press, 1985.

Lynch, Kevin. *What Time Is This Place?* Cambridge, Mass.: MIT Press, 1972.

MacCannell, Dean. *The Tourist: A New Theory of the Leisure Class.* New York: Schocken Books, 1976.

Marin, Louis. *Utopics: Spatial Play.* Atlantic Highlands, N.J.: Humanities Press, 1984.

Marling, Karal Ann. *As Seen on TV: The Visual Culture of Everyday Life in the 1950s.* Cambridge, Mass.: Harvard University Press, 1994.

———, ed. *Designing Disney's Theme Parks: The Architecture of Reassurance.* New York: Flammerion/Centre Canadien d'Architecture, 1998.

Marx, Leo. *The Machine in the Garden: Technology and the Pastoral Ideal in America.* New York: Oxford University Press, 1964.

McLuhan, Marshall, and Bruce R. Powers. *The Global Village: Transformations in World Life and Media in the 21st Century.* New York: Oxford University Press, 1989.

Miniature Rooms: The Thorne Rooms at the Art Institute of Chicago. New York: Abbeville Press, 1983.

Mosley, Leonard. *Disney's World.* Lanham, Md.: Scarborough House, 1985.

———. *The Real Walt Disney: A Biography.* London: Grafton Books, 1985.

Nasaw, David. *Going Out: The Rise and Fall of Public Amusements.* New York: Basic Books, 1993.

Ogilvy, David. *Ogilvy on Advertising.* New York: Vintage Books, 1985.

O'Toole, John. *The Trouble with Advertising: A View from the Inside.* New York: Times Books, 1985.

Peary, Gerald, and Danny Peary. *The American Animated Cartoon: A Critical Anthology.* New York: E. P. Dutton, 1980.

Peiss, Kathy. *Cheap Amusements: Working Women and Leisure in Turn-of-the-Century New York.* Philadelphia: Temple University Press, 1986.

Popcorn, Faith. *Clicking: 17 Trends That Drive Your Business—and Your Life.* New York: HarperCollins, 1997.

237

The Project on Disney. *Inside the Mouse: Work and Play at Disney World.* Durham, N.C.: Duke University Press, 1995.

Rosenberg, Harold. *Discovering the Present.* Chicago: University of Chicago Press, 1973.

Ross, Andrew. *No Respect: Intellectuals and Popular Culture.* New York: Routledge, 1989.

Rybczynski, Witold. *The Most Beautiful House in the World.* New York: Viking Penguin, 1989.

Rydell, Robert W. *All the World's a Fair: Visions of Empire at American International Expositions, 1876–1916.* Chicago: University of Chicago Press, 1984.

Said, Edward W. *Orientalism.* New York: Vintage Books, 1979.

Schickel, Richard. *Intimate Strangers: The Culture of Celebrity.* Garden City, N.Y.: Doubleday and Company, 1985.

———. *The Disney Version: The Life, Times, Art and Commerce of Walt Disney.* New York: Simon and Schuster, 1968.

Schlereth, Thomas J. *Artifacts and the Material Past.* Nashville: American Association for State and Local History, 1980.

Shale, Richard A. *Donald Duck Joins Up: The Walt Disney Studio During World War II.* Ph.D. dissertation, University of Michigan, 1976.

Sklar, Robert. *Movie-Made America: A Cultural History of American Movies.* New York: Vintage Books, 1975.

Smith, David R., ed. *Walt Disney: Famous Quotes.* Lake Buena Vista, Fla.: Walt Disney Company, 1994.

Smith, Henry Nash. *Virgin Land: The American West as Symbol and Myth.* Cambridge, Mass.: Harvard University Press, 1950.

Smoodin, Eric. *Animating Culture: Hollywood Cartoons from the Sound Era.* New Brunswick, N.J.: Rutgers University Press, 1993.

———, ed. *Disney Discourse: Producing the Magic Kingdom.* New York: Routledge, 1994.

Solomon, Charles. *Enchanted Drawings: The History of Animation.* New York: Alfred A. Knopf, 1989.

Sorkin, Michael, ed. *Variations on a Theme Park: The New American City and the End of Public Space.* New York: Hill and Wang, 1992.

Sperling, Cass Warner, and Cork Millner. *Hollywood Be Thy Name: The Warner Brothers Story.* Rocklin, Calif.: Prima Publishing, 1994.

Taylor, John. *Storming the Magic Kingdom: Wall Street, the Raiders, and the Battle for Disney.* New York: Alfred A. Knopf, 1987.

Tebbs, Terry. *The Knott Story.* Las Vegas: Marchant Mint Library, 1992.

Thomas, Bob. *Building a Company: Roy O. Disney and the Creation of an Entertainment Empire.* New York: Hyperion Press, 1998.

———. *Walt Disney: An American Original.* New York: Hyperion Press, 1976.

———. *Walt Disney: Magician of the Movies.* New York: Grossett and Dunlap, 1966.

Tiger, Lionel. *The Pursuit of Pleasure*. Boston: Little, Brown and Company, 1992.

Tschumi, Bernard. *Architecture and Disjunction*. Cambridge, Mass.: MIT Press, 1994.

Turner, Victor. *Dramas, Fields, and Metaphors: Symbolic Action in Human Society*. Ithaca: Cornell University Press, 1974.

Twitchell, James B. *Adcult USA: The Triumph of Advertising in American Culture*. New York: Columbia University Press, 1996.

——. *Carnival Culture: The Trashing of Taste in America*. New York: Columbia University Press, 1992.

Venturi, Robert. *Learning from Las Vegas: The Forgotten Symbolism of Architectural Form*. Cambridge, Mass.: MIT Press, 1977.

Walker, Derek, ed. *Animated Architecture*. London: Architectural Design, 1982.

Walt Disney Imagineering: A Behind the Dreams Look at Making the Magic Real. New York: Hyperion, 1996.

Watts, Steven. *The Magic Kingdom: Walt Disney and the American Way of Life*. New York: Houghton Mifflin, 1998.

Wiencek, Henry. *The World of Lego Toys*. New York: Harry N. Abrams, 1987.

Wilson, Alexander. *The Culture of Nature: North American Landscape from Disney to the Exxon Valdez*. Cambridge, Mass.: Blackwell, 1992.

Wilson-Smith, Timothy. *Delacroix: A Life*. London: Constable, 1992.

Zipes, Jack. *Breaking the Magic Spell: Radical Theories of Folk and Fairy Tales*. Austin: University of Texas Press, 1979.

Zukin, Sharon. *Landscapes of Power: From Detroit to Disney World*. Berkeley: University of California Press, 1991.

ARTICLES AND BOOK EXCERPTS

Achenbach, Joel. "Reality to Be Cancelled?" *Miami Herald*, 13 December 1987, pp. 18–21.

Alexander, Jack. "The Amazing Story of Walt Disney." *Saturday Evening Post* 226, 31 October 1953, pp. 24–25, 80–84, 90, 92.

——. "The Amazing Story of Walt Disney." *Saturday Evening Post* 226, 7 November 1953, pp. 26–27, 99–100.

Allen, Jennifer. "Brave New EPCOT." *New York* 16, 20 December 1982, pp. 40–43.

——. "Tragic Kingdom." *New Republic* 209, 10 and 17 January 1994, pp. 16–17.

Allen, Martha Sawyer. "The Mouse Trap." *Minneapolis Star Tribune*, 10 January 1997, sec. B, pp. 5, 8.

Allen, Robin Lee. "In the Shadows of Mickey's Empire." *Nation's Restaurant News* 26, 23 November 1992, p. 98.

Alo, Patrick. "From the Earth to the Moon and Back Again!" *Disney Magazine* 31, Winter 1995, pp. 26–28.

"The American Dream and the Great Escape." *Economist* 298, 11 January 1986, pp. 83–87.

Anderson, Harry, and Martin Kasindorf. "Disney's Trials in Tomorrowland." *Newsweek* 94, 24 December 1979, pp. 65–66.

Anderson, Kurt. "Look, Mickey, No Kitsch!" *Time* 138, 29 July 1991, pp. 66–69.

Andrews, John. "Culture Wars." *Wired* 3.05, May 1995, pp. 130–138.

Andrews, Nigel. "Euro Disney and the Mouse That Soared." *London Financial Times*, 11–12 April 1992, p. 9.

Anquetil, Gilles, et al. "Invasion Culturelle Américaine: Cette Souris, Est-Elle Dangereuse?" *Le Nouvel Observateur*, 3 January 1986, pp. 20–27.

"Answer That Phone." *Minneapolis Star Tribune*, 15 December 1993, sec. D, p. 4.

"An Answer to Disney." *Minneapolis Star Tribune*, 2 May 1995, sec. D, p. 2.

Anthony, Robert. "Euro Disney: The First 100 Days." Harvard Business School Case #9-693-013, 4 June 1993, pp. 1–23.

Apple, Max. "Uncle Walt." *Esquire* 100, December 1983, pp. 164–168.

Armstrong, Larry. "Disneyland Abroad: Today Tokyo, Tomorrow the World." *Business Week*, no. 2988, 9 March 1987, pp. 68–69.

Aronson, Arnold. "The Total Theatrical Environment: Impression Management in the Parks." *Theatre Crafts* 11, September 1977, pp. 34–39.

"At Play in the Old World." *New York Times*, 23 August 1995, sec. C, p. 19.

Auletta, Ken. "The Human Factor." *New Yorker* 70, 26 September 1994, pp. 54–56, 61–62, 64–66, 69.

Bakeroot, Willy. "Des Myths Devenus Objets." *Projet* 229, 1992, pp. 84–92.

Barry, Dave. "Is Nothing Sacred?" *Miami Herald*, 4 September 1983, pp. 6–9, 18.

Bart, Peter. "Enter the Euro Yank." *Variety* 347, 1 June 1992, pp. 5, 24.

Bayer, Ann. "Happy 40th, Mickey." *Life* 65, 25 October 1968, pp. 57–58, 62.

Bayley, Stephen. "In This Sterile Diorama, Life Is But a Theme." *International Herald-Tribune*, 9 April 1992, sec. 1, pp. 1, 3.

Beckham, Beverly. "Pursuing Donald Duck, Tinkerbell and Wonder." *Patriot-Ledger*, 1 June 1983, p. 3.

Benjamin, Walter. "The Work of Art in the Age of Mechanical Reproduction." In *Illuminations*, ed. Hannah Arendt. New York: Schocken Books, 1969.

Berg, Steve. "Mr. Disney's Neighborhood." *Minneapolis Star Tribune*, 10 December 1995, sec. A, pp. 1, 16–17.

Bergsman, Steven. "In France, Little Flipping Over Euro Disneyland." *Barron's*, 14 October 1991, p. 50.

Bernier, Linda, et al. "Monsieur Mickey or Señor Miqui? Disney Seeks a European Site." *Business Week*, no. 2903, 15 July 1985, p. 48.

Bernstein, Richard. "French Site Chosen for Disney Park." *New York Times*, 19 December 1985, sec. 4, p. 4.

Bieder, Robert E. "Marketing the American Indian in Europe: Context, Commodification and Reception." In *Cultural Transmissions and Receptions: American Mass Culture in Europe*, ed. Rob Kroes, et al. Amsterdam: VU University Press, 1993.

Bierman, James H. "The Walt Disney Robot Dramas." *Yale Review* 66, December 1976, pp. 223–236.

"Big Plans for Theme Parks." *New York Times*, 4 July 1993, sec. 3, p. 6.

"Big Rush for Euro Disney Prospectus." *Times* (London), 9 October 1989, p. 29.

"Big Spenders." *Hollywood Reporter*, finance special issue, 30 January 1998, p. S-10.

Birmingham, Stephen. "Once Upon a Time . . . There Lived the Greatest One-Man Show on Earth . . . in the Magic Land of Hollywood." *McCall's*, July 1964, pp. 98–101, 121.

Birnbaum, Stephen. "Epcot Center: The Newest Wonder at Walt Disney World." *Good Housekeeping* 195, October 1982, pp. 128, 130.

Blake, Peter. "Mickey Mouse for Mayor!" *New York* 5, 7 February 1972, pp. 41–45.

——. "Walt Disney World." *Architectural Forum* 136, June 1972, pp. 24–41.

Blanc, Irene. "Mickey Montre Les Dents." *Paris Match*, 21 December 1989, p. 114.

Bloch, Jeff. "The Honeymooners." *Newsweek*, special issue, Fall/Winter 1991, p. 41.

Bloomfield, Howard. "Mickey Mouse Grows Trees, Too." *American Forests* 82, July 1976, pp. 16–19, 65.

Bly, Laura. "A Happy Debut for 'Le Mickey.'" *Orange County Register*, 13 April 1992, sec. A, pp. 1, 22.

Boehme, Lillian R. "The Magic Kingdom: Is It Really Magic?" *American Opinion* 18, May 1975, pp. 13–20, 85–90.

Boettcher, Marci Schmitt. "Mickey Goes Cruising." *Minneapolis Star Tribune*, 28 April 1995, sec. D, p. 2.

Bonin, Liane. "Tragic Kingdom." *Detour Magazine*, April 1998, pp. 68–72.

"Bonjour, Mickey." *Fortune* 113, 20 January 1986, p. 8.

Boroughs, Don L. "Mickey Mouse Walks Away from a Fight." *U.S. News and World Report* 117, 10 October 1994, p. 103.

Bradbury, Ray. "The Aesthetics of Lostness," in *Yestermorrow: Obvious Answers to Impossible Futures*. Santa Barbara, Calif.: Capra Press, 1991.

———. "L'Homme Qui a Changé Notre Histoire," in "Invasion Culturelle Américaine: Cette Souris, Est-Elle Dangereuse?" *Le Nouvel Observateur,* 3 January 1986, p. 25.

———. "Los Angeles: Orange Without a Navel." *Frontier* 15, February 1964, pp. 7, 9, 15, 17.

———. "The Machine-Tooled Happyland." *Holiday* 38, October 1965, pp. 100–102, 104.

———. "Not Child Enough." *The Nation* 186, 28 June 1958, inside cover.

Bragdon, Claude. "Straws in the Wind." *Scribner's* 96, July 1934, pp. 40–43.

Branch, Mark Alden. "Why (and How) Does Disney Do It?" *Progressive Architecture* 71, October 1990, pp. 78–81.

Brannen, Mary Yoko. "Bwana Mickey: Constructing Cultural Consumption at Tokyo Disneyland." In *Cultures of United States Imperialism,* ed. Amy Kaplan and Donald E. Pease. Durham, N.C.: Duke University Press, 1993.

Brasheres, Charles W. "Walt Disney as Theologian." *Christian Century* 55, 10 August 1938, pp. 968–969.

"Briefs." *New York Times,* 21 March 1990, sec. D, p. 4.

Bright, John. "Disney's Fantasy Empire." *Nation* 204, 6 March 1967, pp. 299–303.

Britt, Russ. "Hollywood's Eyes Are on DreamWorks." *Minneapolis Star Tribune,* 23 October 1995, sec. E, p. 4.

Brizard, Caroline. "Quand Paris Fait de l'Oeil à Mickey." *Le Nouvel Observateur,* 16 August 1985, p. 43.

Brockway, Robert W. "The Masks of Mickey Mouse: Symbol of a Generation." *Journal of Popular Culture* 22, Spring 1989, pp. 25–32.

Brody, Michael. "The Wonderful World of Disney—Its Psychological Appeal." *American Imago* 33, Winter 1976, pp. 350–360.

Brooks, Nancy Rivera. "Disney to Build Movie Studio Tour at Euro Disneyland." *Los Angeles Times,* 17 November 1989, sec. D, p. 1.

Brown, Alan. "Tokyo: Mickey's First Trip Abroad." *Travel and Leisure* 22, August 1992, p. 110.

Brown, Patricia Leigh. "Disney Deco." *New York Times Magazine,* 8 April 1990, pp. 18–22.

———. "In Fairy Dust, Disney Finds New Realism." *New York Times,* 20 July 1989, sec. C, pp. 1, 6.

Browning, E. S. "Disney Gets Many Helping Hands to Sell the New Euro Disneyland." *Wall Street Journal,* 1 April 1992, sec. B, p. 4.

Browning, Peter. "Mickey Mouse in the Mountains: Mineral King Controversy I." *Harper's* 244, March 1972, pp. 65–71.

———. "Mickey Mouse in the Mountains: Mineral King Controversy II." *Harper's* 245, August 1972, pp. 102–103.

Brushaber, George K. "The Secularization of Mickey Mouse." *Christianity Today* 34, 19 March 1990, p. 9.

"Buffett Gives Disney Vote of Confidence in Purchase." *Minneapolis Star Tribune*, 8 March 1996, sec. D, p. 2.

Bukatman, Scott. "There's Always Tomorrowland: Disney and the Hypercinematic Experience." *October* 57, Summer 1991, pp. 55–78.

Burkman, Greg. "The Man Behind the Magic," *Seattle Times*, 11 January 1998, sec. M, p. 12.

"But Is It Art?" *Business Week*, no. 806, 10 February 1945, pp. 72, 76.

Cahn, Robert. "The Intrepid Kids of Disneyland." *Saturday Evening Post* 230, 28 June 1958, pp. 22–23, 118–120.

"California: Spectacular Plus." *Newsweek* 46, 25 July 1955, pp. 32–33.

"California's Lively Steamers." *Mechanix Illustrated*, January 1955, pp. 26–28, 92.

Carey, David. "The Art of the Deals." *Adweek* 33, 1 June 1992, p. 23, eastern edition.

Carr, Harry. "The Only Unpaid Movie Star." *American Magazine* 3, March 1931, pp. 55–57, 122–123.

Carter, Bill. "Merger Has Makings of a TV Juggernaut." *Minneapolis Star Tribune*, 1 August 1995, sec. A, pp. 1, 11.

"Cash Infusion for Euro Disney." *Travel Weekly* 53, 21 March 1994, p. 8.

Castro, Janet. "Mickey Mouse Goes to Paris." *Time* 126, 30 December 1985, p. 62.

"Celebrating Twenty Years of Magic." *Newsweek*, special issue, Fall/Winter 1991, pp. 4–10.

Chaigneau, Jean-François, et al. "Marne au Pays des Merveilles." *Paris Match*, 3 January 1986, pp. 46–51.

Champin, Fleur. "Disney Conquers Europe." *House Beautiful* 134, November 1992, pp. 42–43.

Charlot, Jean. "But Is It Art? A Disney Disquisition." *American Scholar* 8, July 1939, pp. 261–270.

Chavelet, Elisabeth. "Hollywood, L'Envèrs du Succès." *Paris Match*, 12 January 1995, p. 87.

"Cheers and Jeers." *TV Guide*, 9–15 May 1998, p. 13.

Chouffan, Alain. "Tres Chèr Mickey: Les Chiffres du Rêve." *Le Nouvel Observateur*, 2–8 April 1992, p. 41.

Ciardi, John. "Foamrubbersville." *Saturday Review* 48, 19 June 1965, p. 20.

Clancy, Ray, and Bill Frost. "Disney Fantasy Meets Cruel Financial Reality." *Times* (London), 14 October 1991, p. 20.

Cockburn, Alexander. "EPCOT: More Than Just Mickey Mouse." *House and Garden* 155, August 1983, pp. 14, 16, 20, 22.

Cockburn, Andrew. "The New Civil War: Making a Stand." *Conde Nast Traveler* 29, September 1994, pp. 146–150, 183–188.

Cohen, Daniel. "Preview of Disney's World's Fair Shows." *Science Digest* 54, December 1963, pp. 8–15.

Cohen, Risa M. "The Picture of America We Export to the World Is

Not a Flattering One." *Minneapolis Star Tribune,* 26 February 1994, sec. A, p. 19.

Cohen, Roger. "Euro Disney Sees Loss: Disney Profit Rises 33%." *New York Times,* 24 July 1992, p. D3.

———. "The Glories of France in Miniature." *New York Times,* 4 July 1993, sec. 5, pp. 12, 18.

Coleman, Brian. "Euro Disney's First-Period Loss Shrank on Restructuring, Rise in Park Revenue." *Wall Street Journal,* 25 January 1995, sec. A, p. 12.

Constans, Frederic. "Huit Blessés Chez Indiana Jones." *Le Journal du Dimanche,* 15 August 1993, p. 6.

Cooper, Matthew, et al. "Empire of the Sun." *U.S. News and World Report* 108, 28 May 1990, pp. 44–51.

Corliss, Richard. "Hey, Let's Put on a Show!" *Time* 145, 27 March 1995, pp. 54–60.

———. "If Heaven Ain't a Lot Like Disney." *Time* 127, 16 June 1986, pp. 80–82, 84.

———. "Voilà! Disney Invades Europe. Will the French Resist?" *Time* 139, 20 April 1992, pp. 82–84.

———. "You're Under Arrest! Hollywood Goes Florida at the Disney-MGM Theme Park." *Time* 133, 8 May 1989, pp. 102–103.

Cornwell, Regina. "Emperor of Animation." *Art in America* 69, December 1981, pp. 113–120.

Croce, Paul Jerome. "A Clean and Separate Space: Walt Disney in Person and Production." *Journal of Popular Culture* 25, Winter 1991, pp. 91–103.

Crowther, Bosley. "The Dream Merchant." *New York Times,* 16 December 1966, p. 40.

Crumley, Bruce. "Euro Disney's Fragile Condition." *Advertising Age* 65, 5 September 1994, p. 38.

———. "Ogilvy, Mickey & Pals to the Rescue." *Advertising Age* 65, 21 March 1994, p. 42.

Crumley, Bruce, and Christy Fisher. "Euro Disney Tries to End Evil Spell." *Advertising Age* 65, 7 February 1994, p. 39.

Culhane, John. "A Mouse for All Seasons." *Saturday Review* 5, 11 November 1978, pp. 50–51.

———. "The Old Disney Magic." *New York Times Magazine,* 1 August 1976, pp. 10–11, 32–34, 36.

Daniels, Jeffrey. "Theme Parks Put Disney in Third-Quarter Coinland." *Hollywood Reporter,* 27 July 1995, p. 1.

Davis, Sally. "Should We Let Disney Redesign Los Angeles?" *Los Angeles,* July 1974, pp. 45–46, 64–66.

De Chenay, Christophe. "Disney à la Mode de Chez Nous." *Le Monde,* 11–12 April 1992, p. 22.

———. "À Trente-Sept Minutes du Châtelet." *Le Monde*, 12–13 April 1992, p. 10.

DeGeorge, Gail. "A Sweet Deal for Disney Is Souring Its Neighbors." *Business Week*, 8 August 1988, pp. 46–47.

———. "Reanimating Disney World." *Business Week*, 5 December 1994, p. 41.

Delshon, Gary. "Architecture for the Masses." *Sacramento Bee*, 30 September 1990, sec. H, pp. 1, 16.

Demarest, Michael. "Disney's Last Dream." *Time* 120, 4 October 1982, pp. 60–61.

DeMott, John S. "Mickey Mouse on Tokyo Bay." *Time* 121, 18 April 1983, pp. 76–77.

Dennett, Andrea Stulman. "A Postmodern Look at EPCOT's American Adventure." *Journal of American Culture* 12, Spring 1989, pp. 47–53.

De Roos, Robert. "The Magic Worlds of Walt Disney." *National Geographic Magazine* 124, August 1963, pp. 157–207.

De Roux, Emmanuel. "L'Ouverture d'Euro Disney à Marne-la-Vallée." *Le Monde*, 12–13 April 1992, p. 9.

"Disney and France." *New York Times*, 19 June 1986, sec. 4, p. 4.

"Disney Boosts Offering of Zero Coupon Bonds." *Wall Street Journal*, 21 June 1990, sec. C, p. 19.

"Disney Comes to TV." *Newsweek* 43, 12 April 1954, p. 85.

"Disney Does It Again!" *Better Homes and Garden* 61, March 1983, p. 28.

"A Disney Dress Code Chafes in the Land of Haute Couture." *New York Times*, 25 December 1991, pp. 1, 48.

"Disney Firm Selects France as Site for Amusement Park." *Atlanta Constitution*, 19 December 1985, sec. A, p. 12.

"Disney Has a £707 Entry Price." *Times* (London), 6 October 1989, p. 21.

"Disney Impact Greater Than Expected." *Florida Trend: Magazine of Florida Business and Finance*, November 1972, pp. 45–89.

"Disney in Europe." *New York Times*, 13 March 1987, sec. 4, p. 4.

"Disney in France." *New York Times*, 25 March 1987, sec. 4, p. 3.

"Disney £590 Million Finance Secure." *Times* (London), 24 October 1990, p. 26.

Disney, Lillian (with Isabella Taves). "I Live with a Genius." *McCall's* 80, February 1953, pp. 38–41, 103–104, 106–107.

"Disney Looks for Fairy Tale Ending." *Times* (London), 29 July 1991, p. 21.

"Disney Looks to be the Clear Winner in Magic Kingdom." *Times* (London), 9 October 1989, p. 30A.

"Disney Park Considered for Britain." *Times* (London), 1 October 1984, p. 3.

"Disney Park Plans Criticized." *Atlanta Constitution*, 20 December 1985, sec. A, p. 19.

"Disney Plans Next Musical: 'King David.'" *Minneapolis Star Tribune*, 24 December 1995, sec. F, p. 7.

"Disney Plunges Ahead Despite Recent Losses." *Engineering News Record* 231, 22 November 1993, p. 14.

"Disney Premium of 172P." *Times* (London), 7 November 1989, p. 25B.

"Disney Profit Outlook." *New York Times*, 21 March 1991, sec. 4, p. 5.

"Disney Reaps 33% Earnings Jump." *Variety* 348, 27 July 1992, p. 73.

"Disney Renames French Theme Park." *Advertising Age* 65, 19 September 1994, p. 51.

"Disney To Invest in Rockefeller." *Minneapolis Star Tribune*, 17 August 1995, sec. D, p. 3.

"Disney to Sell Stock for Euro Disneyland." *Wall Street Journal*, 6 March 1989, sec. C, p. 16.

"Disney Waxes Roth." *New Yorker* 70, 5 September 1994, pp. 35–36.

"Disney Won't Build Theme Park at Civil War Site." *Minneapolis Star Tribune*, 29 September 1994, sec. A, p. 2.

"Disney World: Pixie Dust Over Florida." *Time* 98, 18 October 1971, pp. 52–53.

"Disneyland." *Life* 39, 15 August 1955, pp. 39–42.

"Disneyland." *McCall's* 82, January 1955, pp. 8–11.

"Disneyland." *Woman's Home Companion*, June 1954, p. 12.

"Disneyland and Disney World." *Theatre Crafts* 11, September 1977, pp. 28–30.

"Disneyland East." *Newsweek* 66, 29 November 1965, p. 82.

"A Disneyland for Hungary?" *New York Times*, 8 August 1988, sec. 4, p. 2.

"A Disneyland of Corporate Promotion." *Business Week*, 26 March 1979, pp. 114, 118.

"Disneyland Paris: Pour Space Mountain, le Show-Biz Redevient Enfant." *Paris Match* 2403, 15 June 1995, p. 39.

"Disney's Epcot Center: A Family Experience." *Black Enterprise* 13, February 1983, pp. 105–106.

"Disney's Moveable Feast." *Newsweek* 78, 6 September 1971, pp. 64–65.

"Disney's Wider World." *Business Week*, 25 December 1965, p. 21.

Dolliver, Mark. "Clinging to a Belief That What's Big Must Be Bad." *Adweek*, 19 January 1998, p. 16.

Donlan, Thomas G. "An Empty Vision." *Barron's* 74, 1 August 1994, p. 51.

Dorst, John. "Miniaturising Monumentality: Theme Park Images of the American West and Confusions of Cultural Influence." In *Cultural Transmissions and Receptions: American Mass Culture in Europe*, ed. Rob Kroes, et al. Amsterdam: VU University Press, 1993.

Dowd, Maureen. "Good News, Mouseketeers: Disney's Taking Over the World." *Minneapolis Star Tribune*, 8 August 1995, sec. A, p. 9.

"Dreams Can Come True." *Minneapolis Star Tribune,* 16 November 1995, sec. A, p. 17.

Dryansky, G. Y. "I'll Take the Playgrounds of Paris." *Conde Nast Traveler* 27, September 1992, p. 34.

Du Bois, Peter C. "More Grumpy News for Euro Disney." *Barron's* 74, 5 September 1994, p. MW12.

Dunlop, Beth. "Disney Reshaping Architecture World." *Miami Herald,* 20 May 1990, sec. I, pp. 1, 2.

Dutka, Elaine. "Dramatic Deal Reverses Series of Eisner Setbacks." *Los Angeles Times,* 1 August 1995, sec. A, p. 14.

Ebenkamp, Becky. "The Show Must Go On . . . the Shelves." *Brandweek,* 16 March 1998, pp. 26–33.

Eddy, Don. "The Amazing Secret of Walt Disney." *American Magazine* 160, August 1955, pp. 28–29, 110–115.

Ehrlich, Henry. "Florida: Preview of the New Biggest Show on Earth." *Look* 35, 6 April 1971, pp. 18–25.

———. "Florida: What Hath Disney Wrought?" *Look* 35, 6 April 1971, pp. 26–28, 31.

"£800 Million for Disney Project in France." *Times* (London), 28 April 1989, p. 28A.

Eisen, A. "Two Disney Artists." *Crimmer's: The Harvard Journal of Pictorial Fiction,* Winter 1975, pp. 35–44.

"Eisner: Disney Pushing to Become 'Aggressive' 'Contender' on Internet." *Minneapolis Star Tribune,* 30 April 1998, sec. D, p. 5.

"Eisner: $565 Million in Stock Options." *Los Angeles Times,* 4 December 1997, sec. A, pp. 1, 36.

Elmer-DeWitt, Philip. "Welcome to Cyberspace." *Time* 146, Spring 1995, pp. 4–11.

Enders, Deborah G. "Old-Fashioned Thrills and Chills." *New York Times,* 4 July 1993, pp. 13, 18.

"Euro Dis Lowers Hotel Prices." *Variety* 352, 25 October 1993, p. 152.

"Euro Disney Agency Decision Near?" *Advertising Age* 65, 14 March 1994, p. 41.

"Euro Disney Brings Paris Plans Forward." *Times* (London), 20 June 1991, p. 26.

"Euro Disney Draws Over 1.5 Million in First Seven Weeks." *Wall Street Journal,* 5 June 1992, sec. B, p. 5.

"Euro Disney Group Cuts Room Rates at Six Hotels." *Nation's Restaurant News* 26, 17 August 1992, p. 2.

"Euro Disney Hotel Closes for Winter." *Los Angeles Times,* 20 September 1992, sec. L, p. 4.

"Euro Disney Immune." *Variety* 346, 10 February 1992, p. 36.

"Euro Disney Looks for New Agency Partner." *Adweek* 34, 29 November 1993, p. 14.

"Euro Disney Makes Money, Finally." *Orlando Sentinel,* 16 November 1995, sec. C, pp. 1, 5.

"Euro Disney Park." *New York Times,* 5 February 1991, sec. 4, p. 5.

"Euro Disney Posts $353 M Loss." *Advertising Age* 65, 7 November 1994, p. 64.

"Euro Disney Re-Creates Top Restaurants." *Nation's Restaurant News* 25, 9 September 1991, p. 16.

"Euro Disney Rescue Plan Is Accepted by Bankers." *Minneapolis Star Tribune,* 15 March 1994, sec. D, p. 3.

"Euro Disney: Small Profit After All." *Herald-Sun,* 16 November 1995, p 2.

"Euro Disney Squashes Stock Rumors." *Nation's Restaurant News* 26, 5 October 1992, p. 14.

"Euro Disney Strikers Reach Accord." *Minneapolis Star Tribune,* 7 July 1998, sec. D, p. 3.

"Euro Disney Taps Steve Burke to be Firm's President." *Wall Street Journal-Europe,* 3 February 1995, p. 5.

"Euro Disney: The Not-So-Magic Kingdom." *Economist* 324, 26 September 1992, pp. 87–88.

"Euro Disney to Build New Town Near Paris-Based Theme Park." *Minneapolis Star Tribune,* 13 March 1996, sec. D, p. 3.

"Euro Disneyland." *Disney Magazine* 29, Winter 1993, p. 58.

"Euro Disneyland." *New York Times,* 8 July 1988, sec. 4, p. 12.

"Euro Disneyland Financing Gains." *New York Times,* 8 July 1988, sec. 4, p. 12.

"Euro Disneyland Off to Not-So-Fun Start." *Chicago Tribune,* 25 September 1988, sec. 7, p. 12F.

"Euro Disneyland Revises Plans." *Wall Street Journal,* 26 October 1990, sec. A, p. 12.

"Euro Disneyland Spending Is Raised." *New York Times,* 4 May 1990, sec. 4, p. 5.

"Euro Disney's $2.3 Billion Expansion Delayed." *Engineering News Record* 228, 15 June 1992, p. 5.

"Euro Disney's Roller-Coaster Ride." *Economist* 332, 3 September 1994, p. 66.

"Euro Disney's Woes Continue." *Business Week,* 1 November 1993, p. 58.

"Europe to Aid Disney Park." *New York Times,* 5 October 1989, sec. 4, p. 19.

"European Preferences." *New York Times,* 2 April 1984, p. 16.

"Ever-Ever Land." *Newsweek,* special issue, Fall/Winter 1991, pp. 38, 40.

"Expansion, Yes. Debt, No." *Forbes* 116, 15 November 1975, pp. 66, 69.

Facts on File. New York: Facts on File, 27 March 1987, p. 205.

"Fair Features Fun and Folksy Informal Charm." *Life* 8, 27 May 1940, pp. 32–33.

"Father Goose." *Time* 64, 27 December 1954, pp. 42–46.

Ferney, Frederic. "L'Amér Look des Anti-Américains." *Le Nouvel Observateur*, 3–9 January 1986, p. 26.

"Fitzpatrick Out at Euro Disney." *Nation's Restaurant News* 27, 25 January 1993, p. 2.

Fleming, Charles. "For Theme Parks It's a Small World." *Variety* 342, 18 March 1991, pp. 1, 110.

Fleming, Charles, et al. "A Goofy Kind of Year." *Newsweek* 122, 18 October 1993, p. 57.

Francaviglia, Richard V. "Main Street, U.S.A.: A Comparison/Contrast of Streetscapes in Disneyland and Walt Disney World." *Journal of Popular Culture* 15, Spring 1981, pp. 141–156.

———. "Main Street, U.S.A.: The Creation of a Popular Image." *Landscape, A Magazine of Human Geography* 21, Spring–Summer 1977, pp. 18–22.

"France and Disney Near Accord." *New York Times,* 21 August 1986, sec. 4, p. 4.

"France, Disney Progress." *New York Times,* 14 March 1987, p. 45.

"France: Euro Disney." *Facts on File.* New York: Facts on File, 19 May 1994, p. 367.

"France Has Survived Mouse Invasion . . . So Far." *Star-Ledger,* 10 April 1994, sec. 8, p. 11.

Franklin, Robert. "4 Big, Familiar American Faces to Appear in Japan Theme Park." *Minneapolis Star Tribune,* 3 February 1995, sec. A, pp. 1, 9.

"French Bonanza for Monsieur Mickey Mouse." *Times* (London), 23 March 1987, p. 6D.

"French Farmers Blockade Euro Disneyland." *Investor's Business Daily,* 29 June 1992, p. 25.

"French Given a Preview of Disney Park." *Atlanta Constitution,* 6 December 1990, sec. F, p. 7.

Frith, Simon. Introduction to *Pop Goes the Culture,* by Craig MacGregor. London: Pluto Press, 1984.

Frow, John. "Tourism and the Semiotics of Nostalgia." *October* 57, Summer 1991, pp. 123–151.

Fumaroli, Marc. "Le Défi Américain." *Le Nouvel Observateur,* 2–8 April 1992, p. 42.

Gaines, Lisa. "Lackluster Financial Results Could Force Euro Disney to Shut Down." *Travel Weekly* 52, 30 December 1993, p. 21.

Galante, Mary Ann. "Mixing Marts and Theme Parks." *Los Angeles Times,* 14 June 1989, pp. 1, 6.

Galluccio, Nick. "The Last Great Dream." *Forbes* 127, 11 May 1981, pp. 87, 89.

Ganley, Elaine. "Euro Disney Learns to Say 'In the Red' in French: Vast Regional Development Plans on Hold." *Star-Ledger,* 10 April 1994, p. 3.

Gardner, John. "Saint Walt: The Greatest Artist the World Has Ever Known, Except for, Possibly, Appolonius of Rhodes." *New York,* 12 November 1973, pp. 64–71.

Gegax, T. Trent. "Booming Amusement Parks: The Theme Is Extreme," *Newsweek,* 30 March 1998, p. 12.

Gershman, Suzy. "The Good, the Bad and the Tacky." *Travel and Leisure* 20, July 1989, pp. 25–30.

Geurand, Jean-Philippe. "La Belle et La Bête." *Actuaciné* 121, October 1992, cover story, unpaginated.

Gibbs, Nancy. "Easy as ABC." *Time* 146, 14 August 1995, pp. 24–30.

Giles, Jeff, and Charles Fleming. "A New Generation of Genies." *Newsweek* 124, 5 September 1994, p. 42.

Giles, Jeff, and Andrew Murr. "The Ride Gets a Little Rougher." *Newsweek* 124, 5 September 1994, p. 43.

Giovanni, Joseph. "At Disney, Playful Architecture Is Very Serious Business." *New York Times,* 28 January 1988, sec. C, pp. 1, 12.

Gitlin, Todd. "World Leaders: Mickey, et al." *New York Times,* 3 May 1992, sec. 2, pp. 1, 30.

Glucksmann, André. "American Magic, in an Homage to Its Roots." *International Herald-Tribune,* 9 April 1992, sec. 1, pp. 1, 3.

Godwin, Nadine. "Disneyland Paris: Getting There Is Part of the Fun." *Travel Weekly* 53, 24 October 1994, p. 37.

———. "Disneyland Paris Is New Address in France for Mickey and Minnie." *Travel Weekly* 53, 24 October 1994, pp. 1, 36, 38–39.

———. "Euro Disney Convention Center to Be Expanded." *Travel Weekly* 53, 17 October 1994, p. 73.

———. "Park Stages Special Events for Meetings Delegates." *Travel Weekly* 53, 17 October 1994, p. 73.

Goldberger, Paul. "Mickey Mouse Teaches the Architects." *New York Times,* 22 October 1972, pp. 40–41, 92–99.

Gooding, Judson. "Of Mice and Men." *Across the Board* 29, March 1992, pp. 40–44.

Goodman, Ellen. "Plastic World." *Literary Cavalcade,* January 1982, pp. 18–19.

"Goofy for Profit." *Orlando Sentinel,* 16 November 1995, sec. C, p. 1.

Gopnik, Adam. "Basic Instinct: Why Are the French Importing Sex?" *New Yorker* 71, 4 December 1995, pp. 98–102.

Gordon, Arthur. "Walt Disney." *Look* 19, 26 July 1955, pp. 28–36, 39.

Gordon, Beverly. "The Souvenir: Messenger of the Extraordinary." *Journal of Popular Culture* 20, Winter 1986, pp. 135–146.

Gordon, Mitchell. "Disney's World." *Barron's,* 14 November 1966, pp. 9, 22–23.

Gottschalk, Earl C. Jr. "Animating Disney's Dream." *Saturday Review* 55, 29 January 1972, pp. 33–35.

Gould, Stephen Jay. "Mickey Mouse Meets Konrad Lorenz." *Natural History* 88, May 1979, pp. 30, 32, 34, 36.

Graham, Jefferson. "Disney Says ABC Won't Be Its Puppet." *USA Today,* 1 August 1995, sec. D, p. 1.

———. "Will DreamWorks' Deal with Network Dissolve?" *USA Today,* 1 August 1995, sec. D, p. 1.

"The Greatest Triple Play in Show Business." *Reader's Digest* 67, July 1955, pp. 69–73.

Greene, Bob. "A Disney Fan's Theme: Parking." *Chicago Tribune,* 17 July 1988, sec. 5, p. 1.

Greenhouse, Steven. "$670 Million Loan Deal for Euro Disneyland." *New York Times,* 26 March 1991, sec. D, p. 5.

———. "Playing Disney in the Parisian Fields." *New York Times,* 17 February 1991, sec. 3, pp. 1, 6.

Grey, Stephen. "It's Euro Birthday Party Time for Mickey." *Daily Express,* 13 April 1993.

Grimsley, Kirstin Downey. "Disney Packs Its Bags." *Washington Post,* 3 October 1994, pp. 1, 16.

Grosswirth, Marvin. "Where Sophisticated Technology Encounters Youthful Fantasies." *Science Digest* 88, October 1980, pp. 76–80.

Grover, Ron. "Theme Parks: This Slugfest Is No Fantasy." *Business Week,* 23 March 1987, p. 38.

———. "Thrills and Chills at Disney." *Business Week,* 21 June 1993, pp. 73–74.

Groves, Derham. "Walt Disney's Backyard." *Excedra: Architecture, Art and Design* 5, 1994, pp. 29–38.

Gubernick, Lisa. "The Third Battle of Bull Run." *Forbes* 154, special issue, 17 October 1994, pp. 67, 70, 72, 74.

Guenther, John. "Norman Rockwell's Reality." *New York Times,* 16 November 1978, p. 26.

Haas, Charlie. "Disneyland Is Good for You." *New West,* 4 December 1978, pp. 13–19.

Hahn, Shannon. "Activist Tells His Life Story in Book." *Minnesota Daily* 97, 9 October 1995, pp. 1, 4.

Halevy, Julian. "Disneyland and Las Vegas . . ." *Nation* 186, 7 June 1958, pp. 510–513.

Handy, Bruce. "Endpaper: Disney Does Broadway." *New York Times Magazine,* 9 October 1994, p. 88.

Harmetz, Aljean. "Disney's 'Old Men' Savor the Vintage Years." *New York Times,* 4 July 1993, sec. 5, pp. 9, 18.

Harrington, Michael. "To the Disney Station: Corporate Socialism in the Magic Kingdom." *Harper's* 258, January 1979, pp. 35–39, 42–44, 86.

Hass, Nancy, and Seema Nayyar. "Learning Its Lessons Well." *Newsweek* 123, 14 February 1994, p. 37.

Hastings, Deborah. "The Player." *Minneapolis Star Tribune,* 17 August 1995, sec. D, pp. 1–2.

Hayes, Jack. "Disney Magic Spreads Across the Atlantic." *Nation's Restaurant News* 25, 28 October 1991, pp. 3, 75.

"HDM's Paris Office Gets Disney Account." *New York Times,* 23 March 1989, sec. D, p. 19.

Heath, Tom. "From Disney: A Scream Gem." *Washington Post,* 14 June 1995, sec. C, pp. 1, 8.

Henderson, Jim. "Euro Disney: Oui ou Non?" *Travel and Leisure* 22, August 1992, pp. 80–85, 110.

Henry, David. "All Eyes on CBS in Light of Disney Deal." *USA Today,* 1 August 1995, sec. B, p. 2.

"Here's Your First View of Disneyland." *Look* 18, 2 November 1954, pp. 82–84, 86–88.

Herzlich, Guy, and Martine Laronche. "Démarchage Tous Azimuts." *Le Monde,* 12–13 April 1992, p. 12.

"Hi Ho, Hi Ho." *Common Cause Magazine* 17, May/June 1991, pp. 10–11.

"Hi-Ho! Hi-Ho! Culture High and Low." *Harper's Bazaar* 275, September 1987, p. 210.

Hiltzik, Michael, and Claudia Eller. "Chemistry Made Talks Quick, Quiet." *Los Angeles Times,* 1 August 1995, sec. A, pp. 1, 14.

Hine, Thomas. "At EPCOT Center, the Message Is Mixed." *Philadelphia Inquirer,* 22 October 1982, sec. C, pp. 1, 8.

———. "EPCOT: It's a Very Carefully Planned Place." *Philadelphia Inquirer,* 21 October 1982, sec. D, pp. 1, 4–6.

Hockenberry, John. "Inside the Mouse." *I.D.: The International Design Magazine,* March/April 1998, pp. 58–65, 96.

Hocker, Cliff. "Forward Spin: If We Help Build It, People Will Come." *Black Enterprise* 25, October 1994, p. 17.

Hofmeister, Sallie, and Jane Hall. "Disney to Buy Cap Cities/ABC for $19 Billion, Vault to No. 1." *Los Angeles Times,* 1 August 1995, sec. A, pp. 1, 15–16.

———. "It's Back to the Future for Disney." *Los Angeles Times,* 1 August 1995, sec. A, pp. 1, 14.

"Honors to Mickey Mouse." *Publisher's Weekly* 129, 1 February 1936, p. 605.

Horovitz, Bruce. "Disney Tops Poll of Best Brand Names." *Los Angeles Times,* 10 July 1991, sec. D, p. 2.

"The House the Mouse Built." *Barron's,* 29 July 1963, pp. 9, 14–15.

"How Disney Will Pay for Cap Cities." *USA Today,* 1 August 1995, p. 1.

Hubler, Eric. "The Many Worlds of Fun in Japan." *New York Times,* 4 July 1993, sec. 5, pp. 12, 17.

———. "This Way to Germany, Canada and the Netherlands." *New York Times,* 4 July 1993, sec. 5, p. 17.

Huey, John. "America's Hottest Export: Pop Culture." *Fortune* 122, 31 December 1990, pp. 50–53, 56, 58, 60.

———. "Eisner Explains Everything." *Fortune* 131, 17 April 1995, pp. 44–48, 52, 56, 58–60, 64, 68.

Hughes, Robert. "Disney: Mousebrow to Highbrow." *Time* 102, 15 October 1973, pp. 88–91.

Humeston, Barbara. "Family Vacations in Central Florida: Disney World Is Just the Beginning." *Better Homes and Garden* 61, November 1983, pp. 205–206.

Ilott, Terry. "Disney Defers Payments to Help ED Stock Price." *Variety* 348, 19 October 1992, p. 54.

Ilott, Terry, and Michael Williams. "Disney Puttin' on the Blitz: Euro Theme Park Partners Find Themselves Picking Up the Tab." *Variety* 346, 2 March 1992, pp. 1, 80.

———. "Euro Disney Predicts Losses for First Year." *Variety* 348, 27 July 1992, pp. 39, 46.

———. "Killing at Euro Disney?" *Variety* 346, 6 April 1992, p. 49.

———. "MCA Plays Catch-Up in Global Parks." *Variety* 342, 18 March 1991, pp. 1, 110.

———. "Report Casts Pall as Theme Park Gets Gall." *Variety* 348, 7 September 1992, pp. 35, 69.

"Imagineering: Audio-Animatronics at the Fair." *Compressed Air* 69, May 1964, pp. 7–9.

"Imagineering: Ford Motor Company." *Compressed Air* 69, September 1964, pp. 20–22.

"Imagineering: General Electric Company." *Compressed Air* 69, June 1964, pp. 16–18.

"Imagineering: Pepsi-Cola Company." *Compressed Air* 69, August 1964, pp. 10–11.

"Intellectuals Attack Euro Disney." *Wall Street Journal*, 7 April 1992, sec. A, p. 10.

"An Interview with Ward Kimball." *Storyboard, The Journal of Animation*, October/November 1991, pp. 16–19, 34.

"It's a Soap World After All." *TV Guide*, 16 March 1996, p. 54.

Ivy, Robert A., Jr. "The New City as a Perpetual World's Fair." *Architecture* 76, April 1987, pp. 50–55.

Iyer, Pico. "In the Land of Mickey-San." *Time* 131, 11 January 1988, p. 51.

"Jack Lang: Fasciné par Orlando." *Le Monde*, 12–13 April 1992, p. 9.

Jackson-Opoku, Sandra. "The Wonders of Disney World." *Essence* 15, June 1984, pp. 34, 38, 43.

Jacobs, Lewis. "Walt Disney: Virtuoso." In *The Rise of the American Film: A Critical History.* New York: Harcourt, Brace and Company, 1939.

Jaffe, Thomas. "Euro Fantasyland." *Forbes* 145, 2 April 1990, p. 204.

James, Barry. "Not Without Qualms, France Cedes Space to Disney's World." *International Herald-Tribune,* 9 April 1992, sec. 1, pp. 1, 3.

Jameson, Frederic. "Postmodernism, or The Cultural Logic of Late Capitalism." *New Left Review* 146, July–August 1984, pp. 53–92.

"Japan's Playland Puts Car Makers in Driver's Seat." *Business Week,* 3 April 1965, pp. 52–54.

Jensen, Oliver. "Fair Girlie." *Life* 9, 29 July 1940, pp. 50–52, 55.

"Jiminy Cricket! Eisner Says Euro Disney May Close." *Minneapolis Star Tribune,* 1 January 1994, sec. D, p. 4.

Johnson, Brian D. "Riding the Movies: There Is Nothing Mickey Mouse About the Huge Expansion of Hollywood Theme Parks." *Maclean's* 104, 11 March 1991, pp. 48–51.

Johnson, David M. "Disney World as Structure and Symbol: Re-Creation of the American Experience." *Journal of Popular Culture* 15, Spring 1981, pp. 157–165.

Johnson, Janis. "New Magic in the Kingdom." *Maclean's* 95, 4 October 1982, p. 56.

Juillard, Jacques. "Invasion Culturelle Américaine: Cette Souris, Est-Elle Dangereuse?" *Le Nouvel Observateur* (3–9 January 1986), p. 21.

Justin, Neal. "Will Power." *Minneapolis Star Tribune,* 18 December 1994, sec. F, pp. 1, 5.

Karp, Richard. "Disney: Trouble in Dreamland?" *Dun's* 101, June 1973, pp. 54–57, 112, 117.

Katayama, Hiroko. "Mouse Madness." *Forbes* 141, 8 February 1988, p. 152.

Keegan, Peter O. "Bucking Japanese Tradition." *Nation's Restaurant News* 26, 23 November 1992, p. 82.

———. "Eight Years Over Tokyo: Japan's Love Affair with Disney Still Going Strong." *Nation's Restaurant News* 26, 23 November 1992, pp. 82, 110.

———. "The Man Behind the Mouse." *Nation's Restaurant News* 26, 23 November 1992, p. 94.

———. "Walt Disney Let Imagination Be His Guide." *Nation's Restaurant News* 26, 23 November 1992, pp. 94, 120.

Kehr, Dave. "It's Not All Ooh-La-La Over French Disney Park." *Chicago Tribune,* 8 June 1991, sec. 1, p. 1.

Kelly, Kevin. "Eno: Gossip Is Philosophy." *Wired* 3.05, May 1995, pp. 146–151, 204, 206–209.

Kelly, Kevin, and Linda Bernier. "It's King Kong Vs. the 'Ravenous Rat.'" *Business Week,* 5 October 1987, p. 54.

"Kids' Dream World Comes True." *Popular Science* 167, August 1955, p. 92.

Kiernan, Michael. "The Tight-Budget, No-Hassle Way to See Disney World." *U.S. News and World Report* 106, 5 June 1989, p. 62.

Kim, James. "A Career Capper for Cap Cities' CEO." *USA Today,* 1 August 1995, sec. B, p. 3.

King, Margaret J. "The American Theme Park: A Curious Amalgram." In *Continuities in Popular Culture: The Present in the Past and the Past in the Present and Future,* ed. Ray B. Brown and Ronald J. Ambrosetti. Bowling Green, Ohio: Bowling Green State University Press, 1993.

———. "Disneyland and Walt Disney World: Traditional Values in Futuristic Form." *Journal of Popular Culture* 15, Spring 1981, pp. 116–140.

———. "The New American Muse: Notes on the Amusement/Theme Park." *Journal of Popular Culture* 15, Summer 1981, pp. 56–62.

"King of Pop, Saudi Prince Teaming Up in Business." *Minneapolis Star Tribune,* 20 March 1996, sec. B, p. 5.

Kirk, Russell. "From the Academy." *National Review* 19, 22 August 1967, p. 911.

Kobliner, Beth. "Next Stop, Euro Disney!" *Money* 21, March 1992, pp. 155–156, 158.

Koepp, Stephen. "Do You Believe in Magic?" *Time* 131, 25 April 1988, pp. 66–73.

Kottak, Conrad Phillip. "Anthropological Perspectives on Contemporary American Culture." In *Cultural Anthropology.* New York: Random House, 1974.

"La Parade des Stars." *Paris Match,* 23 April 1992, pp. 72–75.

Lacey, Edward A. "Electronics at Disney World: How Electronics Is Helping to Make Disney World a Success." *Popular Electronics* 2, August 1972, pp. 44–46.

Lacorne, Denis. "Disneyland et Euro Disneyland." *Esprit* 115, June 1986, pp. 105–113.

La Farge, Christopher. "Walt Disney and the Art Form." *Theatre Arts* 25, September 1941, pp. 673–680.

Landsburg, Mitchell. "Disney Overload." *Minneapolis Star Tribune,* 7 August 1995, sec. D, pp. 1, 4.

——— "Our World Is Turning Into Disney's World." *Minneapolis Star Tribune,* 6 August 1995, sec. A, p. 4.

Larsen, Elizabeth. "Walt's World." *Utne Reader,* March–April 1994, pp. 38, 40.

Latham, Valerie. "Playing on a Theme." *Marketing,* 7 May 1992, pp. 22, 24.

Lawday, David. "Dateline: 'Ow-Dee' to Frère Mickey." *U.S. News and World Report* 112, 13 April 1992, p. 18.

———. "Where All the Dwarfs are Grumpy." *U.S. News and World Report* 108, 28 May 1990, pp. 50–51.

Lawrence, Elizabeth A. "In the Mick of Time: Reflections of Disney's Ageless Mouse." *Journal of Popular Culture* 20, Fall 1986, pp. 65–72.

Leadabrand, Russ. "Mineral King: Go or No Go?" *American Forests* 75, October 1969, pp. 32–35, 44, 46, 48–49.

———. "What About Mineral King?" *American Forests* 73, February 1967, pp. 18–21, 51–52.

Lears, Jackson. "The Mouse That Roared." *New Republic,* 15 June 1998, pp. 27–34.

Leather, Stephen. "European Sell-Out for Disney." *Times* (London), 12 October 1989, p. 25B.

Lebaube, Alain. "Le Syndrome du Maître de l'Univers." *Le Monde,* 12–13 April 1992, p. 10.

Leerhsen, Charles. "How Disney Does It: A Dazzling New Theme Park, Saluting the Movie Biz, Fulfills Walt's Wildest Dream." *Newsweek* 113, 3 April 1989, pp. 48–54.

Leerhsen, Charles, and Fiona Gleizes. "And Now, Goofy Goes Gallic." *Newsweek* 119, 13 April 1992, p. 87.

Lejins, John. "Marceline, Mo.: Disney Had Plans for His Boyhood Home." *Minneapolis Star Tribune,* 25 June 1995, sec. G, p. 6.

Leouffre, Isabelle. "Welcome to France, Mickey." *Paris Match,* 16 April 1992, p. 97.

"Les Français Aiment Les États-Unis." *Le Figaro,* 4 November 1988.

Levy, John. "EPCOT Center, Orlando, Florida." *International Lighting Review* 35, 1984, pp. 2–12.

Lewis, Paul. "A French Disneyland near Paris Is Approved." *New York Times,* 22 March 1987, sec. I, p. 6.

Lewis, Peter. "Disney Advances on Europe." *Maclean's* 98, 8 July 1985, p. 42.

Liddle, Alan. "Guests Walk a Not-So-Fine Line at Euro Disney's Attractions." *Nation's Restaurant News* 26, 23 November 1992, pp. 54, 122.

———. "Vive le Mouse! Mickey Takes on Europe." *Nation's Restaurant News* 26, 23 November 1992, pp. 54, 114.

Lieberman, David. "Disney Buys ABC for $19B." *USA Today,* 1 August 1995, sec. A, p. 1.

———. "Disney Intent on Big Role in World Market." *USA Today,* 1 August 1995, sec. A, pp. 1–2.

"Life Goes to Dali's New Ballet." *Life* 3, 27 November 1939, pp. 90–93.

Lileks, James. "The French Turn Up Their Noses at Disney? Well, Excusez Mouse!" *Minneapolis Star Tribune,* 26 April 1992, sec. F, p. 8.

Lines, Harry. "From Cyclone to Scream Machine: Approaches to Ride Themeing." *Theatre Crafts* 11, September 1977, pp. 40–45, 100–103.

Lingeman, Richard. "Disneyburg Address." *Nation* 259, 11 July 1994, p. 40.

Lipton, Norman C. "Disneyland's Circarama." *Popular Photography* 37, December 1955, pp. 96–97, 182, 184–185.

Liston, James M. "The Land That Does Away with Time." *Better Homes and Gardens* 34, February 1956, pp. 62–63.

Litwak, Leo E. "A Fantasy That Paid Off." *New York Times Magazine,* 27 June 1965, pp. 22–23, 35, 27–28.

Low, David. "Leonardo da Disney." *New Republic* 106, 5 January 1942, pp. 16–18.

Lublin, Joann S. "Will Sneezy Be Making Cold Calls to Sell European Disneyland?" *Wall Street Journal*, 13 September 1989, sec. C, p. 1.

Lyman, Rick. "Euro Disney Attendance Is Disappointingly Mickey Mouse." *Journal of Commerce* 397, 10 August 1993, p. 9A.

MacFadyen, J. Tevere. "The Future: A Walt Disney Production." *Next*, July–August 1980, pp. 24–32.

MacKay, Patricia. "Theme Parks: USA." *Theatre Crafts* 11, September 1977, pp. 26–27, 56, 65–76.

Mahar, Maggie. "Mouse Roars." *Barron's* 74, 28 November 1994, p. 13.

Mancini, Marc. "Pictures at an Exposition." *Film Comment* 19, January–February 1983, pp. 43–49.

Maney, Kevin. "Merger Mania Spreads to Disney World." *USA Today*, 1 August 1995, sec. B, pp. 1–2.

Marcom, John Jr. "Le Défi Disney." *Forbes* 143, 20 February 1989, pp. 39–40.

Marin, Louis. "Disneyland: A Degenerate Utopia." *Glyph* 1, 1977, pp. 50–66.

Marling, Karal Ann. "Disneyland, 1955: Just Take the Santa Ana Freeway to the American Dream." *American Art*, Winter/Spring 1991, pp. 169–207.

———. "Letter from Japan: Kenbei Vs. All-American Kawaii at Tokyo Disneyland." *American Art*, Spring 1992, pp. 102–111.

Martie, Serge. "Les Profits du Rêve." *Le Monde*, 12–13 April 1992, p. 12.

Martin, Mitchell. "Mob Pelts Disney Chiefs." *Washington Post*, 6 October 1989, sec. D, p. 2.

Martin, Richard. "Foodservice Pioneer Nunis Keeps the Dream Alive." *Nation's Restaurant News* 26, 23 November 1992, pp. 58, 132.

———. "Illuminating a Brighter Future." *Nation's Restaurant Review* 26, 23 November 1992, p. 58.

Marx, Wesley. "The Disney Imperative." *Nation* 209, 28 July 1969, pp. 76–78.

Masse, Richard F., and Camille Broussard. "Land Exchange: A Case Study." *Parks and Recreation* 12, December 1977, pp. 26–29, 40–42.

Mattimore, Bryan W. "Strategies of Genius." *Success* 39, October 1992, pp. 26–27.

McCarthy, Michael. "Universal Studios Goes East." *Adweek*, 27 July 1998, p. 29.

McEvoy, J. P. "McEvoy in Disneyland." *Reader's Digest* 66, February 1955, pp. 19–26.

———. "Of Mouse and Man." *Reader's Digest* 41, October 1942, pp. 85–88.

McGeehan, Patrick. "Mergers, Acquisitions on Pace to Record Year." *USA Today*, 1 August 1995, sec. B, p. 2.

———. "Moguls Scout for Mergers at Sun Valley Camp." *USA Today*, 1 August 1995, sec. B, p. 3.

McGuigan, Cathleen. "Après Mickey, Le Déluge." *Newsweek* 119, 13 April 1992, pp. 64–67.

McLuhan, Marshall. "A Garland of Christmases Past and a Glimpse of Christmas Future." *McCall's* 95, December 1967, pp. 97, 163.

McNamara, Brooks. "Come On Over: The Rise and Fall of the American Amusement Park." *Theatre Crafts* 11, September 1977, pp. 32–33, 84–86.

McNary, Dave. "Disneyland's Well-Known Profile Is Given Some Updated Wrinkles." *Minneapolis Star Tribune*, 14 June 1998, sec. G, p. 5.

McReynolds, William. "Disney Plays 'The Glad Game.'" *Journal of Popular Culture* 7, Spring 1974, pp. 787–796.

McUsic, Teresa. "Roy Disney—The Other Man Behind Mickey Mouse." *Minneapolis Star Tribune*, 21 August 1998, sec. D, p. 2.

Mead, Gary, et al. "A Question of the Mouse's Attraction." *London Financial Times*, 13–14 June 1992, p. 5.

Medved, Michael. "The Business." *Sight and Sound* 4, February 1994, p. 4.

Meier, Peg. "A Journey to Orlando's Wonderful (but not Small) World of Disney." *Minneapolis Star Tribune*, 26 February 1995, sec. G, pp. 1, 11–12.

"Meltdown at the Cultural Chernobyl." *Economist* 330, 5 February 1994, pp. 65–66.

Menen, Aubrey. "Dazzled in Disneyland." *Holiday* 34, July 1963, pp. 68–70, 72–75, 106.

Meyer, Michael. "A Charming Prince to the Rescue?" *Newsweek* 123, 13 June 1994, p. 43.

———. "Of Mice and Men." *Newsweek* 124, 5 September 1994, pp. 40–47.

Meyers, Mike. "Experts Ponder: Is This a Merger of Peril or Promise?" *Minneapolis Star Tribune*, 1 August 1995, sec. A, p. 10.

Michaelson, Judith, and Mary Louise Oates. "Fitzpatrick to Head Euro Disneyland." *Los Angeles Times*, 13 March 1987, sec. 6, p. 1.

"Mickey Goes Cruising." *Minneapolis Star Tribune*, 28 April 1995, sec. D, p. 2.

"Mickey Hops the Pond." *Economist*, 28 March 1987, p. 75.

"Mickey, Minnie Back." *Minneapolis Star Tribune*, 11 July 1998, sec. D, p. 2.

"Mickey Mouse Diplomacy." *Minneapolis Star Tribune*, 18 June 1992, p. 2D.

"Mickey Mouse to Le Rescue." *Variety* 346, 17 February 1992, p. 49.

"Mickey Opens in Florida: Disney Moves East." *Life* 71, 15 October 1971, pp. 44–50.

"Mickey Soirée Privée." *Paris Match*, 23 April 1992, pp. 66–75.

"A Mighty Bucks Merger." *Minneapolis Star Tribune,* 1 August 1995, sec. A, pp. 1, 10.

Mikelbank, Peter. "Slipping Paris a Mickey." *Washington Post,* 31 March 1991, sec. F, p. 1.

Miller, Annetta. "Epcot Center: Disney's Dream Come True." *Saturday Evening Post* 254, October 1982, pp. 70–72.

Miller, Bryan. "With a Gallic Touch: 3 French Chefs at Epcot." *New York Times,* 6 January 1988, sec. C, pp. 1, 8.

Miller, Diane Disney. "My Dad, Walt Disney: Small Boy's Dream Come True." *Saturday Evening Post* 229, 17 November 1956, pp. 25–27, 130, 132–134.

———. "My Dad, Walt Disney: Small Boy's Dream Come True." *Saturday Evening Post* 229, 24 November 1956, pp. 26–27, 70, 75, 78, 80.

———. "My Dad, Walt Disney: Small Boy's Dream Come True." *Saturday Evening Post* 229, 8 December 1956, pp. 38–39, 79, 80–82, 85.

———. "My Dad, Walt Disney: Small Boy's Dream Come True." *Saturday Evening Post* 229, 5 January 1957, pp. 24, 80–82.

Miller, Greg, and Jill Leovy. "Burbank Hopes Deal Will Be Icing on Cake." *Los Angeles Times,* 1 August 1995, sec. A, pp. 1, 10.

Miller, Ross. "Euro Disneyland and the Image of America." *Progressive Architecture* 71, October 1990, pp. 92–95.

Miller, Russell. "Past Imperfect." *New Republic* 211, 8 August 1994, pp. 12, 14, 16.

Miller, William Lee. "Marginal Utility in the Magic Kingdom." *New Republic* 145, 21 August 1961, p. 21.

Moore, Alexander. "Walt Disney World: Bounded Ritual Space and the Playful Pilgrimage Center." *Anthropological Quarterly* 53, 1980, pp. 207–218.

Moore, Charles, and Gerald Allen. "You Have to Pay for the Public Life." In *Dimensions: Space, Shape, and Scale in Architecture.* New York: Architectural Record Books, 1976.

Moore, Martha T. "Disney CEO Shows Strengths, Good Timing." *USA Today,* 1 August 1995, sec. B, p. 3.

Morgenstern, Joseph. "What Hath Disney Wrought!" *Newsweek* 78, 18 October 1971, pp. 38–46.

Morison, Elting E. "What Went Wrong With Disney's World's Fair." *American Heritage* 35, December 1983, pp. 70–79.

Morse, Margaret. "An Ontology of Everyday Distraction: The Freeway, the Mall, and Television." In *Logics of Television: Essays in Cultural Criticism,* ed. Patricia Mellencamp. Bloomington: University of Indiana Press, 1990.

———. "Video Installation Art: The Body, the Image, and the Space-in-Between." In *Illuminating Video,* ed. Doug Hall and Sally Jo Fifer. San Francisco: Aperture/Bay Area Video Coalition, 1989.

"The Mother of All Divorces." *Fortune* 131, 17 April 1995, p. 48.

"Mounties Hire Disney to Market Their Image." *Minneapolis Star Tribune,* 29 June 1995, sec. D, p. 3.

"Mouse Madness." *Forbes* 141, 8 February 1988, p. 152.

"Mouse That Roared." *USA Today,* 1 August 1995, sec. A, p. 10.

"The Mouse That Turned to Gold." *Business Week,* 9 July 1955, pp. 72, 74, 76.

"The Mouse That Walt Built—and That Built Walt." *Time* 64, 27 December 1954, p. 45.

"Mouse Trapped in France." *New Statesman and Society* 6, 20 August 1993, p. 6.

Mullard, Claudine. "Eisner le Kid." *Le Monde,* 12–13 April 1992, p. 12.

Munchau, Wolfgang. "Disney Plans Flotation for European Theme Park." *Times* (London), 6 March 1989, p. 27.

"Murphy and Eisner: 2 Success Stories." *Minneapolis Star Tribune,* 1 August 1995, sec. A, p. 11.

Muschamp, Herbert. "Playful, Even Goofy, But What Else? It's Disney." *New York Times,* 5 March 1995, p. 34.

Naylor, Lois Anne. "Doing Disney." *Better Homes and Gardens* 70, January 1992, pp. 108–111.

Neff, Robert. "In Japan, They're Goofy About Disney." *Business Week,* 12 March 1990, p. 64.

Neher, Jacques. "Disney Park Gets European Accent." *Chicago Tribune,* 3 April 1989, sec. 4, p. 1.

Neuffer, Elizabeth. "The World Looks Anew at America." *Boston Globe,* 9 October 1994, pp. 1, 22–23.

"A New Boom: Disneyland East." *Newsweek* 77, 19 April 1971, pp. 103–104.

"The New Civil War: Making a Stand." *Conde Nast Traveler* 29, September 1994, pp. 146–151.

"New Disney Institute Offers Unique Discovery Vacations." *New York Times,* 30 April 1995, summer travel guide, p. 7.

"New Magic in the Kingdom." *Maclean's* 95, 4 October 1982, p. 56.

"New York Opens the Gates to the World of Tomorrow." *Life* 6, 15 May 1939, pp. 19–23.

"Nice Idea, Shame About the Weather." *Economist* 298, 11 January 1986, p. 86.

Nienaber, Jeanne. "The Supreme Court and Mickey Mouse." *American Forests* 78, July 1972, pp. 28–31, 40–43.

"No Mouse in House." *Minneapolis Star Tribune,* 1 July 1998.

Noglows, Paul. "Euro Disney Gives Stateside Stock Near-Term Muscle." *Variety* 347, 20 April 1992, pp. 61–62.

"Not-So-Stately Pleasure Domes." *Economist* 298, 11 January 1986, p. 84.

"Not Such a Small World." *USA Today,* 1 August 1995, sec. B, p. 1.

"Now, Disney World Isn't All Mickey Mouse." *U.S. News and World Report* 93, 13 September 1982, pp. 72–73.

Nundy, Julian. "Disneyland Would Like to Set Trap for Mickey and Company." *Chicago Tribune,* 19 January 1987, sec. 1, p. 12.

O'Brien, Tim. "Year 1: Euro Disney Keeping Its Chin Up." *Amusement Business* 105, 12–18 April 1993, pp. 1, 18.

———. "Euro Disney's New Attractions Aimed at Increasing Attendance." *Amusement Business* 105, 12–18 April 1993, pp. 18, 30.

———. "Germany's Warner Bros. Movie World on Schedule for Late Spring Debut." *Amusement Business* 108, 15–21 January 1996, pp. 17, 24.

"Of Mice, Men and Money." *Economist* 329, 13 November 1993, p. 79.

Okey, Anne K. "Frank G. Wells: In Celebration of an Extraordinary Life." *Disney Magazine* 29, Summer 1994, pp. 12–13.

———. "A New Storybook Land for Euro Disneyland." *Disney Magazine* 29, Fall 1994, p. 31.

"On the Waterfront." *Minneapolis Star Tribune,* 10 August 1995, sec. D, p. 2.

"£1.8 Billion Value on Theme Park." *Times* (London), 21 June 1989, p. 28.

O'Rourke, P. J. "Inside EPCOT Center." *Harper's* 267, August 1983, pp. 42–43.

Orvell, Miles. "Understanding Disneyland: American Mass Culture and the European Gaze." In *Cultural Transmissions and Receptions: American Mass Culture in Europe,* ed. Rob Kroes, et al. Amsterdam: VU University Press, 1993.

O'Steen, Kathleen. "Grand Opening of Euro Disney." *Variety* 347, 20 April 1992, p. 30.

Painton, Priscilla. "Fantasy's Reality." *Time* 137, 27 May 1991, pp. 52–59.

"Paris Site for New Disneyland." *Times* (London), 19 December 1985, p. 7.

Parks, Pam. "Disney's First Family." *Orlando Magazine* 35, October 1981, pp. 64–66.

Pastier, John. "The Architecture of Escapism." *American Institute of Architects Journal* 67, December 1978, pp. 26–37.

Pawley, Martin. "The Last Resort." *Blueprint,* October 1988, pp. 38–39.

Pendleton, Jennifer. "Silver Lining on the Disneylandscape." *Advertising Age,* 24 March 1980, pp. 26–27.

Peterson, Elmer T. "At Home with Walt Disney." *Better Homes and Gardens* 18, January 1940, pp. 13–15, 56.

Petitjean, Gerard. "La Stratégie de la Souris." *Le Nouvel Observateur,* 2–8 April 1992, pp. 40–43.

Peyser, Marc. "Waiting Warily on the Info On-Ramp." *Newsweek* 124, 5 September 1994, p. 46.

Phillips, Andrew. "Where's the Magic?" *Maclean's* 106, 3 May 1993, p. 47.

Podolsky, J. D., and Jane Sims Podesta. "An Uncivil War." *People Weekly,* 18 July 1994, p. 70–72.

Pollack, Andrew. "Sega Takes Aim at Disney's World." *New York Times*, 4 July 1993, sec. 3, pp. 1, 6.

Polta, Anne. "Working on Euro Disney Was Challenge." *West Central Tribune*, 14 March 1992, pp. A1, A8.

Pons, Philippe. "Une Première Réussie." *Le Monde*, 12–13 April 1992, p. 11.

Popkin, James. "Summer in Europe." *U.S. News and World Report* 112, 18 May 1992, pp. 68–70.

———. "Watch Out Mickey: Kong Has Arrived." *U.S. News and World Report* 108, 25 June 1990, pp. 60–63.

Porter, Janet. "Mickey Mouse May Rescue Ferry Firms." *Journal of Commerce* 338, 26 June 1991, sec. A, p. 6.

———. "P & O European Ferries Signs Marketing Pact with Disney." *Journal of Commerce* 338, 5 June 1991, sec. B, p. 3.

Potter, William E. "Walt Disney World: A Venture in Community Planning and Development." *American Society of Heating, Refrigeration, and Air Conditioning* 14, March 1972, pp. 29–32.

Poupard, Bernard. "Marne en Disney: Les Enjeux de Développement de Marne-la-Vallée et de l'Euro Disneyland." *Études* 371, December 1989, pp. 625–638.

Pouschine, Tatiana, and Thomas Bancroft. "Why Not Buy the Real Thing?" *Forbes* 146, 1 October 1990, p. 208.

Powell, Nicholas. "Costume Requirements at Euro Disneyland Called a Mickey Mouse Idea." *Minneapolis Star Tribune*, 10 March 1991, sec. G, p. 5.

"Preview of Disney's World's Fair Shows." *Science Digest* 54, December 1963, pp. 8–15.

Prewitt, Milford. "Disney's 'Imagineers' Turn Fantasy to Reality." *Nation's Restaurant News* 26, 23 November 1992, pp. 62, 118.

———. "Keeper of the Disney Flame." *Nation's Restaurant News* 26, 23 November 1992, pp. 62, 118.

Prial, Frank J. "Dreyfuss, a Driver and Disneyland-by-the-Marne." *New York Times*, 13 August 1985, sec. I, p. 2.

"Prime-Time Passions." *Economist* 336, 5 August 1995, pp. 55–56.

"The Prince." *Money*, October 1998, pp. 108–110.

"Prince Completes Disney Buy." *Travel Weekly* 53, 24 October 1994, p. 77.

"Prince Rescues Euro Disney." *Engineering News Record* 232, 13 June 1994, p. 16.

Prizer, Edward L. "The Disney Decade: Reminiscences, Conversations, Anecdotes and Significant Episodes in the Realization of Walt Disney's Greatest Dream." *Orlando Magazine*, October 1981, pp. 29–63.

Prown, Jules D. "Mind in Matter: An Introduction to Material Culture Theory and Method." *Winterthur Portfolio* 17, Spring 1982, pp. 1–19.

Quiz, Quintus. "That Awful Word 'Art.'" *Christian Century* 53, 22 January 1936, pp. 137–138.

Rafferty, Kevin, et al. "It's A Great Big Beautiful Tomorrow(land) . . ." *Disney Magazine* 30, Winter 1994, pp. 20–23.

"Railroad 'Show Business' on Lake Michigan." *Railway Age* 125, 24 July 1948, pp. 70–87, 97.

Ranard, Andrew. "In Japan, Nothing but Worship for a 'Trendsetter.'" *International Herald-Tribune,* 9 April 1992, p. 3.

Randall, Janice. "In Paris Today, à la Mode Means à l'Américaine." *France Today,* Autumn 1986, pp. 36–39.

Rapoport, Roger. "Disney's War Against the Wilderness." *Ramparts* 10, November 1971, pp. 27–33.

Real, Michael R. "The Disney Universe: Morality Play." In *Mass-Mediated Culture.* Englewood Cliffs, N.J.: Prentice-Hall, 1977.

"A Real Mickey Mouse Outfit." *Times* (London), 24 June 1989, p. 27.

Reckard, E. Scott. "Disney Not Just for Kids." *Minneapolis Star Tribune,* 30 November 1994, sec. D, pp. 1, 4.

Reddy, John. "Disney World—Fun, Fantasy, Reality." *Reader's Digest* 89, December 1973, pp. 196–198, 200, 202, 204.

Reed, Dan. "Mouse Roars." *Minneapolis Star Tribune,* 10 February 1996, sec. D, pp. 1, 3.

Rees, Jenny. "The Mouse That Ate France." *National Review* 44, 11 May 1992, pp. 57–58, 61.

Reeves, Richard. "Parlez-Vous Disney: Mickey Mouse Is Learning French." *Travel and Leisure,* February 1991, pp. 38, 42.

———. "Worlds of Wonder." *Newsweek,* special issue, Fall/Winter 1991, pp. 12–17.

Regan, Mary Beth, et al. "Mickey Does Manassas." *Business Week,* 29 November 1993, p. 46.

"Renowned Hollywood Agent Michael Ovitz Named to No. 2 Position at Walt Disney Co." *Minneapolis Star Tribune,* 15 August 1995, sec. D, pp. 1–2.

Resler, Robb. "Walt Disney World: Epcot Center." *Theatre Crafts* 16, December 1982, pp. 10–11, 12–61.

Reynaert, François. "Des Citrouilles en Or . . ." *Le Nouvel Observateur,* 2–8 April 1992, p. 43.

Riding, Alan. "Only the French Elite Scorn Mickey's Debut." *New York Times,* 13 April 1992, sec. A, pp. 1, 13.

"Riding Out Euro Disney's Razzamatazz." *Marketing,* 27 February 1992, p. 16.

"Robert Fitzpatrick, P.-D.G. d'Euro Disney." *Paris Match,* 16 April 1992, pp. 96–97.

Roberts, Robin. "On the Move with Epcot." *Saturday Evening Post* 255, November 1983, pp. 90–91.

Robins, Alexandra. "Mickey Goes to France: Totally Awesome for Kids." *Los Angeles Times,* 3 May 1992, sec. L, pp. 1, 14.

Robins, Marjorie. "Mickey Goes to France: Awfully American for Grown-Ups." *Los Angeles Times,* 3 May 1992, sec. L, pp. 1, 14.

Robinson, Phillip. "Harsh Reality Dents the Disney Fantasy." *Times* (London), 26 January 1991, p. 29.

———. "Leading Role for Kermit at Disney." *Times* (London), 21 February 1990, p. 27.

Ross, Irwin. "Disney Gambles on Tomorrow." *Fortune* 106, 4 October 1982, pp. 62–68.

Rossanigo, di Carlo. "Topolino & Soci Sbarcano in Europa." *Fortune,* June 1991, pp. 126–131.

Rossant, John, et al. "How Disney Snared a Princely Sum." *Business Week,* 20 June 1994, pp. 61–62.

Rothchild, John. "EPCOT: It's a Stale World After All." *Rolling Stone,* September 1983, pp. 33–34, 36–38.

Rothenberg, Sheila, and Robert S. Rothenberg. "Walt Disney World: Not Just for Kids." *USA Today* 119, November 1990, pp. 78–83.

Rudnitsky, Howard. "Creativity with Discipline." *Forbes* 143, 6 March 1989, pp. 41–42.

Rudolph, Barbara. "Monsieur Mickey." *Time* 137, 25 March 1991, pp. 48–49.

Rush, Diane H. "Disney 'Imagineers' Come to Florida." *Business and Economic Dimensions Magazine,* January 1971, pp. 1–6.

Rustin, Richard E. "A Disney Venture Dwarfs the Market in London Trading." *Wall Street Journal,* 25 October 1989, sec. C, p. 12.

Rykwert, Joseph. "Is Euro Disney a Substitute for Paris?" *Times Literary Supplement,* no. 4668, 18 September 1992, pp. 6–7.

Said, Edward W. "Orientalism: The Cultural Consequences of the French Preoccupation with Egypt." In *Egypt: Al-Jabarti's Chronicle of the French Occupation,* ed. Robert Tignor. New York: Markus Wiener Publishing, 1993.

Salz-Trautman, Peggy. "Can Bugs Top Mickey's Act?" *World Press Review* 41, March 1994, p. 36.

Sample, Robert L. "The Exciting World of Epcot Center." *Administrative Management,* November 1982, pp. 49–52.

"San Francisco Opens Its Golden Gate Exposition with Wild West Gallop." *Life* 6, 6 March 1939, pp. 11–15.

Sasseen, Jane. "Disney's Bungle Book." *International Management* 48, July–August 1993, pp. 26–27.

"Saudi Prince Buys Into Euro Disney." *Advertising Age* 65, 6 June 1994, pp. 49, 54.

"Saudi Prince May Reduce Park Stake." *New York Times,* 3 February 1995, sec. D, p. 5.

"Saudi Prince to Buy Shares in Euro Disney Offering." *Travel Weekly* 53, 13 June 1994, p. 55.

"Saudi's Disney Investment May Ease a Few Minds." *Minneapolis Star Tribune,* 3 June 1994, sec. D, p. 3.

Sayle, Murray. "Of Mice and Yen." *Harper's* 267, August 1983, pp. 36–39, 42–45.

Schiffres, Manuel. "When You Wish Upon a Stock." *Changing Times* 44, April 1990, p. 24.

Schmickle, Sharon. "Their Soul Is in the Soil: French Love for the Farm Fuels Trade War." *Minneapolis Star Tribune,* 8 April 1993, sec. A, p. 1.

Schneider, Steven. "The Animated Alternative." *Art in America* 69, December 1981, pp. 113–120.

Schoemer, Karen, and Andrew Murr. "An Endless Stream of Magic and Moola." *Newsweek* 124, 5 September 1994, p. 47.

Sears, John F. "Bierstadt, Buffalo Bill, and the Wild West in Europe." In *Cultural Transmissions and Receptions: American Mass Culture in Europe,* ed. Rob Kroes, et al. Amsterdam: VU University Press, 1993.

"Sega's American Roots." *New York Times,* 4 July 1993, sec. 3, p. 6.

Sertl, William J. "Hollywood Divine." *Travel and Leisure* 19, December 1989, pp. 140–146, 192–196.

Serwer, Andrew E. "Analyzing the Dream." *Fortune* 131, 17 April 1995, p. 71.

"Seville: Reine du Monde." *Paris Match,* 30 April 1992, pp. 46–51.

"Shares in Euro Disneyland." *Wall Street Journal,* 6 October 1989, sec. A, p. 9.

Sheffe, Edward D. "EPCOT: Making the City of Tomorrow Known Today." *Madison Avenue,* April 1983, pp. 98–99.

Shellhorn, Ruth P. "Disneyland: Dream Built in One Year through Teamwork of Many Artists." *Landscape Architecture* 46, April 1956, pp. 124–136.

Short, David. "A Year of TV Births and Quota Rows." *European,* 28 December–3 January 1996, p. 19.

"Show Business: How to Make a Buck." *Time* 70, 29 July 1957, pp. 76, 78.

"Showmen: The Magic Kingdom." *Time* 87, 15 April 1966, p. 84.

Simon, Carey, and Charlene Marmer Solomon. "Disneyland and Other Diversions." *Publisher's Weekly* 239, 27 April 1992, pp. 63–64, 70.

Sims, Calvin. "Makeover at Disney." *Minneapolis Star Tribune,* 3 May 1994, sec. D, pp. 1, 8.

Sivell, George. "Autumn Target Set for $1 Billion Euro Disneyland Flotation." *Times* (London), 26 May 1989, p. 27A.

———. "Disneyland Opens at 887p in Grey Deals." *Times* (London), 25 October 1989, p. 31.

———. "Disneyland Postpones £1 Billion Flotation." *Times* (London), 25 April 1989, p. 25B.

———. "Mickey Mouse Weaves a Magic Deal." *Times* (London), 29 May 1989, p. 23B.

———. "Trading to Start in Disneyland." *Times* (London), 24 October 1989, p. 25.

Skapinker, Michael. "Mickey Mouse Outfit Suffers Culture Shock." *London Financial Times*, 23 April 1992, p. 19.

Sklar, Robert. "The Making of Cultural Myths: Walt Disney." In *The American Animated Cartoon: A Critical Anthology*, ed. Danny and Gerald Peary. New York: Dutton, 1980.

Sloan, Allan K. "Europe Is Ripe for Theme Parks." *Los Angeles Times*, 22 August 1990, sec. D, p. 3.

Sloan, Gene. "Mickey at Sea." *USA Today*, 31 July 1998, sec. D, pp. 1–2.

Slotkin, Richard. "Buffalo Bill's 'Wild West' and the Mythologization of the American Empire." In *Cultures of U.S. Imperialism*, ed. Amy Kaplan and Donald E. Pease. Durham, N.C.: Duke University Press, 1993.

Smith, Shanna. "Where the Buffalo Roam." *Disney Magazine* 30, Fall 1995, pp. 26–28.

Solomon, Charlene Marmer. "How Does Disney Do It?" *Personnel Journal* 68, December 1989, pp. 50–57.

Solomon, Jolie, et al. "Disney: A Sudden Surrender in Virginia." *Newsweek* 124, 10 October 1994, p. 46.

———. "Mickey's Trip to Trouble." *Newsweek* 123, 14 February 1994, pp. 34–39.

Sorkin, Michael. "See You in Disneyland." *Design Quarterly* 154, Winter 1992, pp. 5–13.

"Spain Tries to Prove It's a Mickey Mouse Place." *Times* (London), 29 May 1985, p. 8C.

"Spreading from Disney World: A Spectacular Boom in Florida." *U.S. News and World Report* 72, 12 June 1972, pp. 60–63.

Steiner, Michael. "Walt Disney, the Mythic Frontier, and the Architecture of Reassurance." Paper delivered at the annual meeting of the American Studies Association, Pittsburgh, 10 November 1995.

Stephens, Suzanne. "Manifest Disney." *Architectural Record* 180, June 1992, pp. 54–59.

———. "That's Entertainment." *Architectural Record* 178, August 1990, pp. 72–79, 121.

Stevens, Elizabeth Lesly. "Mouse-ke-fear." *Brill's Content* 1, December 1998–January 1999, pp. 94–103.

Stevenson, Richard W. "Movie Theme Park Planned for Disneyland in France." *New York Times*, 17 November 1989, sec. B, p. 6.

Stoltz, Jack H. "Steamboat 'Round the Bend." *Senior Scholastic* 69, 8 November 1956, p. 7T.

"Storm Clouds Over Disney Land." *Business Week*, 1 November 1993, p. 43.

Styron, William. "Slavery's Tragedy Would Be Cheapened by Disney's Theme Park." *Minneapolis Star Tribune*, 7 August 1994, sec. A, p. 27.

"Succession Becomes Issue at Disney." *Minneapolis Star Tribune,* 19 July 1994, sec. D, p. 3.

Summers, Diane. "Disney's Cast of Thousands." *London Financial Times,* 18 February 1991, p. 10.

Sutton, Horace. "Babes in Disneyland." *Saturday Review* 50, 10 June 1967, pp. 80–82.

———. "Mickey's Global Mission." *Saturday Review* 3, 7 February 1976, pp. 53–55.

Swengly, Nicole. "Of Mice and Marketing Men." *Times* (London), 24 October 1990, p. 18.

Tagliabue, John. "A Comic-Strip Gaul Battles Disney." *New York Times,* 15 August 1995, p. 3.

———. "Step Right Up, Monsieur! Growing Disneyfication of Europe's Theme Parks." *New York Times,* 23 August 1995, sec. C, pp. 1, 19.

Tempest, Rone. "U.S. Has Designs on Europe and Finds Itself Welcome." *Minneapolis Star Tribune,* 16 May 1993, sec. F, p. 4.

Tempest, Rone, and Joel Havemann. "Euro Disney Proves It Is 'A Small World After All.'" *Sunday Punch* (Ikeja, Nigeria), 20 September 1992, unpaginated.

"That Mouse Will Really Roar Now." *Minneapolis Star Tribune,* 1 August 1995, sec. D, p. 1.

"That's Live Entertainment: On Stage in the Parks." *Theatre Crafts* 11, September 1977, pp. 46–51, 76–84.

"Theme Parks: Hearts, Brains, Jobs." *Economist* 328, 4 September 1993, p. 33.

Thomas, Bob. "Uncle Walt's Greatest Stand: How There Almost Was No Disneyland." *Los Angeles,* December 1976, pp. 162–165, 204–209, 250–253.

Thompson, Terri. "Housing Gets the Disney Treatment." *Business Week,* 3 June 1985, pp. 72–74.

Thompson, William Irwin. "Looking for History in L.A." In *At the Edge of History.* New York: Harper & Row, 1971.

Tighe, Chris. "Queuing for Flawed Fantasy." *London Financial Times,* 13–14 June 1992, p. 5.

Tilles, Daniel. "Letter From Paris: Changing Times." *Adweek,* 23 March 1998, p. 21.

———. "Letter From Paris: The French Exception." *Adweek,* 20 April 1998, pp. 24, 26–27.

———. "Letter From Paris: Operation Euro." *Adweek,* 11 May 1998, pp. 24, 26.

Tillier, Alan. "Disney Is Not Funny in France." *Times* (London), 16 March 1986, p. 56G.

Toy, Stewart. "An American in Paris." *Business Week,* 12 March 1990, pp. 60–61, 64.

———. "Euro Disney's Prince Charming?" *Business Week,* 13 June 1994, p. 42.

———. "Is Disney Headed for the Euro-Trash Heap?" *Business Week,* 24 January 1994, p. 52.

———. "Mouse Fever Is About to Strike Europe." *Business Week,* 30 March 1992, p. 32.

Toy, Stewart, et al. "The Mouse Isn't Roaring." *Business Week,* 24 August 1992, p. 38.

Treichler, Robert. "Mickey Mouse Goes Continental." *World Press Review* 38, July 1991, p. 41.

Truesdell, Bill. "Epcot Center." *Travel/Holiday* 158, October 1982, pp. 28–30.

Tully, Shawn. "The Real Estate Coup at Euro Disneyland." *Fortune* 113, 28 April 1986, p. 172.

Turner, Richard. "Euro Disney's Fitzpatrick Denies Report that 3,000 Workers Quit Over Low Pay." *Wall Street Journal,* 27 May 1992, sec. B, p. 10.

Turner, Richard, and Peter Gumbel. "Major Attraction: As Euro Disney Braces for Its Grand Opening, the French Go Goofy." *Wall Street Journal,* 10 April 1992, sec. A, pp. 1, 14.

Tuttle, Alexandra. "The French Dance to Disney's Looney Tunes." *Wall Street Journal,* 13 April 1992, sec. A, p. 16.

"Utell, Euro Disney Sign Deal." *Travel Weekly* 52, 21 January 1993, p. 43.

Vaughan, Vicki. "Euro Disney Designers Work to Avoid Culture Clash." *Journal of Commerce,* 2 May 1991, sec. B, pp. 1, 8.

Vial, Charles. "Les Comptes de Fées: Euro Disney Ouvre Ses Portes à Marne-la-Vallée." *Le Monde,* 12–13 April 1992, pp. 1, 11.

Virilio, Paul. "Cataract Surgery: Cinema in the Year 2000." In *Alien Zone: Cultural Theory and Contemporary Science Fiction Cinema,* ed. Annette Kuhn. New York: Verso, 1990.

"Visit by Walt Disney." *Herald* 7 (published by students of The Edison Institute, Greenfield Village), 26 April 1940, pp. 2, 6, 18.

"Visualizing Disneyland with Sam McKim." *"E" Ticket* 18, Spring 1994, pp. 8–21.

Wagner, Grace. "It's a Small World After All." *Lodging Hospitality* 48, April 1992, pp. 26–27, 30–32, 34, 46.

Walker, Martin. "Disney's Saccharin Turns Sour." *World Press Review* 41, March 1994, p. 36–37.

Walkup, Carolyn. "Cheers, Some Fears Greet Minn. Debut of Biggest US Mall." *Nation's Restaurant News* 26, 17 August 1992, pp. 1, 4.

Wallace, Kevin. "Onward and Upward with the Arts: The Engineering of Ease." *New Yorker* 39, 7 September 1963, pp. 104–129.

Wallace, Mike. "Mickey Mouse History: Portraying the Past at Walt Disney World." *Radical History Review* 32, March 1985, pp. 33–57.

Waller, Gregory A. "Mickey, Walt, and Film Criticism from Steamboat Willie to Bambi." In *The American Animated Cartoon: A Critical Anthology.* ed. Danny and Gerald Peary. New York: E. P. Dutton, 1980.

Waller, Martin. "Disney Prepares for Market Debut." *Times* (London), 18 September 1989, p. 24.

———. "Euro Disneyland Price Is 707p." *Times* (London), 6 October 1989, p. 23.

———. "Men of Vision Seek £580 Million in the Mud of Euro Disneyland." *Times* (London), 14 September 1989, p. 29A.

———. "Mickey Mouse Stakes for Sale." *Times* (London), 13 September 1989, p. 25H.

———. "Taste of Chocolate for Mickey Mouse." *Times* (London), 27 December 1989, p. 21.

"Walt and the Professors." *Time* 39, 8 June 1942, pp. 58, 60.

"Walt Disney, 65, Dies on Coast; Founded an Empire on a Mouse." *New York Times,* 16 December 1966, pp. 1, 40.

"Walt Disney Builds Half-Pint History." *Popular Science,* February 1953, pp. 118–119.

"Walt Disney: Great Teacher." *Fortune* 26, August 1942, p. 156.

"Walt Disney (1901–1966): Imagineer of Fun." *Newsweek* 68, 26 December 1966, pp. 68–69.

"Walt Disney's Giant Little Railroad." *Look,* 25 September 1951, pp. 17, 19–20, 22–24.

"Walt Disney's Snow White and the Seven Dwarfs, Part I." *Good Housekeeping* 105, November 1937, pp. 35–38, 221–226.

"Walt Disney's Snow White and the Seven Dwarfs, Part II." *Good Housekeeping* 105, December 1937, pp. 35–38, 162–168.

"Ward Kimball: The Wonderful World of Walt Disney." In *You Must Remember This,* ed. Walter Wagner. New York: G. P. Putnam's Sons, 1975.

Wasserman, Arnold. "Fun and Loathing at EPCOT." *Industrial Design Magazine* 30, March–April 1983, pp. 34–39.

Watson, Catherine. "Bonjour Pardner: Continent Will Get Goofy (and Mickey and Donald) with Euro Disney Opening." *Minneapolis Star Tribune,* 29 March 1992, sec. G, pp. 1–2.

———. "A Theme Park Built on Blood and Bones." *Minneapolis Star Tribune,* 5 December 1993, sec. G, p. 1.

Webb, Michael. "The City in Film." *Design Quarterly* 136, 1987, pp. 1–33.

Weinraub, Bernard, and Geraldine Fabrikant. "Turmoil at Disney: The Sequel." *New York Times,* 13 March 1995, sec. C, pp. 1, 6.

"Welcome to France, Mickey." *Paris Match,* 16 April 1992, pp. 90–95.

Wells, Melanie. "A Triumph for 'Old' Media." *USA Today,* 1 August 1995, sec. B, p. 3.

"What Other Newspapers Are Saying." *Chicago Tribune,* 4 April 1987, sec. 1, p. 11.

"Where Business Presents Tomorrow." *Nation's Business* 69, November 1981, pp. 64–66.

Whitaker, Frederic. "A Day with Disney." *American Artist* 29, September 1965, pp. 44–48, 66–67, 72.

Whyte, Kenneth. "The Carsen Show." *Saturday Night* 108, February 1993, pp. 48–52, 62–64, 66–69.

"The Wide World of Walt Disney." *Newsweek* 60, 31 December 1962, pp. 48–52.

Wiener, Jon. "Disney World Imagineers a President." *Nation* 257, 22 November 1993, pp. 605, 620, 622–623.

Wilkening, David. "250,000 More People, 125,000 New Jobs." *Orlando Magazine* 35, October 1981, pp. 62–63.

Williams, Michael. "Euro Disney Awash in Red Ink." *Variety* 351, 19 July 1993, p. 38.

———. "Euro Disney Goes to Bat in Bond Market." *Variety* 343, 24 June 1991, p. 66.

———. "Euro Disney Stock Falls After Release of Figures." *Variety* 347, 8 June 1992, pp. 30, 34.

———. "Le Mouse Gets His First Candle." *Variety* 350, 12 April 1993, pp. 35, 47.

———. "Mart Trips Mousetrap as French Dis Disney." *Variety* 347, 1 June 1992, pp. 1, 89.

———. "No Mickey Mouse Opening for Star-Studded Euro Disney Bow." *Variety* 347, 20 April 1992, pp. 33, 42.

———. "Suit May Halt Euro Disney in Its Mouse Tracks." *Variety* 343, 6 May 1991, pp. 327, 332.

Wilsher, Peter. "Financial Cracks in the Concrete Jungle." *Management Today*, September 1992, pp. 90–95.

Wilson, Alexander. "The Betrayal of the Future: Walt Disney's EPCOT Center." *Socialist Review* 84, November–December 1985, pp. 40–54.

Wittstock, Melinda. "Not Enough Disney to Go Around." *Times* (London), 23 October 1989, p. 25.

———. "Road Runner Catches the Disney Float." *Times* (London), 21 October 1989, p. 17.

Wolin, Richard. "The Anti-American Revolution." *New Republic,* 17 and 24 August 1998, p. 35.

Woller, Barbara. "For ABC Executive, Future Promising in Tomorrowland." *USA Today*, 1 August 1995, sec. B, p. 3.

Wolters, Larry. "The Wonderful World of Walt Disney." *Today's Health* 40, April 1962, pp. 26–31, 69–72, 75–76.

"A Wonderful World: Growing Impact of the Disney Art." *Newsweek* 45, 18 April 1955, pp. 60–64.

Woodson, Weldon D. "Through the Jungles of Disneyland." *American Forests* 62, January 1956, pp. 20–22.

"World's Fair." *Life* 6, 13 March 1939, pp. 33–49.

"Worlds of Wonder," *Newsweek*, special issue, Fall–Winter 1991, p. 15.

"Yes, Virginia, There Is a Walt Disney." *Forbes* 113, 15 February 1974, pp. 30–31.

"Zell, Disney to Invest in Rockefeller." *Minneapolis Star Tribune*, 17 August 1995, sec. D, p. 3.

Zimmerman, Gereon. "Walt Disney: GIANT at the Fair." *Look* 28, 11 February 1964, pp. 28–32.

Zoltak, James. "Disneyland Banks on Entertainment As Well As Attractions to Lure Crowds." *Amusement Business* 108, 15–21 January 1996, pp. 17, 23.

Zuber, Martha. "Mickey-sur-Marne: Une Culture Conquérante?" *French Politics and Society* 10, Summer 1992, pp. 63–80.

COMPANY REPORTS AND NEWSLETTER ARTICLES

"The Cast Members' New Smile." *En Coulisse* 3, 15–30 October 1992, p. 2.

"Christmas Season Press Event—November 20/22." *En Coulisse* 3, 15–30 November 1992, p. 4.

"Club Bénévole." *En Coulisse* 3, 15–30 November 1992, pp. 5–6.

"Club Bénévole." *En Coulisse* 3, 15–30 June 1993, p. 6.

"Communiqué: Communication Interne," 23 June 1993, p. 1.

Comprehensive Euro Disney Media Plan, base plan, October 1992–September 1993.

"Constructive Marvels." *En Coulisse* 3, 1–15 May 1993, p. 12.

"Décollage." *En Coulisse* 3, 1–15 February 1993, p. 1.

"Deux Cow-Boys à Euro Disney." *En Coulisse* 3, 1–15 October 1992, p. 8.

"Disney à la Mode de Chez Nous." *En Coulisse*, no. 3, September 1993, p. 4.

"Disney Institute." *Walt Disney World Eyes and Ears*, 13 July 1995, pp. 1, 4.

"Disney's Wild Animal Kingdom Guided by Prestigious Panel." *Walt Disney World Eyes and Ears*, 13 July 1995, p. 2.

"Et Si On Se Faisait Un Peu de Cinéma?" *En Coulisse* 3, 1–15 December 1992, pp. 1–3.

"Euro Disney Communiqué Special," 12 October 1992.

"Euro Disney Continues Strategic Reexamination." *En Coulisse Communiqué*, 8 July 1993, p. 1.

Euro Disney Information Presse, "Euro Disney S.C.A. Announces Fiscal 1992 Results, Proposed Dividend and Deferral of Management Fee to the Walt Disney Company," 19 November 1992, pp. 1–3.

Euro Disney Information Presse, "The Impact of Euro Disney on the

Economy and Tourism After Six Months in Operation," 30 October 1992, pp. 1–3.

"The Euro Disney Look." Paris: The Euro Disney Resort, 1992.

Euro Disney Media Plan, memo by Anne Marie Verdin and Nathalie Moride, January 1993.

"Euro Disney Resort Quiz." *En Coulisse* 2, 15–31 March 1992, p. 3.

"Euro Disney: Un Nouveau Élan." *En Coulisse* 3, 15–30 October 1992, pp. 4–5.

"Euro Disneyland, Le Vent En Poupé." *En Coulisse* 3, 1–15 February 1993, p. 2.

"A European Team." *En Coulisse* 3, 1–15 May 1993, p. 2.

"Évolution." *En Coulisse*, no. 3, September 1993, p. 3.

"Fan Mail." *En Coulisse* 3, 1–15 October 1992, p. 5.

"Five Thousand Smiles." *En Coulisse* 3, 1–15 October 1992, p. 5.

"Fun Facts." *En Coulisse* 3, 1–15 May 1993, p. 8.

"Going to Bat for Quality." *En Coulisse* 3, 15–30 June 1993, p. 5.

"Golf Euro Disney." *En Coulisse* 3, 15–30 October 1992, p. 8.

"Happy Birthday Euro Disney Resort." *En Coulisse* 3, 1–15 May 1993, pp. 6–7.

"Houba!" *En Coulisse* 3, 15–31 January 1993, p. 8.

"How to Raise a Reindeer." *En Coulisse* 3, 1–15 December 1992, pp. 4–5.

"Info." *En Coulisse Hebdo*, no. 2, 18–25 August 1993, p. 1.

"Interview: Changing of the Guard." *En Coulisse* 2, 15–30 September 1992, p. 5.

"Interviews." *En Coulisse* 3, 1–15 November 1992, pp. 4–5.

"La 'Dream Team' en Tournée à Travers la France." *En Coulisse* 2, 15–30 September 1992, p. 8.

"Le Château en Gâteau: Good Enough to Eat!" *En Coulisse* 3, 15–30 April 1993, p. 2.

"Le Marche Britannique: Des Disneyphiles!" *En Coulisse* 3, 1–15 May 1993, p. 2.

"Le 29 Juin: Bienvenue Sur Endor!" *En Coulisse* 3, 15–30 June 1993, p. 2.

"Les Filleuls de Mickey: Un An Déjà." *En Coulisse* 3, 15–30 April 1993, p. 4.

"Lettre de Robert Fitzpatrick," *Euro Disney Communiqué Special*, 15 January 1993.

"A Living Legend." *En Coulisse* 3, 15–30 June 1993, pp. 1–2.

"Marsupilami's First Visit: Houba!" *En Coulisse* 3, 15–30 April 1993, p. 4.

"Mickey's World Tour." *En Coulisse* 3, 1–15 February 1993, p. 2.

"Milestone Met!" *Op Sheet*, no. 17, 25 April–1 May 1993.

"Nestlé: La Collection Magique." *En Coulisse* 3, 1–15 June 1993, p. 5.

"New Program: Show Time." *En Coulisse* 3, 1–15 December 1992, p. 3.

"The Old Mill Gets a Face-Lift." *En Coulisse* 3, 15–30 June 1993, p. 2.

"Olé!" *En Coulisse* 2, 1–15 September 1992, p. 4.

"Passage du Flambeau." *En Coulisse* 3, 1–15 October 1992, p. 3.

"Promoting Euro Disney in Germany." *En Coulisse* 3, 15–30 June 1993, p. 4.

"Prospectus: Euro Disney, S.C.A." 17 June 1994, p. 1.

"Publicité: L'Émotion Retrouvée." *En Coulisse* 2, 15–30 September 1992, p. 8.

"Rencontre Avec Roy Disney." *En Coulisse* 3, 15–30 April 1993, p. 2.

"Sortie Officielle." *En Coulisse* 3, 1–15 November 1992, p. 8.

"Sous le Signe de la Nuit." *En Coulisse* 3, 1–15 June 1993, pp. 1–2.

"Tourisme: Une Année Difficile." *En Coulisse*, no. 2, August 1993, p. 4.

"Unconventional." *En Coulisse* 3, 1–15 November 1992, p. 3.

"Une Image en Pleine Mutation." *En Coulisse*, no. 1, July 1993, p. 3.

"Walt Disney Attractions Amsterdam—Opening Up the Dike," *En Coulisse* 3, 15–31 May 1993, p. 4.

"West Side Store." *En Coulisse* 2, 1–15 September 1992, p. 4.

"What's News." *En Coulisse* 3, 15–31 December 1992, p. 5.

TELEVISION REPORTS, FILMS, AND VIDEOS

Bird, Lance, and Tom Johnson. *The World of Tomorrow*. 1981. Film.

"Disneyland 1955 Grand Opening." 17 July 1955. Videotape, Walt Disney Imagineering Research Center, Glendale.

"The Disneyland Story." 27 October 1954. Videotape, Walt Disney Imagineering Research Center, Glendale.

"The Disneyland Story, Pre-Opening A-Roll." 10 July 1955. Videotape, Walt Disney Imagineering Research Center, Glendale.

"Disneyland, U.S.A." 1955. Videotape, Walt Disney Imagineering Research Center, Glendale.

"Disneyland's 10th Anniversary." 3 January 1965. Videotape, Walt Disney Imagineering Research Center, Glendale.

"E! Entertainment Report" (Amy Powell). February 1996. KARE 11 News.

"Euro Disney Grand Opening" (hosted by Don Johnson and Melanie Griffith). 11 April 1992. CBS.

"The Experimental Prototype Community of Tomorrow." 10 November 1966. Videotape, Walt Disney Imagineering Research Center, Glendale.

"Florida Press Conference." 15 November 1965. Videotape, Walt Disney Imagineering Research Center, Glendale.

"Indiana Jones George Lucas Reel." 5 May 1993. Videotape, Walt Disney Imagineering Research Center, Glendale.

"Rolly Crump: What Do You Do For Yourself?" WED Scrapbook, videotape HI-8MM #31573, Walt Disney Imagineering Research Center, Glendale.

INTERVIEWS

Interviews with members of Walt Disney Imagineering, conducted at Walt Disney Imagineering headquarters in Glendale, Calif.

Stewart Bailey, 17 July 1995
Tony Baxter, 6 July 1995
Susan Bonds, 29 June 1995
Barry Braverman, 7 July 1995
Bobby Brooks, 17 July 1995
Ron Chesley, 6 July 1995
Rolly Crump, 26 June 1995
Tim Delaney, 6 July 1995
Glenn Durflinger, 5 July 1995
Tom Figgins, 17 July 1995
Bruce Gordon, 10 July 1995
John Hench, 22 June 1995
Nancy Hickman, 27 June 1995
Erik Jacobson, 6 July 1995
Joe Lanzisero, 27 June 1995
Sam McKim, 26 June 1995
Tom Morris, 27 July 1995
David Mumford, 29 June and 10 July 1995
Jan Sircus, 17 July 1995
Marty Sklar, 23 June 1995
Edward Sotto III, 28 June 1995
Randy Webster, 10 July 1995

Other Interviews

Bruce D. Becket, AIA, president, Bruce Becket and Associates, Glendale, Calif., 13 July 1995.
Wing Chao, senior vice president, Walt Disney Design and Development Company, Burbank, Calif., 7 July 1995.
Bill Cottrell, retired Imagineering president, at his home, 12 July 1995.
Marvin Davis, retired Disney Imagineer, at his home, 26 July 1995.
Morgan "Bill" Evans, retired Disney landscape designer, Glendale, Calif., 30 June 1995.
Ward Kimball, retired Disney animator, at his home, 14 July 1995.
David R. Smith, Walt Disney Archives director, Burbank, Calif., 12 July 1995.
Thomas Thomas, exhibits artist, Gene Autry Western Heritage Museum, Los Angeles, Calif., 28 June 1995.
Card Walker, retired Disney chairman, at his home, 27 July 1995.
Bob Weis, former Disney Imagineer, Glendale, Calif., 14 July 1995.

Index

275

289